ASIA IN WESTERN FI

Asia in
Western fiction

edited by
Robin W. Winks and
James R. Rush

UNIVERSITY OF HAWAII PRESS
HONOLULU

Published in North America by
University of Hawaii Press
2840 Kolowalu Street
Honolulu, Hawaii 96822

Reprinted 1991

Published in the United Kingdom by
Manchester University Press
Oxford Road
Manchester M13 9PL

Library of Congress Cataloging-in-Publication Data
Asia in Western fiction/edited by Robin W. Winks and James R. Rush.
    p.   cm.
  ISBN 0-8248-1293-X
  1. Asia in literature. 2. Asians in literature. 3. Imperialism in literature.
4. Colonies in literature. 5. European fiction—History and fiction.
6. American fiction—History and criticism.
I. Winks, Robin W. II. Rush, James R.
PN3352.A84A8   1990
809.3'9352095—dc20   89-20149

Printed in Great Britain by Bell and Bain Ltd., Glasgow

CONTENTS

CONTRIBUTORS

Ainslie I. Embree is Professor of History and Director of the Southern Asian Institute at Columbia University. His publications include *Charles Grant and British Rule in India, and India's Search for National Identity*; he is Editor-in-Chief of the *Encyclopedia of Asian History*.

Theodore Nicholas Foss was co-founder of the Institute for Chinese–Western Cultural History at the University of San Francisco. Currently he is Assistant Director of the Center for East Asian Studies, Stanford University. His research explores eighteenth-century scholarship on China by Jesuits, including cartography and the use of Chinese-language sources.

Gavin R. G. Hambly is Professor of History at the University of Texas at Dallas. He is author of *Cities of Mughul India*, editor of *Central Asia*, and a contributor to *Comparative History of Civilization in Asia* and *The Cambridge Economic History of India*, vol. 1. He is co-editor of *The Cambridge History of Iran*, vol. 7 (forthcoming).

Donald F. Lach is Bernadotte E. Schmitt Professor Emeritus of Modern History, University of Chicago. He is the author of *Asia in the Making of Europe*, vols. 1–2, and a Fellow of the American Academy of Arts and Sciences.

Donald Lammers is Director of the Honors College at Michigan State University. He is author of *Explaining Munich: The Search for Motive in British Policy*, and is currently working on aspects of the diplomatic and scholarly career of Sir Charles Eliot.

Robin Jared Lewis is Associate Dean and Lecturer in South Asian Studies at the School of International and Public Affairs of Columbia University. He is author of *E. M. Forster's Passages to India*, and served as Executive Editor of the *Encyclopedia of Asian History*.

Luree Miller is a travel writer and biographer. Her most recent books on the Himalaya area include *On Top of the World: Five Women Explorers in Tibet*, and a children's book, *The Black Hat Dances: Two Buddhist Boys in the Himalayas*.

Since 1946, *Morton J. Netzorg* has been co-proprietor, with his wife, of the Cellar Book Shop, which specialises in materials about South-East Asia and the Pacific. His works include *Backward Turn Backward: A Study of Books for Children in the Philippines 1866–1945*, and an annotated bibliography entitled *The Philippines in World War II and to Independence: December 8, 1941–July 4, 1946*.

Milton Osborne is head of the Asia–Pacific Branch of the Australian government's Office of National Assessments. He is the author of several books on the Indo–China region and of *Southeast Asia: An Illustrated Introductory History*.

James R. Rush is a historian of South–East Asia. His work includes *Opium to Java: Revenue Farming and Chinese Enterprise in Colonial Indonesia*,

1860–1910, and articles on contemporary South–East Asian affairs for the Universities Field Staff International.

Jonathan D. Spence is George B. Adams Professor of History at Yale University. His most recent book is *The Question of Hu*. He is also author of *Emperor of China, The Death of Woman Wang, The Memory Palace of Matteo Ricci* and other books about China.

C. Mary Turnbull is a Fellow of the Royal Historical Society and has recently retired as Professor of History at the University of Hong Kong. Her works on Asia include *A History of Singapore, 1819–1988* and *A History of Malaysia, Singapore and Brunei*, both of which have been published in revised editions in 1989, and *The Straits Settlements, 1826–67: Indian Presidency to Crown Colony*.

Robin W. Winks, is Randolph W. Townsend Jr Professor of History and Master of Berkeley College at Yale University. He is the author of *Cloak and Gown: Scholars in the Secret War, British Imperialism, A History of Malaysia* (with John Bastin), *The Idea of an American Imperialism: Argumentative Essays in Comparative History* (forthcoming) and numerous other books on British, North American and other subjects.

GENERAL INTRODUCTION

Imperialism was more than a set of economic, political and military phenomena. It was a habit of mind, a dominant idea in the era of European world supremacy which had widespread intellectual, cultural and technical expressions. The 'Studies in Imperialism' series is designed to explore, primarily but not exclusively, these relatively neglected areas. Volumes have appeared, or are planned, on education, disease, the theatre, juvenile literature, natural sciences, art and sexuality, among others. But, in redressing the balance in favour of such multi-disciplinary and cross-cultural studies, it is not intended that the economic, political and military dimensions should be ignored. The series seeks to demonstrate that these can be fully understood only in their wider cultural context and that imperialism had profound effects on dominant as well as on subordinate societies.

Studies of imperial literature clearly have an important place in such a programme. Surely no area of the world has excited the imagination of Europeans and Americans as profoundly as has Asia. Since the late Middle Ages there has been an insatiable appetite for travel books dealing with Eastern cultures in all their richness and diversity, most of them fiction masquerading as fact. In these, as in later more explicitly fictional works, Westerners have projected their fears and ambitions, dreams and desires onto Asia. The East has been repeatedly reconstructed from generation to generation to illustrate arguments about alternative systems, philosophies or life-styles. From Milton's Satanic 'gorgeous East' whose kings were showered with 'barbaric pearl and gold' to Montesquieu's idealised *Lettres Persanes:* from Coleridge's or Fitzgerald's dreamy Orient to the erotic exoticism of Pierre Loti or Laurence Hope; from Lafcadio Hearn's visions of Japan to the countless writings with Asian settings of the twentieth century – authors both literary and popular have used Asia either to explore their fantasies and throw off Western restraints or to discover a mystic spirituality and different moralities. In this they have mirrored the constant search of the architect, artist, musician and craftsman for a new aesthetic, fresh design values, an extension to the language of their craft. The East has been appropriated and prefabricated for Western use and exercise of power, but at times it has also had a transforming effect, creating genuinely syncretic art forms.

Past studies of the Orient in Western literature and the arts have tended to concentrate on specific areas of the East as experienced by particular occidental cultures. This volume seeks to examine fictional representations of India, the Himalayan regions, Indo-China, Malaysia, Indonesia, China, Japan and the Philippines in the writings of British, French, Dutch and Americans among others. It provides a unique geographical, chronological and linguistic range within a specifically historical perspective and, in doing so, offers a remarkable breadth of insight into the complex grappling of West with East.

J. M. M.

ACKNOWLEDGEMENTS

Donald Lach and Theodore Nicholas Foss's 'Images of Asia and Asians in European fiction, 1500–1800' is also published in Thomas H. C. Lee (ed.), *China and Europe in Sixteenth to Eighteenth Centuries, Images and Influences* (Hong Kong: The Chinese University of Hong Kong Press, 1990). The editor thanks the Press for the co-publication.

James R. Rush's 'Journeys to Java: Western fiction about Indonesia 1600–1980' was originally published in *UFSI Reports*, No. 13, 1987 (Universities Field Staff International).

Milton Osborne's 'Fear and fascination in the tropics: a reader's guide to French fiction on Indo-China' was Occasional Paper No. 11 in the series *Wisconsin Papers on Southeast Asia*, Center for Southeast Asia Studies, University of Wisconsin, 1986.

Morton J. Netzorg's 'The Philippines in mass-market novels' originally appeared in the *Philippine Quarterly of Culture and Society*, 9, 1981.

Donald Lammers's 'Taking Japan seriously: some Western literary portrayals of the Japanese during the climax of their national self-assertion' appeared initially in Warren I. Cohen (ed.) *Reflections on Orientalism* (1983), Michigan State University: Asian Studies Center, South Asia Series No. 33; East Asia Series no. 8.

Many of the essays in this volume were originally written for a symposium entitled 'Asia in Western-Language Fiction', sponsored by The Asia Society with funding from the Rockefeller Foundation.

In the Introduction, Robin W. Winks has quoted from Ezra Pound: *Personai*. Copyright © 1926 by Ezra Pound. Reprinted by permission of New Direction Publishing Corp.

In Chapter 6, Luree Miller has quoted from *Himalayan Concerto* by John Masters. Copyright © 1976 by John Masters. Reprinted by permission of Brandt & Brandt Literary Agents, Inc.

In Chapter 7, Jonathan Spence has quoted from *The Singapore Grip* by James G. Farrell, reprinted by permission of Weidenfeld & Nicolson; *Braving the Elements* by James Merrill, © James Merrill 1972, reproduced by permission of Atheneum Publishers, an imprint of Macmillan Publishing Co.; *The Chinese Love Pavilion* by Paul Scott, reprinted by permission of Eyre & Spottiswoode; *A Single Pebble*, © John Hersey, reprinted by permission of Alfred A. Knopf Inc.; *The Great Wall of China* by Franz Kafka, reprinted by permission of and © Martin Secker & Warburg and Schocken Publishing House Ltd.; and *The Good Woman of Setzuan* by Bertolt Brecht, from *Parables for the Theatre: Two Plays by Bertolt Brecht*, revised English versions, by Eric Bentley, © Eric Bentley 1948, 1961, 1963 (original copyright renewed 1976), reprinted by permission of the University of Minnesota Press.

[ix]

In Chapter 8, C. Mary Turnbull has quoted from 'Mad Dogs and Englishmen' by Noel Coward, © the Noel Coward Estate; and 'Macao' by W. H. Auden, reprinted by permission of Faber & Faber Ltd and Random House.

-

CHAPTER ONE

Introduction

Robin W. Winks and James R. Rush

> O fan of white silk,
> clear as frost on the grass-blade.
> You also are laid aside.
>
> Pound

Ezra Pound, perhaps more than any other Western writer, faced the problem of transmitting Chinese thought into terms which would be meaningful to readers with Western literary sensibilities. Here he sought to reduce from ten lines to three a translation (introduced in 1901 by H. A. Giles) of a poem overlaid with tones of nostalgia, as the West would understand the term. Pound saw the original meaning clearly, in all its ambiguity, and he reduced 'The Fan Piece' for her Imperial Lord virtually to *haiku*, expressing the differences between the rights of an imperial lord who may simply lay aside a lady, that is, truly neglect her, while romantically yearning for the time when she still had favour in his eyes and lay beside him.[1] In these lines Pound also shows us just how difficult it is for Western readers truly to see – as opposed to look at – Asia without fastening onto that which is seen in stereotypes which originate from Western needs and experiences.

Any reader who has ever visited Asia knows that the great bulk of Western-language fiction about Asian cultures turns on stereotypes. Of course, neither cliché nor stereotype is necessarily wrong. Indeed, expressions often become cliches by virtue of embodying some universally recognised truths, while the stereotype, despite being a term normally thought to encompass prejudicially negative attitudes, may promote sympathy (as in Pearl Buck), especially when the thrust is away from purely intellectual understanding and towards compassion. No doubt Asian writing on the West is no less given to stereotypes, though because of the different roles played by a self-conscious

[1]

literature in most Eastern societies, the effect is not the same.

Those of us who are interested in Asia most likely began with views which were in some sense wrong. If our initial contact was in books, and as children, at least we shall have encountered Asia through the falsity of simplification. Later we probably experienced a more sophisticated level of falsification in the many romantic novels of empire, the adventure stories and travel tales, all of which made the cultures of Asia romantic, exotic and intriguing for us in our teens. Old *National Geographics* discovered in a grandfather's study, glimpses of Chinese scrolls when taken to our first museum or art gallery by a parent, Second World War comic books which show slavering Japanese ready to ravish white maidens as Tojo, Hitler and Mussolini looked on, or a little-understood visit to a movie house to see Wang Lung complete the cycle of his days and return to the good earth from which he sprang – these and hundreds of other early encounters shaped the way we in the West conceived Asia. Slowly, perhaps, our perceptions become more nearly true, in the sense that they coincide with some definition of reality which would be acknowledged by the Asian society itself; slowly some learn an Asian language, live within and assimilate to an Asian culture, become in some small measure 'Asian' themselves. But for every person who makes such a mental journey, there are thousands who do not pass beyond the barriers (or even over the bridges) of popular literature.

There are, of course, many sources of stereotypes, and literature is only one. It may not be the most important. However, at a certain level of society, among an educated readership, the most direct point of contact with, say, India is likely to be through Rudyard Kipling, E. M. Forster or perhaps M. M. Kaye. Each of these writers gives us a different India, of course, and each uses India to a personal purpose. The more astute reader will know this and examine that purpose; while the reader primarily seeking entertainment may simply absorb the colour, the sights and sounds that the author wishes to transmit and will shape attitudes from that absorption. How often does one hear the conventional wisdom that *Passage to India* is the 'finest book on India' ever written by a Westerner, when the book is in a fundamental sense not about India at all? We may recognise that Moby Dick is not about a whale hunt, but for many readers the use of an unfamiliar locale leads them to invest the sense of place communicated by such a book with largely Western meanings.

How should we expect knowledge to be otherwise? Of course, Western writers see Asia from a Western perspective. The question is, in what ways – not whether – such writers distort reality, and whether these ways matter in any important sense. The answer is usually that they matter when the distortions lead to unsympathetic or uninformed responses to Asian cultures; or that they matter if they deaden awareness or lead to false expectations. Yet surely they matter as much if they exaggerate awareness, lead to unthinkingly romantic or benign responses to these cultures or subvert the function of literature itself, blunting our critical sensibilities. Having admitted as much, one is at once caught up in the problem of subjectivity. Kipling knew well that the East was East, the West was West, and the twain would never meet, though he meant something rather different by this assertion from that which his detractors argued: not that Asia and the West might never co-operate, but that each would, must, remain within its own system of integrity, for to merge one's approach to life with that of another culture is to lose one's identity, no longer to be 'East' or 'West' as one becomes a cosmopolite speaking for no one except oneself.

The following collection of essays attempts to explore the problem of entering Asian societies through Western (and predominantly English) fiction, since this is the major port of entry for most schoolchildren, university students and, indeed, one suspects, most adults. There are many other ports of entry: service in war, for government, or in business; through the eyes of the missionary, the anthropologist, the linguist, the explorer, or the modern traveller; motion pictures and television; even the neighbourhood Chinese restaurant. However, most who journey to these ports come armed with books and most often fiction – James Clavell's *Shogun* on the flight to Tokyo, the latest Robert Ludlum *en route* to Hong Kong, one of Paul Scott's *Raj Quartet* while checking into the Taj Mahal Hotel in Bombay – which creates or reinforces expectations which, in turn, colour the actual experience of Asia. Over the years motion pictures and television may have displaced fiction in this regard, but if the long view is taken, perceptions of Asia in the West have surely been shaped more persistently by fiction, broadly construed, than by any other medium.

From this conviction grew the Asia Society's Western-language fiction project. With a generous grant from the Rockefeller Foundation, which wished to see what one might learn about specific cultures from a survey of the fiction purporting to be 'about' those cultures, the society sponsored a seminar on how one might best prepare a volume such as this; this was followed by a series of talks by writers of modern fiction set in Asia; by Milton Caniff (creator of 'Terry and the Pirates' and 'Steve Canyon' who influenced millions of teenage readers and servicemen with his cartoon sketches of the Dragon Lady), and by writers of travel literature and makers of films. In the meantime, the authors whose essays appear here (as well as some others) were commissioned to examine the broad body of fiction as it related to a specific Asian nation (or peoples). Essays on sweeping cultural perceptions, on the role of the British in South Asia and the Far East, and on problems inherent in a genre (thriller fiction, travel writing, children's literature) were also initially seen as important, though, in the long run as a matter of practicality, these subjects were eliminated lest the volume grow too unwieldy. The editors hope the selection of essays will be of value to the teacher in search of 'sound' literature to give to a primary or secondary school student, as well as to the general public and to the scholar.

During the seminar the editors learned much about the West's own stereotypes of itself. They were told that essays must not discuss how novels dealt with sexual matters as many teachers (and the parents of their students) would find this offensive; they were told that there simply were no 'good' novels about certain cultures; they learned that Asian readers do not hold in high regard some of the most revered works of Western writers; most important, they learned that we too had established stereotypes for literature, since the categories of knowledge, attitude and technique which the editors asked each writer to address proved unsuitable in many instances. An essayist saw that poetry was more important than prose; a writer recognised that only the cheapest or most sensational literature was read in the West in any large measure; a scholar saw that special problems arose when, for example, an English-language reader first encountered Indo-China through an English translation of a French novel. Over all lay the awareness that many readers would be profoundly influenced in their approach to such literature by the realities of Western foreign policies. In the end, therefore, the editors outlined the general problem with which they wished the essays to deal, individually and taken collectively, and left each author to approach that problem through the particularities of the literature at hand.

Needless to say, this literature varies enormously in quality, tone and purpose. There are, for example, markedly few important – in the sense of being important literature – novels by Westerners set in the Philippines, while there are many set in India or China. There is, of necessity, some overlap between the literatures, for Joseph Conrad did not write solely of the islands which have become Indonesia, and even had he done so, his themes are universal; thus, at times, different authors had to approach the same writers and even the same books, from a different angle. Many writers cannot be contained within the bounds of a political entity, for intellectual history, social theory and literary sensibilities know little of political boundaries.

Though generally organised by national identities, in conscious reflection of the manner in which The Asia Society was organised through national councils, the essays quickly demonstrated that one of the greatest stereotypes of all is that of literature bearing any direct relationship to nationhood. However, the essays also save us from the countervailing notion that all Asian cultures are, at bottom, alike, all 'Third World', 'underdeveloped', 'developing', 'lesser developed', or part of some skewed geography called, briefly, the 'North–South dialogues'. Literature which is truly universal in its underlying themes serves well our sense of humanity, but serves badly our need for an awareness of the rich particularity of cultures.

There are parallels here with stereotypes in Western fiction on African or Arab cultures.[2] We all know of how Desdemona saw Othello; we have (one presumes) reflected on *The Nigger of the Narcissus*, and thought about the modern sensitivity to Helen Campbell Bannerman's 'little Black Sambo' – not, in fact, about Africa at all, but set in India and virtually without racist taint if read truly rather than simply reacted to.[3] However, we may not have explored the way in which an entire set of novels from the 1920s preconditioned Western readers to certain responses where Africa was concerned: now forgotten books such as Maran's *Batouala*, Gaston Joseph's *Koffi*, Delavignette's *Toum*, or Southon's *Yellow Napoleon*. Nor may we have seen the relationship of Graham Green's *Heart of the Matter*, or even the work of G. A. Henty, H. Rider Haggard and John Buchan, to the 'more serious' work of Conrad in *Heart of Darkness*.

The origin of stereotypes which Asia shares with Africa is the need for writers to fit their stories into literary presuppositions. Some very great works of literature may support the worst prejudices, whether intentionally or through persistent misapprehensions by generations of readers. Indeed, literature is not to be judged by its 'fairness' to the people who populate its pages, and truly great literature read by simple minds may fail utterly even when the intent is to communicate a sense of common humanity. Conrad, in particular, is so full of sub-texts that even the most attentive reader may, at times, miss his point. If, today, we respond rather differently to the prevailing (and fashionable) melancholy of Geothe's *Sorrows of Young Werther*, how are we to understand the intention of the artist in, say, Henri Fauconnier's *Soul of Malaya*? Where there is a body of critical literature, by which we may find our way into the culture for which a work of art was intended, we may understand in a fuller sense, but what of those readers who cannot read Goethe – or Kipling – in the context of their time or in the original language, and who take immediate stereotypes to heart? And what of those authors who, like Fauconnier, Scott or Clavell, lack critical texts and commentaries by which the less attentive might be led to understand what the authors truly intended (or rather what a modern critic believes they truly intended)? If it is true that the Japanese and the French dream of different matters, or that Japanese and American pornography are concerned with different brutalities, how is a Western reader actually to use Western fiction, or more difficult yet, to apply Western translation of an Eastern text?[3]

In Africa one begins with Babar, the king of the elephants. In Asia perhaps one begins with Tin-tin, that never-ageing Belgian reporter whose creator, Hergé, may have introduced more modern-day European children to the Himalayas than any other writer. One then moves through Kipling's *Jungle Book*, Ian Fleming's 'James Bond' and the adventure tales of John Masters. At some point one reaches that which the academy deems 'literature'. The stereotypes become muted, the colours run and the sense of complexity increases; yet we, as readers, may find that, despite all intention, *Passage to India* leaves us unattracted to Indians, and that John Hersey's *A Single Pebble* suggests to a reader not Chinese dedication, sensitivity and humanity, but Chinese single-mindedness, disregard for life and fatalism. The stereotypes are within us: the literature all too often merely feeds those we wish fed. How many children recognise that Babar is a socialist king?

This need to find in what we read support for what we wish to believe is hardly unusual. There is an imperialism of the mind which is fed by what it sucks up, and even authors with the best of intentions may fall foul of those nearly unconscious and generally unexamined needs. Books which are 'authentic' may not be what most readers seek. What is the difference between Kipling's Mowgli and 'Jungle Jim' Corbett? What is the continuum through a Mark Derby, a David Dodge and a Gavin Black (all thriller writers) to Anthony Burgess, Han Suyin or Paul Theroux (all 'serious' writers), other than having Malaysia in common as a geographical focus? How does one come to comprehend that an image may take on the force of truth, even replace a truth? How may one read Camões as the epic poet of the Portuguese empire without diminishing Asia? How may one read Camoes against Asia without diminishing him? These questions cannot be answered here, but they must be asked by the reader as each essay is examined.

This book attempts to explore only one of the major sources of written Western stereotypes of Asian cultures. There are many others – those ports of entry which remain unvisited here. There is the vast body of missionary literature, by which missionology took shape and through which those who had dedicated themselves to helping others sought to justify man's ways to God. There is the enormous burden of exploration, adventure and travel writing, which, by its very nature, falsifies since no traveller cares to return without a good story to tell. Even the journals of early explorers, though taken to be historical sources, distorted that which was recorded: Pigafetta, who sailed with Magellan, asserted the existence of an island named Aruchete, in the East Indies, though he knew its inhabitants (whom he described as being a cubit high, and having ears so large that they used one as a pillow and the other as a blanket when they slept) only from the memory of a woodcut he had seen in a German cathedral. Vasco da Gama, expecting to find Christian churches in South Asia, insisted that a Hindu temple in Calicut was evidence that Christians had passed that way. The very map of the world was shaped to stereotypes: the Near East, Middle East and Far East being near, middle and far primarily with respect to an island off the coast of Western Europe. Artists first saw South Pacific islands in terms of the *beau sauvage,* and contemporary canons of the picturesque controlled how they depicted native cultures, the *karst* formations of China or the bazaars of India. The seraglio, the slave girl, the culture of the Persians or of the Khmer, all were transmuted by the artist's special talents into new, intense images for the West.[4] When a Western readership first encountered Montesquieu's *Persian Letters* (published anonymously in 1721), it read these 'letters' as a commentary on the West, just as Toqueville intended his *Democracy in America* to be a commentary on contemporary France. When Montesquieu showed how intelligent and rapacious men could always find excuses for limiting liberties, he and his readers knew he was using a fictional Persia to comment upon Europe; yet within a century his tales were taken as being true as well for the land from which the letters were said to have originated. They thus became a 'source' for entry-level knowledge on the Middle East.

Nor did 'scientific' writers escape from applying stereotypes to Asian cultures. Anthropologists, finding static culture necessary to their mode of study, and attempting to account for the rapid submission of entire populations to Western rule, described a 'primitive mentality', or wrote broadly of *How Natives Think* – the title of Lucien Levy-Bruhl's influential work, first published in French in 1910 – and thus encouraged the assumption that all Africans, all Chinese or all Malays were alike. The first Asian displays in Western museums, the first attempt to represent Indian art, the first labels placed on New Guinean pudenda flaps when displayed in London,

[7]

B

the cup of tea by the fireside and the firecracker at Guy Fawkes night or Independence Day, each reinforced loosely-held, little examined views of Asian societies. Taken together, such scratches on the Western mind remained at the periphery, untended, almost unconscious motes swimming before the reader as he first took up *The Good Earth, the Bridge Over the River Kwai* or Lafcadio Heran to enter for the first time what the reader believed to be China, Burma or Japan.[5] In so simple, so complex, ways Western images of Asia were shaped.[6] Here, therefore, in this volume a body of writers seek to examine how one very important strand – literary fiction – contributed to those images.[7]

R. W. W.

Some popular European images of Asia, especially of the Muslim world and of India, are very old and are derived from periods of Eastern strength and dynamism *vis-à-vis* the West. But most of the literary images addressed in this volume emerged in the long period during which Europe first sought and then achieved domination of Asia. The stories which bore them were by-products of the historical processes of exploration, trade and conquest; of imperial administration and foreign residence; and of other forms of European and American assertiveness over Asia and Asians which have characterised the modern era.

Eventually, most of Asia was colonised outright, and much of the rest was made subject to a powerful Western presence. Unequal treaties governed relations between Western countries and Thailand and China, and along the China coast Westerners were privileged occupants of Treaty Ports; Macao was a Portuguese colony, Hong Kong a British one. The British were, in fact, everywhere: India (including present-day Pakistan and Bangladesh); Ceylon (Sri Lanka); Burma; Malaya, Sarawak (of the White Rajahs) and North Borneo (now combined in Malaysia) and Singapore. The Dutch held the massive Indies (now Indonesia); the French, Indo-China; and the Americans, the Philippines, which they acquired from Spain in 1898. From 1897 Germany too claimed an Asian sphere of influence. In understanding this period of near total European ascendency, and its literature, it is important to remember that as Westerners took in Asia, they observed it, judged it and reduced it to cliches and stereotypes from a perspective of singular strength and privilege and, until rather late in the game, largely unexamined confidence. The West's penetration of Asia was thorough, and, for Asians, impossible to reciprocate.

Asia thus became the stage for episodes of modern Western history.

Western fiction set in Asia recounts these episodes, and fantasies of them, in tales of conquest and of bending East to West; in trivial stories of the petty worlds of overseas Europeans; and of much in between. In them, Europeans and Americans move among Asians with relative ease and affluence, as did many of the authors (and Tintin, for that matter), embodying the power of the dominant races – even if, like George Orwell, this disgusted them. What is more, through fiction and fictionalised accounts of travel abroad vast numbers of 'stay-at-homers' could participate vicariously as Europe embraced the world. Donald F. Lach and Theodore Nicholas Foss tell us that even in the seventeenth century: 'The literary man could travel from Calicut to Peru, to Zipangu without leaving his chair.' Later, story books by G. A. Henty, and scores of others, prepared young Englishmen to join in the great enterprise of subduing and ruling vast Asian (and African) populations. As Edward W. Said has asserted persuasively, imperialism has shaped our fictions of Asia.

This is reflected not only in the range of stereotypes depicting Asians as cruel and treacherous, childlike and, as Robin Jared Lewis writes, 'inherently unable to rule their own lives', even if possessed of a kind of medieval nobility (images which made taking up the White Man's Burden seem heroic) but also in common literary themes. One of the most familiar is the contrast and tension between a place or state of order and safety, on the one hand (the West, home, the settled colony, the garrison, the club and the company of 'one's own kind') and a troubled hinterland, on the other (the East, far from home, the frontier, the native world, 'out there' and, of course, 'them'). Crossing from one to the other often rewards protagonists with conquest, praise, wealth and sexual gratification, but doing so is also dangerous, confusing and sometimes disillusioning. A vast segment of this literature involves the exploration of Asian interiors – whether they be real frontiers, like Kim's adventures with British and Russian spies in the 'the mountains' in Kipling's *Kim*; mystical ones, like Adela Quested's unnerving encounter with the 'inarticulate world' of the Marabar caves in Forster's *Passage to India*; or metaphysical ones, like Joseph Knecht's apprenticeship with Elder Brother in the Bamboo Grove in Hesse's *The Glass Bead Game*. Or they could be sexual explorations, sometimes gloriously fulfilling but more often in these stories unaffectionate, trivial and tragic. As Alec Waugh observed in *Hot Countries*, the real romance of modern Asia (he wrote in 1930 and specifically of Malaya) involved not men and women, but work; work aimed at developing 'a strange and hostile country into a happy and prosperous dependency.'

Western fiction about Asia reveals that many of these explorations were superficial. In the Philippines, as Morton J. Netzorg shows, American fiction seldom rose above mass-market adventures and romances. And Milton Osborne describes the French as repulsed by, and otherwise indifferent to, the Vietnamese. Thus, there are plenty of cliché-ridden yarns of conquest, adventure, lust, booty and espionage in the many and strange lands of the East that fail, as D. N. Lammers points out with respect to Japan, to 'take Asia seriously'. But, as these essays also reveal, there are many that do not.

Ultimately, Asia gave domineering Westerners much to brood about. On one level there was the dark side of Western behaviour in Asia: the expansionist, acquisitive and racist urges depicted by Dekker (Multatuli), Forster, Orwell and many others. At another level, positive admiration and self-doubt. arose in response to the apparently superior virtues of Asian religions and ways. Not surprisingly, deeper and more complex Western responses occurred when Europeans confronted Asia's older, culturally dominant civilisations in India and China, and, for the Dutch, Java. China, with its rational and durable civic philosophy, its size and complexity, and its refined, civilised arts (and, as Jonathan D. Spence notes, its very opacity to would-be knowers) has drawn serious Western minds to thought – and literature – for centuries. And judging from Western fiction, India, multifarious and overwhelming India, has thrown up to Western observers the richest variety of alternative spiritual visions, and has most often provoked crises of personal and cultural identity. As Ainslie T. Embree tells us, there are many spiritual 'searchers' among the Western characters in modern novels of India. But it is in turn of the century *Kim* that the question of identity arising from the interpenetration of East and West is raised most powerfully, as Kipling's Irish-born, Indian-bred boy hero, at once a 'sahib' yet just as fully 'native' must ask himself: 'Who is Kim?' and 'What is Kim?'.

By the time of *Kim*'s arrival – the peak of high colonialism and the high tide of racial exclusivity throughout the colonial world – East and West had long since met and begun mixing at many levels. Westerners often found the results unattractive and depicted them so in stories: Kipling's Hurree Babu (of *Kim*) is among the few Westernised Indians shown favourably in the fiction of British India; Europeans who 'went native' were scorned throughout Asia. As for Eurasians, the offspring of East–West liaisons, they are invariably depicted in stories as weak, cowardly and inferior, as in Somerset Maugham's Borneo story, 'The Yellow Streak'. Inevitably, however, some individuals of mixed Asian–Western descent and culture became writers of fiction themselves, and added their special insider's perspective to our catalogue of literary images of Asia. Among those discussed in this book are the prolific Han Suyin, for her novels of Nepal (Luree Miller), Malaya and the overseas Chinese (Jonathan D. Spence) and Hong Kong (C. Mary Turnbull), and the *Indische* writers of the Netherlands Indies, Maria Dermout and E. Du Perron (James R. Rush).

A more important insider's perspective, in the long run, is that of Western-educated Asian writers. Morton J. Netzorg introduces us to the Filipino literary man and nationalist Jose Rizal, who wrote novels in Spanish in the late nineteenth century, and to later Filipino writers whose work is entirely in English. And in the essays by Luree Miller, Ainslee T. Embree, C. Mary Turnbull and Jonathan D. Spence, we meet other modern Asians as interpreters of their own societies through English-language literature; the Indians R. J. Narayan and Bhabani Bhattacharya, for example, and the Hong Kong Chinese Timothy Mo. For many writers of fiction today in India, Malaysia, Singapore and the Philippines, English is the preferred medium, the novel and short story the preferred forms – direct consequences of East meeting West in former colonies. (The facts that modern Indonesian writers overwhelmingly choose to write in the national language and that the vast majority of Western literature about Indonesia was until recently written in Dutch account for the dearth of literary images of Indonesia in the English-reading world; and this, in turn, helps to explain the relative invisibility of this huge tropical Asian society in the Western awareness.)

The emergence of this new genre of Western-language literature in Asia is not wholly a post-colonial phenomenon; but it is largely so, occurring as modern Asian nation states assert themselves ever more effectively over the once overbearingly powerful West. In this literature the old tension between East and West, between safe havens and alluring but dangerous frontiers, is often internalised as conflict between generations, between (Asian) tradition and (Western-driven but also Asian) modernity. But as Embree points out, many of the older interpretations of Asia survive, indeed still thrive, in these modern stories. Now, however, the old cliches may cut many ways. In the play *M. Butterfly* (1988) by David Hwang, a Chinese-American playwright, the classic tragedy of an East–West love affair is reversed when the Chinese mistress to a Western diplomat ultimately reveals herself to be a cunning and consummately manipulative *he*.

Thus, while older literary stereotypes of Asia and Asians persist, as reincarnated in popular spy fiction, Rambo movies and *Noble House*-type blockbusters, new and more complex visions constantly appear alongside them, adding subtle and confusing designs, and cumulatively truer ones, to the mosiac of literary images we call upon when we think of Asia.

A caveat to the reader: although this is a book about fictions, only one of its authors, Robin Jared Lewis, is a student of literature, formally speaking. Luree Miller is a biographer and travelwriter who lived for seven years in the Indian subcontinent; Morton J. Netzorg, who was born and raised in the Philippines, is a bookseller and bibliophile. The rest of us are historians.

J. R. R.

Notes

1 See Wai-lim Yip, *Ezra Pound's Cathay*, Princeton, 1969, p. 61.

2 See an able examination of *European and African Stereotypes in Twentieth-Century Fiction*, London, 1980, by Sarah L. Milbury-Steen, which provides parallel support for some of the broad conclusions expressed here.

3 See Nicolas Kiessling, 'The nightmare, melancholy and creativity', *Dreamworks: An Interdisciplinary Quarterly*, IV, summer 1981, 284-7. Eugene Eoyang prepared a superb statement about the problem of translation in relation to China for The Asia Society series.

4 For example, on the problem of Western perceptions of India as seen through art, consult Partha Mitter, *Much Maligned Monsters: History of European Reactions to Indian Art*, Oxford, 1977.

5 Harold R. Isaacs, who attended the seminar in which this project was launched has written perceptively, and in the end pessimistically, of this process in *Scratches on Our Minds*, reissued as *Images of Asia: American Views of China and India*, New York, 1962.

6 There are other books which attempt this task in a different or more limited fashion. The most useful are D. C. R. A. Goonetilleke, *Developing Countries in British Fiction*, London, 1977; M. M. Mahood, *The Colonial Encounter: A Reading of Six Novels*, London, 1977; Martin Green, *Dreams of Adventure , Deeds of Empire*, New York, 1979; Alan Sandison, *The Wheel of Empire: A Study of the Imperial Idea in some Late Nineteenth and Early Twentieth Century Fiction*, London 1967; and Wallace Hildick, *Children and Fiction*, London 1970. On children's literature see also Bob Dixon, *Catching Them Young: I. Sex, Race and Class in Children's Fiction* and II. *Political Ideas in Children's Fiction*, London, 1977, which though strident, contains many good ideas; Lai Nam Chen, *Images of Southeast Asia in Children's Fiction*, Singapore, 1981; and Richard Usborne, *Clubland Heroes*, London 1953. Jonah Raskin, *The Mythology of Imperialism*, New York, 1971 provides a good essay on Forster (and a bad one on Kipling). Country-specific studies include Brijen K. Gupta, *India in English Fiction, 1800–1980*, Metuchen, N. J., 1973; Benita Parry, *Delusions and Discoveries: Studies on India in the British Imagination, 1880–1930*, London, 1972; Allen J. Greenberger, *The British Image of India: A Study in the Literature of Imperialism*, London, 1969; and – one of the few books to look at the writings of missionaries as literature – Helen G. Trager, *Burma through Alien Eyes: Missionary Views of the Burmese in the Ninetenth Century*, New York, 1966. Other relevant titles, especially on Japan and China, are cited in the essays on those literatures.

7 At various stages Christopher S. Gray and Datus Smith helped with editorial chores. The manuscript was prepared for publication by The Asia Society, but the society abandoned both its publication branch and its national councils shortly before the manuscript, at that time in a much different form, was submitted for approval. Consequently, some of the twenty participants in the original project had their essays published elsewhere and some few of the original contributions were never revised for publication. Subsequently James Rush took the project in hand and completed the revision of the manuscript in its present form.

CHAPTER TWO

Images of Asia and Asians
in European fiction, 1500–1800

Donald F. Lach and Theodore Nicholas Foss

> In Xamdu did Cublai Can build a stately Palace encompassing sixteen miles of plaine ground with a wall wherein are fertile Meddowes, pleasant springs, delightfull Streames and all sorts of beasts of chase and game, and in the middest thereof sumptuous house of pleasure, which may be removed from place to place.

Reading these words from Samuel Purchas's *His Pilgrimage* (1613), Samuel Taylor Coleridge fell into a short, deep, drug-induced sleep and, upon waking, composed his famous poem 'Kubla Khan' (1798) in a frenzy of inspiration. Many other writers of earlier generations, after consulting travelogues, were similarly moved to use the East as backdrops for their compositions and to decorate their fictitious characters and imaginary places with mysterious, enchanting or comical names of Asian origin. To writers of fiction, the travel books offered between two covers ideas and sources on many peoples and places. The literary man could travel from Calicut, to Peru, to Zipangu without leaving his chair.

The first of the great travel collections to include substantial information on Asia, the medieval overland travels as well as the voyages of discovery, was compiled by Giovanni Battista Ramusio, a Venetian humanist and civil servant. His *Delle navigationi et viaggi (Of Navigations and Voyages)* (1550–56) in three huge volumes became the model for subsequent travel collections and a rich storehouse of material for authors of imaginative literature to draw upon. Richard Hakluyt, the Oxford geographer and close student of Ramusio's work, brought together an English treasury of materials on Asia in the second edition of his *Principall Navigations* (1600). This immense anthology, called by Froude 'the epic of the English nation,' was reprinted and amplified substantially by Samuel Purchas in *Hakluytus Posthumous, or Purchas His Pilgrimes* (1625). While Hakluyt and Purchas collected in England, the De Bry family put together in Frankfurt a multi-volume travel collection entitled *Collectiones peregrinationum in Indiam orienalem et occidentalum (Collection of Travels in the East and West Indies)* (1590–1634). The illustrations in the De Bry collection, supplemented by the maps and engravings in the atlases being prepared by other printers, provided literati of the seventeenth century with a visual and semi-realistic acquaintance with the places, peoples and prospects of the East.

From the middle of the sixteenth century to the middle of the seventeenth century the writers of Catholic Europe had available in handy sizes the collections issued by the Society of Jesus of the letters sent to Europe by its missionaries in the East. With the passage of time Jesuit scholars and others prepared histories of the Christian mission in Asia based on the Jesuit letters in which serious attention was paid to indigenous religious practices and social customs, subjects sometimes not treated in the travel accounts of merchants and sailors. Fresh material on Asia in Dutch, German, English, French and Latin collections and histories poured from the presses in the seventeenth and eighteenth centuries.[1] Latin translations of certain Chinese classics were published in Paris in 1685; the Sanskrit classics did not begin to be translated until almost a century later. A miscellany drawn from the abundant materials sent to Europe by the Jesuits in China was published by J.B. Du Haldde in his encyclopedic *Description géographique, historique, chronologique, politique de d'Empire de la Chine et de la Tartarie Chinoise* (1735). In the eighteenth century the documentation on China available in Europe exceeded greatly in bulk and quality the information published on Japan, India and the rest of Asia. The 'Sinomania' of eighteenth-century Europe was inspired by a plethora of written works as well as by a craze for Chinese *objets d'art*.

To Europe before 1500 Asia was a world apart, a region of magic, mystery and opulence. India, though it had never been completely isolated from European contacts, was none the less perceived as a land peopled by Amazons, monsters and devils, as well as by wise and ascetic brahmins. Through the medieval romance the deeds of Alexander the Great, both real and fictional, brought to Europe additional examples of the wonders of India. Indian stories and moral tales meanwhile migrated overland to Europe through the languages of the Middle East. As they travelled westwards the themes, plots and characters of the originals altered to appeal to local beliefs, customs and tastes; in Europe they were incorporated into song, drama and story, often in Christian or European disguise. The ethical messages in the tales of India were also acclimatised and incorporated into mystery and miracle plays, sermon books and the 'mirrors for princes'. Medieval legend placed Prester John in India and made him an ally of the Christian world in its struggle against Islam.

Until the thirteenth century the rest of Asia, unlike India, was practically unknown in Europe; only vague references to the Serica or Sinica of the Romans helped to keep alive a sketchy knowledge of China's existence. The Mongol invasions of Europe in 1240–41 opened overland relations which brought to Europe the revelation of Cathay. The facts about Cathay related by Marco Polo and Sir John Mandeville were often as marvellous as the fables about India. Little wonder that the Europeans of the Renaissance were inclined to confuse such authentic travel accounts with the fictional romances in prose and poetry which were so popular then! Confusion sometimes became befuddlement, for the travellers often embroidered their factual accounts with traditional fancies so as to make their exploits more colourful, while European writers of romance inserted authentic materials into their fictional writings to make them more credible.

The romance is the literary form which best illustrates the transition from the mythical India of the Middle Ages to a more realistic Asia. Medieval stories of chivalry and love were broadened in the crusading era (eleventh to fourteenth centuries) to include characters, scenes and information from outside Europe. The Cathay of the medieval travellers was introduced into the Italian romance of the fifteenth century by Matteo Maria Boiardo, the author of a long romantic poem, *Orlando Innamorato (Orlando in Love)*, based on the epic of Roland, the model chivalric hero. In Boiardo's hands, Cathay and the Orient were used to provide a secular and pagan setting for the exploits of Roland, the Christian knight. Boiardo invented the character called Angelica, the pagan princess of Cathay and an immoral adventuress, who conquers in the story the chaste heart of Roland. His European and Asian characters are distinguished from each other not by language or appearance but by their pagan and Christian beliefs. Being pagans, his Oriental characters need not exhibit Christian virtues or Islamic perfidy. They are rich, warlike and secular in their interests. Lodovico Ariosto, who continued Boiardo's incomplete romance in his *Orlando Furioso* (definitive edition published in 1532) brought Cathay and Angelica into the broader stream of European romance.

In the Iberian peninsula the history of the modern prose romance of chivalry begins in 1508 with the publication of the anonymous *Amadis De Gaula (Amadis of Gaul)*. Over the following century fifty new chivalresque works appeared in Spanish and Portuguese. While Amadis ventured only as far east as Turkey, the *Emperor Calrimudo*

(1520) of Joao de Barros, who was later to become the most eminent historian of Asia, sings the praises of the Portuguese conquests in India and foresees the opening of the distant East Indies and China by the valour of Portuguese arms. In the meantime, Ariosto was adding information on Asia from contemporary maps and geographical descriptions to his *Orlando.* In these early romances Asia is still a land of rare gems, sumptuous living, and the home of magic and the healing arts. It is a place of escape, somewhere between the real and imaginary worlds, where marvels and extraordinary deeds might be expected to take place, or where there might even flourish a community of the sort idealised by Sir Thomas More in his *Utopia* (1516), or by Tommaso Campanello in his *City of the Sun* (1602).

The sensual and profligate character of the romances stimulated churchmen and moralists of the latter half of the sixteenth century to denounce them. In later incarnations, such as Luis Barahona de Soto's *Las lágrimas de Angélica (The Tears of Angelica)* (1581), Boiardo's tempestuous Angelica becomes an unhappy and moral young woman plagued with misfortune. Cervantes, on the other hand, denounces the romances of chivalry, except for a few, and in *Don Quixote* (1608) asks:

> What mind, that is not wholly barbarous and uncultured, can find pleasure in reading of how a great tower full of knights sails away across the sea like a ship with a fair wind, and will be tonight in Lombardy and tomorrow morning in the land of Prester John of the Indies, or some other that Ptolemy never described nor Marco Polo saw?

A semi-factual literature extolling or commenting upon the opening of Asia appeared in parallel to the sixteenth-century romances of chivalry. The Spanish literary caravel of Bartolome de Torres Naharro called *Propalladia* (1517) was designed to bring through comedies news of distant lands and peoples to a public eager for victories and spectacles. Rabelais's satirical romance of *Gargantua and Pantagruel* (published between 1532 and 1562) takes Panurge and Pantagruel on an imaginary north-west voyage to Cathay, a utopia to the east of India where he locates the Oracle of the Divine Bottle. In 1577 Christopher the Armenian published the *Peregrinaggio (Travels)*, or travels of the three princes of Serendip, in which their stories of happy accidents are laid in 'the golden isle' of Ceylon, a place which is suitably remote, wealthy and exotic.[2] In his epic *Sepmaines* (1578,1584) Guillaume de Salluste, Sieur du Bartas, celebrates Asia as the homeland of humanity and of infinite varieties of beasts and plants. Bernardino Balbi, in his long Italian poem called *La nautica* (1585), denounces as barbaric some of the religious and social customs of the Hindus; and Guillaume Bouchet in his French *Les Serees (The Chinese)* (1584–1608) expresses an opinion commonly held in Europe that the warriors of the East are weak, timid and cowardly, and too inclined to depend on overwhelming numbers rather than on individual acts of courage. But it was also Bouchet who had one of his discussants argue that Asians should be painted the colour they are and with the features they possess. India appears in the *Faustbuch* (1587) as the earthly paradise and in Christopher Marlowe's *Tamburlaine the Great* (1590) as a golden land peopled by warlike, fratricidal and lustful hordes. Conversely, George Puttenham, the father of English literary criticism, credits the high civilisations of Asia with possessing sophisticated poetic traditions of their own and with having invented the pattern poem. These examples show, as do the histories and other factual literature, that the medieval view of Asia persisted, but with realistic shadings being added on the basis of more recent information.

The eclipse of the romance of chivalry in the Baroque era was followed by the rise of the heroic – gallant romance and the novel. *I l magno Vitei (The Great Vitei)* (1597) of Ludovico Arrivabene was the first lengthy prose romance to celebrate Asian rulers and their nations. Vitei, the 'first king of China', is portrayed as the exemplar of the excellent prince and the perfect captain who rules over the most virtuous nation ever known. In following his career, Arrivabene comments on Vitei's military exploits against China's neighbours, his inventions, his learning and his virtue. Arrivabene sprinkles the landscape of Asia with natural marvels, both real and fabulous. But more than anything else this Italian homily expresses the view, later to become more popular, that Europe has much to learn from China, the model society.

Moral issues about overseas expansion were raised by the clerics, literati and scholars of Europe from the earliest years of the sixteenth century. Dramatists and poets warned that the riches of the East were breeding hatred, corruption and weakness among the Portuguese themselves. The youth of the nation was dying uselessly for pepper and glory in distant lands or in shipwrecks caused by the avaricious overloading of the vessels returning from the East. Two genres of Portuguese literature developed in the latter half of the sixteenth century which celebrated the overseas military triumphs and maritime exploits of the nation; these siege dramas and shipwreck narratives also contained messages to the people at home of the heavy costs in life and in moral living to the Portuguese in Asia. While in the East, the best of Christians often became rapacious, cruel and selfish. Missionaries and other churchmen inveighed vainly against the deprivation of their charges in Asia and warned that the moral fibre of the nation was being steadily weakened.[3]

Fernao Mendes Pinto (1509–83) was one Portuguese who learned from twenty years of personal experience in Asia about its hardships and temptations. In 1557 he returned to Lisbon and five years later began writing the account of his adventures in the East. The composition of his *Peregrinacao* (Travels) went slowly for he was old and tired and was frequently interrupted by others who consulted him as a source on the Portuguese empire. His book was completed by the time of his death but it was not printed until 1614. No work about Asia had a greater impact on seventeenth-century European literature than Pinto's reminiscences. It appeared in two Portuguese editions and in seven Spanish, three French, two Dutch, two German and three English translations. While its contents have a strong base in fact, it was generally read for its entertainment value and for its ethical message. Some of Pinto's contemporaries accepted his story as authentic; others held that it was fantasy and 'too good to be true'.

Pinto's *Peregrinacao* is, in fact, an amalgam of truth and fiction. Where his memory failed or his good sense commanded, Pinto did not hesitate to complete a picture from his lively imagination. He endeavoured in this way to provide the reader with his general impressions of Asia's wealth, cities, peoples and customs; he also sought to reveal the personal moral dilemma which he experienced during the course of his travels. He was repelled by the actions of his fellow Christians and by their violence towards innocent Asians. Greed, avarice and pride combined to drive the Portuguese to more venal sins. He let his readers know also that the Asians were hospitable, charitable, God-fearing and moral. The example of Asia, as he saw it, might help Europe to confront its own delinquency and to begin its own moral rehabilitation.

Both Arrivabene and Pinto saw China with its unmatchable historical longevity, its highly organised society and its exemplary princes as models of governance and lay morality. Martin Opitz, the father of German Baroque poetry, wrote during the Thirty Years War *Lob des Krieges-Gottes (Praise of the Gods of War)* (1628), his major poem, in which he avers that it was Mars who sent Europeans over the sea route to China's rich shore where porcelains, printed books and artillery are made. But even while Opitz celebrated China's peaceful technical achievements, the War God was beginning to split the Middle Kingdom apart. The Manchus began in the 1620s to attack the ailing Ming rulers and the civil war in China spread until the dynasty fell in 1644. Mars was also at work in Japan, whose Tokugawa rulers had driven out the Spaniards and the Portuguese by

1640 and left the Dutch as their only European contact.

News of the Manchu Conquest was relayed to Europe by the letters and books of the Jesuits in China, such as Marino Martini, and by the reports of Dutch merchants and emissaries, such as John Nieuhof.[4] While many observers in Europe deplored the victory of the barbarous Manchus over the civilised Chinese of the Ming, some of the German writers of novels and picaresque romances were inclined to pay it little heed or to congratulate the Manchus.

The first European novel about the Manchu conquest was Christoph Hagdorn's *Aeyquan* (1670), a courtly romance in German played against a Chinese background. Aeyquan, Hagdorn's hero, is an Asian knight errant and son of the Mogul emperor of India who supposedly helped the Manchus capture Peking and received as a reward an important post at the Ch'ing court. The historical account essentially follows the *De bello Tartarico (On the Tartar War)* (1654) of Father Martini with additions from Dutch materials.[5] Written in a courtly and heroic style, this Baroque novel borrowed its form from Gautier de la Calprenedes's *Cassandra* (1642–45), a classic French novel in the heroic style. Hagdorn's work, however, brought to this genre the idea of using *contemporary* events in remote places as the backdrop for chivalric deeds and romantic love. Compared to Hagdorn's, the depiction of China in Arrivabene's *Il magno Vitei* is flat, dull and without contemporary meaning. To Hagdorn, the Manchu conquest was a victory over a dynasty which deserved its unhappy fate.

Hagdorn's *Aeyquan* became a prototype for several courtly novels prepared by other authors writing in German during the last years of the seventeenth century. In *Der asiatische Onogambo* (1673) of Eberhard Werner Happel, an Asian prince who becomes emperor of the Manchu dynasty after many heroics, tribulations and love sagas, invites the Jesuit Adam Schall to instruct him about his new empire. The triumph of the Christian mission in China, casually remarked upon by Happel, soon became the subject of a huge novel by Rudolf Gasser, a Capuchin father of Switzerland. In his *Aussforderung (Challenge)* of 1686–89, Gasser depicts the Chinese as being quite different from Europeans in colour, language, dress and beliefs – an emphasis he undoubtedly received from his perusal of the Jesuit sources on which his allegorical novel is based.

Gasser's contemporaries in writing novels about China turned away from his idealised utopia to a more realistic and worldly depiction. Daniel Caspar von Lohenstein, a leading author of the courtly romance, included in his *Arminius* (1689–90) an encyclopedia of curious knowledge; this novel celebrates the valiant prince, criticises the irrational beliefs of the Brahmins in cows and the transmigration of souls, deprecates their practice of selling holy water from the Ganges, and accounts for the extreme enmity of the Manchus and Chinese by reference to their differing environmental backgrounds and to the stars which guide them.[6]

Less pretentious is the Baroque novel of Heinrich Anselm von Ziegler called *Asiatische Banise (Banise, the Asiatic)*, though it is likewise based on research in ancient and contemporary sources. The author of the first European novel set in Pegu (Burma), Ziegler in his note to the reader lists as his main source Francisci's collection of materials on the East Indies. While he set out to celebrate the valiant and heroic Banise, it was Chaumigrem, the arch-villain, who appealed to readers. From the viewpoint of German literary history, Ziegler's was the last of the Baroque novels planned on a lavish scale and stuffed with relevant and irrelevant erudition. It was also the last of the heroic – gallant novels set in Asia.

The Manchu conquest, and Martini's description of it, was dramatic enough to inspire a number of European playwrights. While visiting the Low Countries in 1658, Samuel Chappezeau, a French author, published at Leyden a tragic comedy called *Armetzar ou les amis ennemis (Armetzar or the Friendly Enemies)*. The first French drama laid in China, *Armetzar's* plot is based in part on Chappezeau's long novel entitled *Ladice ou les victoires du Grand Tamerlane (Ladice or the Victories of Tamerlane the Great)* (Paris, 1650), that centres on the friendship between the son of Tamerlane, the Mongol conqueror of the fourteenth century, and the son of the Chinese emperor. The emperor himself is depicted as being kindly and well-meaning but ineffective in war. Chappezeau's work conveys the impression that China is not an impersonal and idealised state but one in which changing events affect the lives of real human beings just as they do elsewhere.

The tragedy of the Manchu conquest likewise appealed to contemporary Dutch playwrights. The great poet Joost van den Vondel (1587–1679) published in 1667 his drama in verse called *Zunqchin*. Here he dramatises the suffering of the Ch'ung-cheng emperor in the last hours before his suicide. While Vondel worked on his play, a younger Amsterdamer, Antonides van der Goes, wrote a similar tragedy called *Trazil of overrompelt-Sina (Trazil, or China taken by Surprise)* and published it in 1685. In both dramas the message is conveyed that Peking, like ancient Troy, fell to predatory conquerors who used treachery, betrayal and deceit to win the city. Writing at a time when the Dutch Empire in Asia was growing and flourishing, both poets warn that no empires endure forever and that their successes and failures are governed by fortune rather than by man.

[21]

The English dramatists, who were likewise inspired by the empire their country was building in Asia, also brought to their public a message of the universal significance of contemporary events in Asia. In 1676 both Elkanah Settle and John Dryden published plays based on current happenings. In Settle's *The Conquest of China by the Tartars*, the Manchus and Chinese were not engaged in a battle of barbarism against civilisation but in courtly and aristocratic intrigue for control of the empire. Dryden's *Aureng-Zebe* is a play about contemporary India, where British commercial interests and prospects were greater than elsewhere in Asia. Based on the English translation (1671) of Francois Bernier's *Historie de la dernière revolution des Etats du Grand Mogol (History of the Last revolution of the States of the Great Moghul)*, Dryden's rhymed drama set in Agra in 1600 depicts the Mogul emperor as a supremely kind, heroic and reflective ruler who deserves the empire which he governs.

English and French authors of romance were less inventive in the use they made of Asia than the Iberian and German writers of the seventeenth century. Perhaps this was so because they satisfied their public's taste for the curious by imaginary voyages into the cosmos, beneath the earth, into the Orient or to deserted islands. Domengo Gonsales, Bishop Godwin's *The Man in the Moone* (1638), descended from his lunar adventure to a mountain located in the terrestrial China near 'the high and mighty city of Pachin [Peking]' where he is entertained by a Mandarin and meets the Jesuit authority on China, Father Pantoja. *La terre australe connue* (1676) of Gabriel Foigny takes place in a totally imaginary Australia whose virtuous inhabitants are hermaphrodites. Foigny uses his imaginary people as rationalistic critics of the low moral and religious conditions obtaining in the bisexual societies of Europe and Asia. In similar fashion, F.M. Mission in his *Vogage de. . . Francois Leguat* (1707) used the Chinese community of Batavia on Java to argue his point that poverty can be eliminated by social solidarity; he describes their religious rites as background to his Protestant satire of the Catholic Church. Mission's fiction follows closely the popular accounts of real French travellers such as Mocquet, Dellon and Tavernier, as does that of Simon Tyssot de Patot. In Tyssot de Patot's imaginary *Vogages. . . de Jacques Masse*, Dellon's account of the Inquisition at Goa is used to launch a violent attack on the Catholic priesthood and to condemn the irrational tortures visited upon rational and tolerant Asians by the Portuguese.

The insatiable appetite for travel books on the East enabled a French opportunist to perpetrate a marvellous hoax. Taking the name George Psalmanazar, he posed first as a native Japanese and later as a more exotic Formosan. He composed a historical and geographical account of his assumed native land, *Description of Formosa* (1740), which included a mock alphabet and grammar. Here he depicts Formosa as a land rich in gold and silver, and under the governance of Japan. In great and fictitious detail, he fabricates elaborate religious rituals for the Formosans. His Formosans are indefatigable in labour, good soldiers who love war, loyal, industrious and cunning, truthful and disdainful of merchants. This literary spoof illustrates what an enterprising rogue perceived might be believed about Asia by the European of the early eighteenth century. While there were those who suspected him of being a charlatan, others engaged him to teach the Formosan language!

European writers of the seventeenth century also began to use Asian scenes and characters in their comedies. A farce attributed to Moliere called *Les Indes (The Indies)* was played at Paris in 1661. In the popular theatre of the French fairs and of the Italian comedy, burlesques of Oriental customs and beliefs began to appear more frequently in the century's last decades. At the *Comédie Française,* so popular with the dandies of Louis XIV's France, many spectacles were put on before lavish and exotic Oriental settings. Marc-Antoine Legrand in his satire *La Foire Saint-Laurent (The St. Laurent Fair)* (1709) had Indians, Chinese, Persians and Turks on the stage and in the chorus, and had Europeans disguise themselves in Oriental costumes. Through such vehicles the Romanesque Orient and the Oriental buffoon were brought into the French popular theatre. Between 1715 and 1775 at least twenty-one different plays appeared in France burlesquing Orientals and their customs.[7]

Most seventeenth-century and early eighteenth-century court pageants, ballets, harlequinades and dramas presented an opulent and confused image of Asia. Monkeys danced around Chinese porcelain columns, Japanese princes cavorted on stage with Indian knights. Such entertainments were extravagant fluffs depicting Asia as brittle, beautiful and frivolous. The popularity of chinoiserie in art helped to inspire the excesses of the authors and designers of such spectacles. While the trappings portrayed an imagined Asia, the underlying plots involved subjects of universal appeal, especially affairs of the heart. The gorgeous East was often chosen as a literary backdrop, as many authors admitted, because readers could be expected to suspend disbelief when the scene was laid far from home.

By 'setting the scene in a remote situation', Daniel Defoe, in his ever popular *The Life and Adventures of Robinson Crusoe* (1719), explored the theme of the European in his relation to men in the state of nature. Like his continental precursors in writing novels of seafaring adventure, shipwreck and life on a 'desert isle', Defoe utilised for his geography and local colour many of the available travel books. In *The Further Adventures of Robinson Crusoe*, published less than four months after the initial work, Defoe has his popular adventurer say:

> I must confess it seemed strange to me when I came home and heard our people say such fine things of the power, riches, glory, magnificence and trade of the Chinese, because I saw and knew that they were a contemptible herd or crowd of ignorant sordid slaves, subjected to a government qualified only to rule such a people.[8]

Defoe also deprecates Chinese military acumen, wonders how such a huge empire could be conquered by such 'contemptible fellows' as the Tartars (Manchus), and concludes by describing the Great Wall as a 'mighty nothing'.[9] Much of Defoe's anger was probably related to the anti-Asian feeling then being fomented by the English textile workers in their campaign against the imports from Asia. The author of *The Weavers' Complaint* (1719) put it this way:

> Ev'ry jilt of the town
> Gets a calico gown;
>
> . . . .
> 'Tis a test of the brains of the nation
> To neglect their own works,
> Employ pagans and Turks,
> And let foreign trumpery o'er spread 'em.

Many authors of the first half of the eighteenth century ignored or misunderstood the differences between the cultures of the Near and Far East. They lumped together various countries and labelled the lot 'the Orient'. Antoine Galland's (1646–1715) translation of *The Tales of the Thousand and One Nights* (1704–17), a collection of Near Eastern romantic fairy stories, sparked a fad for Oriental tales. Other authors composed tales in imitation of the Persian originals, but with little care for keeping peoples and cultures straight. One such author, Thomas Simon Gueulette, wrote a series of stories set in the most distant parts of Asia. His *Thousand and One Quarters of an Hour, or the Tartarian Tales; his Chinese Tales, or the Marvellous Adventures of the Mandarin Fum-Hoam;* and his *Sultans of Guzarat, or The Dreams of Men Awake (Mogul Tales)* drew from sources as varied as the Bible, contemporary Western novels, translations from European languages and Gueulette's own imagination.

Most Oriental romances, however, presented anything but an accurate depiction of the 'customs of the East'. The scores of collections which followed the Europeanised *The Tales of the Thousand*

and One Nights preserved an undifferentiated Asia peopled with stock characters: genii, magicians, captive maidens in seraglios, magnificent mandarins and autocratic sultans in settings of fabulous wealth. When the eighteenth-century European reader picked up a volume of Oriental tales he expected to be transported to a place of fantasy, a fairyland of stock exotica, where characters use elusive and quaintly overblown rhetoric and employ magic and enchantment liberally.

All this went on at a time when substantial and accurate information on Asia was being conveyed to the European reading public. The Jesuits portrayed China in their voluminous publications as a well-governed land of Confucian orthodoxy, home of the *sage chinois.* This view led many writers, such as the philosopher Leibniz or the free-thinker La Mothe Le Vayer (who remarked facetiously, 'Saint Confucius, pray for us') to compare European society unfavourably with a superior Chinese model. Jesuit works on the Confucian social order inspired various literary trends in Europe. Christoph Wieland's political novel *Der goldene Spiegel (The Golden Mirror)* (1772), a product of Enlightenment interest in rational government, enlightened despotism and Confucianism presented a model government in a fictitious and far away country – not China by name but China by inspiration. In some satirical didactic works, such as the numerous discourses by Voltaire, an Asian visitor – usually Chinese – is the mouthpiece through which the author highlights the failings of European life and civilisation. Tobias Smollett's *History and Adventures of an Atom* (1769), like Gilbert and Sullivan's *Mikado* of a century later, satirised public affairs in England by contrasting them with those in little-known Japan. Smollett detailed the metempsychosis of an atom which relates its former experiences in Japan. 'Many of the names and much of the matter' on Japan, Smollett admits, came from Engelbrecht Kaempfer's *History of Japan* (1727–28) through the massive *Modern Part of the Universal History,* which Smollett had helped to compile and edit.[10] He was particularly intrigued by the similar geographic and cultural relationships which insular England and Japan have to the Eurasiatic contin-ent.

Since so many letters, travelogues and reports had been sent back by Europeans who actually had travelled in Asia, it became almost inevitable that European authors would seize upon the idea of writing fictional letters by exotic 'outside' critics of European society. After all, there had been a number of Asian visitors who had travelled to the West, among them Japanese embassies of 1585 and 1614, envoys from Eastern princes, and converts such as the young Chinese Michael Shen-Futsung in the 1680s and Arcadius Hoang in 1720s.

The device of the fictive letter was popular from the late seventeenth century on as European authors used imaginary Easterners as correspondents: Marana's *Turkish Spy* (1687); Montesquieu's *Two Persians* (1721); the *Lettres chinoises* (1739) of J. B. Boyer, Marquis d'Argens; Elizabeth Hamilton's *Translations of the Letters of a Hindo Rajah* (1797). Many of the letters were attributed to Chinese: Horace Walpole's *A Letter from Xo-Ho, a Chinese Philosopher at London, to his friend Lien Chi at Pekin* (1957); Frederick the Great of Prussia's *Relation de Phihihu (The Account of Phihihu)* (1760), six satirical letters of a 'Chinese official' which lampoon among others, 'the Grand Lama of Rome'. The writers' fictitious epistles created an Asian commentator who had little of Asia almost as European as the society being criticised.

The Marquis d'Argen's Chinese in Paris, Sieou-tcheou by name, comments upon his own countrymen. With the *Lettres chinoise* the Chinese are characterised variously as being phlegmatic in temperament, litigious, afraid of the Japanese, as well as deists who pay great honour to men of learning. They are fond of playing tricks on travellers. The Chinese ideal of a pretty woman, he comments, is quite different from that of a European. In making this last observation Sieou-tcheou repeats the words of the Jesuits Le Comte and Du Halde almost verbatim:

> That which the Chinese chiefly admire, as making a perfect Beauty, is a large Forehead, short Nose, small Eyes, a Mouth middle sized, and Hair black, for they cannot bear to see it yellow or red; however there must be a certain Symmetry and Proportion between all the Parts to render them agreeable.[11]

Probably the most effective Asian critique produced was Oliver Goldsmith's *Citizen of the World: or Letters from a Chinese Philosopher Residing in London to His Friend in the East* (1762). Since Goldsmith's letters appeared originally in the periodical *Public Ledger*, over a two-year span, he had the opportunity to change the attitude of his Chinese commentator Lien Chi Altangi in response to the reception given the letters by readers of the early issues.[12] Goldsmith had read Voltaire's opinions of China, but almost all of his facts on Chinese subjects he derived from the Jesuit missionary works of Le Comte and Du Halde. Hardly a page was written without consulting these works.

Lien Chi Altangi observes in one letter that the English currently pride themselves on holding things Chinese in highest regard, although they are truly ignorant of even the most elementary information on China. He sees everywhere a Sinomania which he condemns as being vulgar and debasing to the spirit and subtlety of his culture. His taste was offended, as he relates in the story of his visit to the home of an English 'lady of distinction'. She expressed surprise at Lien Chi Altangi's lack of 'Chineseness':

> Lord (she said), have you nothing pretty from China about you; something that one does not know what to do with: I have got twenty things from China that are of no use in the world. Look at these jars, they are of the right pea-green: these are the furniture!
>
> Dear madam, said I, those, though they may appear fine in your eyes, are but paltry to a Chinese; but as they are useful utensils, it is proper they should have a place in every apartment.
>
> Useful! sir, replied the lady; sure you mistake, they are of no use in the world.
>
> What! are they not filled with an infusion of tea as in China? replied I.
>
> Quite empty and useless upon my honour, Sir.
>
> Then they are the most cumbrous and clumsy furniture in the world, as nothing is truly elegant but what unites use with beauty.
>
> .   .   .   .
>
> Pray, sir examine the beauties of that Chinese temple which you see at the end of the garden. Is there any thing in China more beautiful?
>
> Where I stand I see nothing, madam, at the end of the garden that may not as well be called an Egyptian pyramid as a Chinese temple; for that little building in view is as like the one as t'other.

Goldsmith's Chinese not only satirises European mores he also ridicules contemporary European stereotypes of China.

The Sinomania among creative writers of the eighteenth century extended beyond porcelain to the country of Confucius and to its artistic tastes. As a reaction to the neo-classical vogue emerging in Europe certain writers celebrated the antiquity of China and claimed it a more worthy model than Greece or Rome. The most ancient civilisation in the world and still enduring, China was extolled for its rational order, secular morality and refined sense of taste.

> Of late, 'tis true quite sick of Rome and Greece,
> We fetch our models from the wise Chinese,
> European artists are too cool and chaste,
> For Mand'rin only is the man of taste.
>
> (James Cawthorne, *Essay on Taste*, 1756)

However, what is that good taste? Europeans manufactured chinoiseries, composed unreal images, imported objects for which they misunderstood the usages, called these things Chinese and then applauded the Chinese for having good taste! It was the vogue for chinoiserie which elevated the Chinese to a man of taste in European eyes. When the fad waned in the later years of the eighteenth century, the European opinion of the Chinese became hypercritical. Chinese taste was characterised as 'coarse' and 'unnatural' by Johann Gottfried Herder, and Goethe wrote in 'Der Chineser in Rom' (the Chinese in Rome) (1796):

> In Rome I saw a stranger from Pekin,
> Uncouth and Heavy to his eyes appeared
> The mingled piles of old and modern time.
> 'Alas!' he said, 'what wretched taste is here!
> When will they learn to stretch the airy roof
> On light plastered shafts of varnished wood
> Gain the fine sense and educated eye,
> Which only finds in lacquer, carvings quaint,
> And variegated tintings, pure delight?'
> Hearing these words unto myself I said,
> Behold the type of many a moon-struck bard
> Who vaunts his tissue, woven of a dream
> 'Gainst nature's tapestry, that lasts for aye
> Proclaims the sick the truly sound, and this
> That he, the truly sick, may pass for sound.[13]

As the bizarre and the sage Chinese began to fade from Europe's imagination in the latter half of the eighteenth century, the Asian began again to be depicted as human – nothing less, nothing more. Inspired by translations of genuine Asian fictional works, and above all by the balanced, accurate and encyclopaedic work of Du Halde, authors began to compose more realistic and humanised word portraits of Asians. Ludwig August Unser's 'Vou-ti bey Tsin-nas Grabe, eine Elegie im chinesischen Geschmack' ('Vou-ti at the Grave of Tsin-nas, an Elegy in the Chinese Taste') was based quite loosely upon an incident mentioned in Du Halde's work. In Unzer's poem the main character, Vou-ti, emerges as a sensitive individual capable of deep and simple human emotion at the death of his beloved. Unlike his predecessors, Unzer strove to understand his character as a Chinese, as one who possessed distinctive attitudes towards death and religion. While Unzer claimed that his poem was written in the Chinese manner, he had few models to follow other than the brief translations in Du Halde. The great literature of the T'ang and Sung was largely unknown in Europe. Judged by contemporaries an embarrassingly poor poem stylistically, Unzer's 'Vou-ti' none the less marked the beginning of another change towards the Asian in fiction.[14]

Certain European authors of the later eighteenth century began to perceive a China beyond the monolithic Confucian moral order so often extolled in the Jesuit accounts. Karl Sigismund, Freiherr von Seckendorf, who composed an unpublished non-satirical moral admonition called 'Der chinesische Sittenlehrer', ('The Chinese Moralist') was also struck in passing by a reference in Du Halde's *Description. . . de la Chine*, retelling the delightful dream of the Taoist Chuang-tzu.[15] In 'Das Rad des Schicksals'('The Wheel of Fate') (1784) Seckendorf starts with the metempsychotic reverie of Chuang-tzu, in which the philosopher wonders if in reality he is a butterfly dreaming he is Chuang-tzu or Chuang-tzu dreaming he is a butterfly. On the basis of this dream Seckendorf tried to compose a piece in what he assumed to be an authentic Chinese manner. Chuang-tzu consults his Taoist teacher Lao-tzu, giving Seckendorf an occasion to present some of the tenets of Taoism as he dimly understood them. Here, as in Unzer's poem, Seckendorf attempted to present a story which is truly Chinese. At the same time, he became one of the first to portray Chinese popular religion in a work of fiction.

Until the eighteenth century Europeans had little knowledge of the nature and content of Asian fiction. No piece of South or East Asian fiction was available in a Western language at the dawn of the century. When translations finally began to appear, the Asian for the first time was allowed to speak for himself rather than through a Western writer. As a result, the distinctive character and the humanity of the individual Chinese or Indian began to replace the stereotypic Asian everyman. Du Halde brought translated excerpts, poetry, philosophical discourses, a few stories and a Chinese play to the attention of European readers as part of his *Description. . . de la Chine* (1735). The play, originally from the Yuan dynasty, was called *Choa Shih ku erh (Orphan of the House of Chao)*. In the translation of the French Jesuit missionary to China, Joseph-Henri-Marie de Premare, the play depicts the Chinese respect for virtue and familial loyalty. Du Halde, however, criticised it for failing to follow the eighteenth-century French dramaturgical standards of unity of time, place and action. Other European writers – Voltaire, Mestastasio, Goethe – as well as minor English playwrights undertook to improve the Chinese original in 'Orphans' of their own. While the story remained in its European adaptations a tale of political intrigue and eventual heroic revenge, every writer felt that the Chinese original needed substantial revision. The plot was altered, characters shuffled and little thought was wasted upon accuracy in depicting China of the thirteenth century. Authors and their audiences had certain expectations about drama and about China, and did not wish to have their images confused by something truly Chinese.

Later in the century more serious attempts were made to understand Asian literature for its own sake. *Hau Kiou Choaan (Hao ch'iu chuan, The Fortunate Union)*, a 'copious abstract' of an anonymous

Chinese popular novel, appeared in England in 1761, telling of the love and the trials experienced by a handsome virtuous young scholar and beautiful intelligent girl. The Anglican Bishop Thomas Percy edited the translation he found among the papers of an East India Company merchant James Wilkinson. Since it was the first genuine Chinese novel to be even partially translated and printed in a European language, doubt was cast upon its authenticity. In fact, *Hau Kioou Choaan,* a typical Chinese novel, was quite different from the wild and magical pseudo-Oriental tales. The central theme of the eventual triumph of true love was, of course, not uncommon in European fiction in Asian settings, but *Hau Kiou Choaan* was valued by Percy because, in his opinion, it gave the 'true character of a living people'. Percy was enough of a scholar to annotate the translation, drawing from works such as Du Halde's for notes on everything from family life to pagodas and Confucianism. He hoped that the translation and the notes 'taken together might be considered as forming a concise, and not altogether deflective account of the Chinese'.

While a few translations of Asian fiction had begun to open the European consciousness to the Asian as revealed in his own fictional writings, it was the emergence of the European scholar of Asia and his translations which would fundamentally alter Europe's image of the Asian. At the end of the eighteenth century, as Britain began to expand its Empire in India and as companies of France and Britain began to send scholars to the east, Europeans residing in the East studied the languages and literatures there. Abraham Hyacinthe Anquetil-Duperron became deeply interested in Asian languages and civilisation while in India from 1755 to 1761. Later he produced a French version of the Zoroastrian Parsee text *Zend-Avesti* (1771). English linguist diplomats such as William Jones also began to appreciate the richness of Indian literature and to produce translations of significant works as well as commentaries on Asian societies. Charles Wilkins, under the instructions of William Jones, produced in 1785 the first translation in English prose of the classic epic poem of Hinduism, the *Bhagavad-gita.* In the introduction to the translation, with a note of surprise at finding it so, the *Bhagavad-gita* is characterised as 'a performance of great originality, of sublimity of conception, reasoning, and diction almost unequalled' and one which could not be judged by Western standards.

The European concepts of Asia as a geographical entity changed little in fiction over the course of the three centuries examined here. Asia remained remote and generally undifferentiated, except for China. By the eighteenth century numerous images of Asian peoples were alive and competing with one another. The Asian, including the

Chinese, was portrayed variously as harlequin or sage, slave or despot, with qualities which ranged from capricious and hedonistic to rational, benevolent and ethical. The chameleon-like image of the Asian changed in literary creations as a response to the historical conditions prevailing in Europe *and* Asia at a given time. Renaissance, Baroque and Enlightenment writers certainly conceived of the Asian in terms set by their own European mental and artistic bents. But it was not the European environment alone which moulded these literary conceptions. Cataclysms in Asia – the Manchu Conquest of China or the rise of the Mogul Empire in India – contributed their share to transforming or shading the European images. The particular sources from which the imaginative writers drew also added distinctive colourings. In the Jesuit letters, histories and translations China was portrayed as an ethical, social and rational model; in the writings of the Protestant merchants, who competed with the Chinese in East and South-East Asian markets, the Chinese were sometimes represented as connivers and cheats.

The European authors of fiction were often uncertain as to how they should assess the veracity of their sources or reconcile the conflicts in them. To some the factual travels of Pinto were fictional; for others the fabrications of Psalmanazar were authentic. Still there were those, perhaps a majority of the authors, who were not at all concerned about the authenticity of their sources. Asia, from Ariosto to Gueulette, was a pagan backdrop between the real and imaginary worlds, where marvels might be expected and where readers could suspend judgement and accept the incredible. In the early romances, Europeans were distinguished from Asians by their beliefs and ethics and not by language, colour or behaviour. From Arrivabene to Wieland, the Chinese were extolled as exemplars from whom the Europeans had much to learn about governance, social order and natural morality.

Still there was always something queer and unreal about Asians and their qualities, products and practices. As warriors they were feeble, no match for Europeans, and victorious only when in combat with other Asians. Their arts and crafts, while universally admired and often emulated, were seen as being more decorative than substantial, more feminine than masculine. Since Asians were so unpredictable to Europeans, they soon became comic figures in European plays and skits. 'Once he had become the butt of jokes, it was not long before the Asian became the object of derision and satire. The hostility to Asians which first became obvious in the eighteenth century was linked to certain more practical considerations, such as the craze for Indian textiles and China goods which drained precious metals from Europe and produced unemployment there, as well as by a growing suspicion of the Jesuits and their starry-eyed stereotype of China. While many authors admired China's ancient and enduring civilisation, the neo-classicists of the late eighteenth century derided its institutions and arts, and compared them unfavourably with the glories of Greece and Rome.

Beginning in the mid-seventeenth century, a tendency developed of depicting the Chinese as real human beings with a different but not a bizarre culture. The Manchu Conquest of China, seen as a victory of barbarism over civilisation, stimulated the writers of the Baroque era to begin treating of human suffering in China, including the tragedy of the last Ming emperor. The translation of the Confucian classics reinforced for Europeans the assertions of the Jesuits about the high level of Chinese thought. Sympathy and understanding were eclipsed in the early eighteenth century by the 'Sinomania' which swept Western Europe, and it was not revived to any appreciable degree until later in the century when a more substantial documentation on China and the Chinese became available. Once a few translations of authentic Chinese fiction appeared, several European authors wrote what they conceived to be imitations of Chinese works in which they tried to let the Chinese speak for themselves. By the end of the century a few Europeans began to understand that Asian writings could not be fairly judged by Western standards.

While fiction produced competing images, in which Asians were adulated, ridiculed or humanised, it should not be assumed that imaginative literature alone created these representations. Perhaps even more important to the popular imagination was the picture of Asia and the Asian conjured up from the available textiles, porcelains and lacquer-works, and from the European engravings in travel books and histories. The 'willow pattern world' of China which pervaded the imagination of Europe during the first half of the eighteenth century was created only in small measure by writers of fiction. In the previous two centuries as well imaginative fiction relayed to Europe a changing conception of Asians derived from the images in non-fictional narratives, maps and the visual arts. In brief, the writers of fiction reflected the stereotypes implicit in their often-conflicting and limited sources; quite frequently they used their own fertile imaginations to reconcile, colour or alter the competing images inherited from the past or transmitted by contemporaries.

Notes

1 For example: E.Francisci, *Ost- und West-Indischer wieauch sinesischer Lust- und Stats-Gerten*, Nurnberg, 1668; E.W. Happel, *Thesaurus exoticorum*, Leyden, 1688; J. Nieuhof, *The Embassy of the Dutch East Indian Company to the Tartar Cham.* translated 1669.

2 Although some scholars have doubted it, Christopher was a real person and the translator of these Persian tales from an old story cycle. See S. V. R. Cammann, 'Christopher the Armenian and the three princes of Serendip', in A. O. Aldridge (ed.), *Comparative Literature: Matter and Method Urbana*, III. 1969, pp. 227–56.

3 On 'moral Asia' see Henry Y. K. Tom, 'The wonderful voyage: Chivalric and moral Asia in the imagination of sixteenth-century Italy, Spain, and Portugal', Ph.D. dissertation, Univ of Chicago, 1975, Pt II.

4 See E. Van Kley, 'News from China: Seventeenth-century European notices of the Manchu Conquest', *Journal of Modern 'History*, XLV, 1973, 561–82.

5 See E. Van Kley, 'An alternative muse: The Manchu Conquest of China in the literature of sevnteenth-century Northern Europe', *European Studies Review*, VI, 1976, 32–3.

6 See Lohenstein, *Arminius*, I, pp. 594–607, 617, 659–66; II, p. 489.

7 See P. Martino, *L'Orient dans la littérature française au XVIIe et au XVIIIe siècle*, Paris, 1906, p. 33.

8 Moynadeir edn of 1903, II, p. 258.

9 Moynadeir edn, II, pp. 271–2.

10 L. L. Martz, *The Later Career of Tobias Smollett*, New Haven, 1942, pp. 94–101.

11 Jean-Baptiste Du Halde, *A Description of the Empire of China. . .* 2 vols, London, 1738–41, I: pp. 281–2, quoting L. Le Comte, *Nouveaux mémoires sur l'état présent de la Chine*, 2 vols, Paris, 1696.

12 Note the names: Lien Chi Altangi is similar to one of Walpole's characters; Fum Hoam, Lien's correspondent in China, is the name of the Mandarin in Gueulette's *Chinese Tales*.

13 Translation from J. S. Cobb, *Goethe*, New York, 1902, Vol. III.

14 For more on Unzer and other German poets, see E. Selden, 'China in German poetry from 1773 to 1833', *University of California Publications in Modern Philology*, XXV, 1941–44, 141–316.

15 Goldsmith was also inspired to write on this dream of Chuang-tzu. See his *Citizen of the World.*

Reading list

Appleton, William W., *A Cycle of Cathay: The Chinese Vogue in England during the Seventeenth and Eighteenth Centuries*, New York, 1951.

Baudet, Henri, *Paradise on earth: Some Thoughts on European Images of Non-European Man*, New Haven, 1965.

Camoens, Luis de, *The Lusiads* (Translated by W. C. Atkinson), Harmondsworth, 1952.

Cawley, Robert R., *Unpathed Waters: Studies in the Influence of the Voyagers on Elizabethan Literature*, Princeton, 1940.

Conant, Martha P., *The Oriental Tale in England in the Eighteenth Century*, New York, 1908.

Cornelius, Paul, *Languages in Seventeenth and Early Eighteenth-Century Imaginary Voyages*, Geneva, 1965.

Dawson, Raymond, *The Chinese Chameleon: An Analysis of European Conceptions of Chinese Civilization*, London, 1967.

Dufresnoy, Marie-Louise, *L'Orient Romanesque en France* (1704–1789), Montreal, 1946.

Echeruo, Michael J. C., *The Conditioned Imagination from Shakespeare to Conrad: Studies in the Exo-cultural Stereotype*, London, 1978.

Gove, Philip B., *The Imaginary Voyage in Prose Fiction: A History of its Criticism and a Guide for its Study with an Annotated Check List of 215 Imaginary Voyages from 1700 to 1800*, New York, 1941.

Honour, Hugh, *Chinoiserie: The Vision of Cathay*, London, 1961.

Kley, Edwin Van, 'The effect of the discoveries on Seventeenth-century Dutch popular culture', *Terrae Incognitae*, VIII, 1976, 29–43.

Lach, Donald F., *Asia in the Making of Europe*, Vol. 2, Bk 2, Chicago, 1977.

Lowes, John Livingston, *The Road to Xanadu: A Study in the Ways of the Imagination*, Boston, 1955.

Martino, Pierre, *L'Orient dans la littérature français en XVIIe et XVIIIe siècles* (1906), Geneva, 1970.

Nelson, William, *Fact or Fiction: The Dilemma of the Renaissance Storyteller*, Cambridge, Mass., 1973.

Olschki, Leonardo, *Marco Polo's Asia*, Berkeley, 1960.

Reichwein, Adolf, *China and Europe: Intellectual and Artistic Contacts in the Eighteenth Century*, London, 1925.

Remy, A. F. J., *The Influence of India and Persia on the Poetry of Germany*, London, 1901.

Rowbotham, A. H., *Missionary and Mandarin: The Jesuits at the Court of China*, Berkeley, 1942.

Selden, Elizabeth, 'China and German poetry from 1773 to 1833', *University of California Publication in Modern Philology*, XVI, 1941–44, 141–316.

Steadman, John M., *The Myth of Asia*, London, 1970.

Tscharner, E. H. von, *China in der deutschen Dichtung bis zur Klassik*, Munich, 1939.

Willson, Amos L., *A Mythical Image: the Ideal of India in German Romanticism*, Durham, NC, 1964.

CHAPTER THREE

Muslims in English-language fiction[1]

Gavin R. G. Hambly

I begin with the assumption that there exists in both Western Europe and the USA a set of luridly coloured, highly distorted, yet widely held impressions of the Middle East, and of Muslims in general. These stereotypes have almost universal validity in the sense that they are as much accepted by those with personal experience of the area – businessmen, educators, journalists and members of the diplomatic, defence or intelligence-gathering communities – as they are by their 'stay-at-home' fellow countrymen, for whom knowledge of the area is supplied by episodic and disjointed coverage in television news programmes or on the front page of a daily newspaper. Obviously, there are exceptions, but these are not my concern here. These stereotypes, formed early in life, are rarely erased by subsequent serious study or personal encounters. This is especially true of Americans, but it is hardly less so among Europeans. The difference is that while American awareness of Muslims is relatively recent and for most Americans the Middle East seems extraordinarily remote, European perceptions of the Muslim world are centuries old, originating in medieval Christendom's encounter with Islam in the age of the Crusades. The centuries of European imperial expansion only reinforced and confirmed earlier prejudices. This European legacy, rooted in hatred and fear which later turned to scorn and derision, has been taken over by Americans virtually intact.[2]

It follows, then, that assumptions and prejudices regarding Muslims today, although undoubtedly moulded by the reporting of world events in the news media, owe much to stereotypes of Muslim society long embedded in the imagination, and, most conspicuously, in the imaginative fiction of the West. Today, this tradition is expressed mainly through cinema, television or in the lurid romances available on railway bookstalls or supermarket stands, in which the vicious terrorist or the corrupt oil-rich businessman are recurring Middle Eastern 'types'. Behind such stock figures in contemporary genres of entertainment, however, there lies a pattern of writing on the Middle East and Islam in nineteenth and early twentieth-century fiction extending back to Sir Walter Scott and the beginnings of the historical novel, and even earlier, to remote images of the Saracen foe of medieval Christendom. Not that the images were invariably hostile: a recurring motif is the natural dignity, generosity and manly faith of the Muslim gentleman, as contrasted with the duplicity or hypocrisy of the Christian crusader, cleric or (in a later age) proconsul. As early as the time of the First Crusade (c.1099), the chronicler William of Tyre could not withhold a grudging admiration for the enemies of his faith. He termed Alp Arslan, the conqueror of the Byzantines at Manzikert (1071), a magnificent foeman and described the later Seljuq Sultan, Qilij Arslan, as 'a valiant man of much subtlety'.[3] The anonymous author of the contemporary *Gesta Fran-corum* (Deeds of the Franks) went even further:

> What man, however experienced and learned, would dare to write of the skill and prowess and courage of the Turks. . .they have a saying that they are of common stock with the Franks, and that no men, except the Franks and themselves, are naturally born to be knights. This is true, and nobody can deny it, that if only they had stood firm in the faith of Christ. . .you could not find stronger or braver or more skilful soldiers.[4]

Thus, the stereotypes were never consistent, derived as they were from a multi-faced and ambiguous historical experience. Nineteenth- and early twentieth-century European attitudes had been shaped by assumptions made by earlier generations. During the opening phases of the Crusading epoch (the twelfth and thirteenth centuries), Islam, according to the Christian theologians, was yet another pernicious heresy. Gradually, the perception of this spiritual evil merged with the recognition of the military threat which a resurgent Islam presented, as the Latin principalities in the Holy Land were one by one extinguished, and as the Ottomans advanced into the Balkans. The fall of Constantinople in 1453 and the Ottoman thrust towards the heart of Central Europe only confirmed long-standing fears, which even the Christian victory at Lepanto in 1571 did little to allay. Only with the failure of what was to prove the last Ottoman assault on Vienna in 1683 did Christendom begin to feel secure from the Muslim menace.[5]

Obviously, this was not the entire story of Christian–Muslim interaction during the medieval and early modern periods, but it was the aspect which loomed largest in the popular imagination of

Europe, an ongoing story of conflict and violence which quite obscured other patterns of communication: the picturesque embassies, the almost unbroken commercial exchanges, and the two-way trade in material objects, fashions, vocabulary and ideas. At the same time, it was during these early centuries of contact that there emerged in the European mind two pervasive and related images of Islamic society. These were of slavery, which, in one form or another, was ubiquitous throughout the Muslim world; and of sexual licence, the latter rooted in the early polemics of Christian schoolmen.[6]

To take slavery first, by the end of the sixteenth century confrontation between Christians and Muslims in the Mediterranean world was characterised by raids upon each other's shores, piracy and the capture of, and the trafficking in, men and women. Such conditions were taken for granted – no one could remember things being different. Europeans, even those living far from the Mediterranean, were well informed about the sufferings of the thousands of Christians captured by Muslim corsairs, who languished in the *bagnios* (slave prisons) of Algiers or Tripoli or who were lashed to the oars in Turkish galleys – although it goes without saying that Muslim captives fared no better at Christian hands.

Public concern was such as to make alms-giving for the relief of Christian prisoners of the Corsairs, or for their ransom, a major aspect of sixteenth- and seventeenth-century charity. Cervantes was only one among many who experienced Muslim captivity at first hand and lived to tell the tale, while many a church in the coastal regions of Southern Europe displayed the chains of former Christian galley-slaves hung on its walls in thanksgiving for their release.[7] As for the fate of female slaves immured within a pasha's seraglio, horror at the contemplation of such a life was not infrequently diluted by a voyeuristic thirst for information regarding polygamy as an institution. European readers had long been regaled by travellers' tales of harem life and concubinage such as the Muslim ruling elite were presumed to indulge in. Alleged Muslim sexual excess was a topic which had long before fascinated the clerical writers of medieval Europe, and it was one which over the centuries fuelled the fires of prejudice, as when Rodrigo, in Shakespeare's *Othello*, referring to Othello, speaks of 'the gross clasps of a lascivious Moor'. The causes of this obsessive preoccupation with Muslim sexuality are not hard to understand: unlike the celibate Jesus, the prophet Muhammad had been a married man with several wives; the Koran allowed a circumscribed form of polygamy; divorce, for men, was easily obtained; and the realities of ubiquitous household slavery led inevitably to widespread concubinage. With polygamy went, for the affluent, purdah (the seclusion of women from the prying eyes of men) and the seraglio or harem, with eunuchs in attendance to guard their precious charges and to protect their master's honour. Pederasty too was alleged to be common.

In short, Europeans supposed that the sexual appetites of Muslim men, whether for wives or slave girls, women or boys, were insatiable, and if travellers' tales were to be believed, reality far exceeded the most imaginative fiction, as exemplified by the allegedly lubricious translations of Sir Richard Burton. In 1889, observing that the Shah's entourage on his state visit to London included several wives and a catamite, a Victorian statesman duly noted the contrast with the home life of his own dear Queen; while as late as the 1940s and 1950s, the alleged sexual exploits of King Faruq made front-page news in the British gutter-press. Of more enduring significance, throughout the nineteenth century, the eroticism as well as the exoticism associated with the Levant and North Africa was splendidly portrayed – and preserved – by a fashionable genre of painting devoted to Middle Eastern subjects. While many of these subjects were landscapes, with picturesque vistas of bazaars, mosques and ruins, others, with such titles as 'The Slave Market', 'The Circassian Captive', 'Odalisques at the Bath House', or 'The Sultan's Favourite' and ranging from masterpieces by Delacroix to decors for high-class bordellos, were unmistakably titillating but reinforced the stereotype of a society steeped in sexual depravity.

If Muslim men were regarded as irredeemably licentious, their women, from sultana to dancing girl, were assumed to be little better. Europeans were fascinated by the fantasy of 'dusky charms' concealed behind the veil, particularly after translations of *The Thousand and One Nights* circulated widely among Western readers. In his magnificent *Eothen* (1844), Alexander Kinglake evokes this particular fantasy in circumstances which were to become a stock situation of novels with a Middle Eastern setting:

> as you make your difficult way through a steep and narrow ally, shut in between blank walls, and little frequented by passers, you meet one of those coffin-shaped bundles of white linen that implies an Ottoman lady. Painfully struggling against the obstacles to progression interposed by the many folds of her clumsy drapery, by her big mud-boots, and especially by her two pairs of slippers she works her way on full awkwardly enough, but yet there is something of womanly consciousness in the very labour and effort with which she tugs and lifts the burden of her charms: she is closely followed by her women-slaves. Of her very self you see nothing, except the dark luminous eyes that stare against your face, and the tips of the painted fingers depending like rosebuds from out of the blank bastions of the fortress. She turns, and turns again, and carefully glances around her on all

sides to see that she is safe from the eyes of Mussulmans, and then suddenly withdrawing the *yashm*ak (veil), she shines upon your heart and soul
with all the pomp and might of her beauty. And this, it is not the light,
changeful grace that leaves you to doubt whether you have fallen in love
with a body or only a soul; it is the beauty that dwells secure in the perfect-
ness of hard, downright outlines, and in the glow of generous colour. There
is fire, though, too – high courage, and fire enough in the untamed mind, or
spirit, or whatever it is which drives the breath of pride through those
scarcely parted lips.[8]

What made Muslim women fascinating was the knowledge that they
were forbidden fruit. Unseen behind the veil, or the seraglio walls,
they were imagined to be ravishingly beautiful and, as a consequence
of the assumed frustrations of their confined existence, probably
available for a furtive *affaire*, especially with a European. Harem
intrigue is one of the most frequent motifs in novels with a Middle
Eastern setting, and in this, as in other respects, James Morier's
Adventures of Hajji Baba of Ispahan (1824) set a fashion. *Hajji Baba*
contains two such harem episodes, one tragic and the other with a
happy outcome. Both emphasise the helplessness of women in
Muslim society and their status as playthings of men. A century
later, James Elroy Flecker's *Hassan* (1922), a work with obvious
echoes of *Hajji Baba*, also has a harem episode central to the action
of the play. Hassan was to inspire a Broadway musical, *Kismet*, and a
movie (1955).

In these incidents, from *Hajji Baba* to *Hassan*, are to be found the
basic ingredients of the numerous tales of escape, or attempted
escape, from the harem, many of which, as in Morier's *Ayesha, The
Maid of Kars* (1834), involve either a European woman or European
men assisting in the liberation of a Muslim woman. Such imaginary
escapades could be rendered light-heartedly on stage, as in Mozart's
Die Entführung aus dem Serail (The Elopement from the Seragio)
(1782) or Rossini's *L'Italiana in Algieri (The Italian Girl in Algiers)*
(1813), or even Weber's *Oberon* (1826), but generally liaisons between
European men and Muslim women were portrayed in fiction as being
brief and tragic. In this, the novels of Pierre Loti (1850–1923) serve as
an epitome, juxtaposing the 'civilised' European with the 'savage'
child of nature. Such bitter–sweet encounters, once so fashionable
among suburban readers, now survive mainly in the opera house, in
Delibes' *Lakhmé* or Puccini's *Madame Butterfly*.

That the outcome of such relationships had to be tragic was
implicit in prevailing racial and imperial ideologies. The native
woman was the embodiment of unrestrained sexuality, and to submit
to her embraces was to pass from a world of civilised values and

[39]

c

order to one of primitive and self-destructive passion. The degeneration of Willems as a result of his infatuation with the Malay girl, Aissa, in Conrad's *An Outcast of the Islands* (1908–9) exemplified the consequences of surrender to native mores and morals. Kipling, too, explored this theme and in several short stories underlined the danger and anguish of such liaisons, although he was less concerned with the destructive consequences for the white man than for the human suffering involved. An early story, 'Beyond the Pale' (*Plain Tales from the Hills*, 1888), dealt with an Englishman's brief association with a Hindu widow, resulting in her mutilation by her kinsfolk, and Kipling makes his point very clear from the outset:

> A man should, whatever happens, keep to his own caste, race and breed. Let the White go to the White and the Black to the Black. Then, whatever trouble falls is in the ordinary course of things – neither sudden, alien nor unexpected.[9]

A later story describes with understanding and sympathy the *affaire* of an English official and a Muslim girl, the tragic love of John Holden and Ameera in 'Without Benefit of Clergy' (*Life's Handicap*, 1891). It is among Kipling's best stories, but the final message is unmistakable: 'East is East, and West is West, and never the twain shall meet. . .'

Perjorative stereotypes of Muslim sexuality, including the widespread allegation of 'unnatural vices', were reinforced by a number of additional unfavourable stereotypes as a consequence of the advance of the colonial powers into the heartlands of the Muslim world during the nineteenth century and early twentieth century. Encounters resulting from this advance coloured the writing of journalists, travellers and colonial officials, whose much-read publications (of which *Blackwood's Magazine* contains numerous illustrations) provided the raw materials for sedentary writers of romance. In some, perhaps many, of these publications the borderline between fact and fiction was never clearly drawn (Sir John Malcolm's *Sketches of Persia* of 1828, and Sir Percy Sykes's *The Glory of the Shia World* of 1910 are two such examples), but either way the result was the confirmation of long-held prejudices by supposedly authentic, firsthand experience. Furthermore, for more informed readers, Islam was becoming a 'problem', the consequence of the reluctance of Muslims to surrender themselves quietly to European tutelage. Their obdurate resistance could be explained either in terms of social Darwinism (a decaying and degenerate civilisation unwillingly giving way to a superior one) or, more romantically, in terms of a preordained conflict between East and West – Persia against Greece, Parthia against Rome, Saracens against Crusaders – to be resolved at last in favour of the contemporary West. Islam was seen to be not only incurably obscurantist as a religious system but also as offering a more uncompromising opposition to westernisation than, say, nineteenth century India or China.

The incorrigible wickedness and ingratitude of Muslims, when offered the helping hand of the West, can be clearly traced in the pages of the European press decade after decade throughout the nineteenth century: Ottoman atrocities in the Balkans; the assassination of a Russian ambassador in Tehran in 1828 and the East India Company's envoy in Kabul in 1841; the torture and execution of Colonel Stoddart and Captain Connolly in Bukhara in 1843; the treachery and massacres of the First Afghan War; and Muslim participation in the Indian Mutiny of 1857. Then there was the attack on the British legation in Kabul in 1879; the Bulgarian Atrocities of which Gladstone made much in his Midlothian campaign of 1879; and, perhaps most famous of all, General Gordon's death at Khartoum in 1885. These were only the more dramatic of numerous incidents in which missionaries, merchants and ambassadors encountered the relentless hostility and atavistic violence of Muslims.

These events coloured nineteenth-century and early twentieth century European perceptions of the Muslim world, and provided the models for virtually all fictional writing about it. Thus, treachery, cruelty and murderous revenge were the traits almost automatically ascribed to Muslim fictional characters: traits which might be elevated to a kind of satanic grandeur, as in Kipling's 'The Ballad of the King's Mercy' and 'The Ballad of the King's Jest' (*Ballads and Barrack Room Ballads*, 1892). That such behaviour was frequently the result of prior European aggression was generally ignored or glossed over, while little attempt was made to differentiate the characteristics of various categories of Muslims – Arabs, Afghans, Indians, Persians, Sudanese or Turks. Collectively, all were assumed to be motivated by a blind and irrational hatred for Christians, and it is surely significant that the distinction between European and Asiatic or Middle Easterner was generally expressed in terms of Christian versus Muslim.

Exemplification of such assumptions pervade the pages of the widely read and highly popular novels of G. A. Henty (1832–1902), as in *With Kitchener in the Soudan, At Aboukir and Acre, To Herat and Cabul, In Greek Waters, A Knight of the White Cross, The Dash for Khartoum* or *The Tiger of Mysore*. In *With Clive in India* (1884), for example, the young English hero, Charlie, comments on a message brought in from the future Nawab Mir Jafar on the eve of the battle of Plassey: 'I expect that he does not know what he means himself. These Asiatics are at any time ready to turn traitors, and to join the strongest', to which his commanding officer, Major Eyre Coote, replies: 'Yes, these Mohammedan chiefs are indeed crafty and treacherous rascals. The whole history of India shows that gratitude is a feeling altogether unknown to them and that whatever favours a master may have lavished upon them they are always ready to betray him if they think that by so doing they will better their position.'[10]

Yet, despite his native jingoism, Henty tried to stick close to the facts available to him, and this is illustrated in his observations in the same book relating to the outcome of Plassey and the murder of the former Nawab, Siraj al-Dawla:

> Suraja Dowlah was undoubtedly a profligate and rapacious tyrant. In the course of a few months he alienated his people and offended a great number of his most powerful chiefs. The war which he undertook against the English, although at the moment unprovoked, must still be regarded as a patriotic one, and had he not soiled his victory by the massacre of the prisoners, which he first permitted and then approved, the English would have had no just cause of complaint against him. From the day of the arrival of Clive at Calcutta he was doomed. It is certain that the nabob would not have remained faithful to his engagements when the danger which wrung the concessions from him had passed. Nevertheless the whole of the circumstances which followed the signature of the treaty, the manner in which the unhappy youth was alternately cajoled and bullied to his ruin, the loathsome treachery in which those around him engaged with the connivance of the English, and lastly the murder in cold blood, which Meer Jaffier, our creature, was allowed to perpetrate, rendered the whole transaction one of the blackest in the annals of English history.[11]

Although addressed primarily to schoolboys, Henty's writings served as the catalyst for a whole series of adventure 'yarns' – *Blackwood's Magazine*'s tales from the outposts of empire, stories of the French Foreign Legion and the tradition of historical romances associated with the name of Rafael Sabatini. Perhaps three of the most characteristic examples of the genre are Sir Arthur Conan Doyle's *The Tragedy of the Korosko* (1898) and A. E. W. Mason's *The Four Feathers* (1902) – both set in the Sudan – and John Buchan's *Green-mantle* (1916), a story of Muslim intrigue and fanaticism pitted against the civilising mission of the British Empire, and read by generations of Anglo-Saxons on both sides of the Atlantic.

Nineteenth-century and early twentieth century writers of historical fiction implanted firmly in their readers' minds the abiding notion of Islam as a backward religion and way of life, but a few authors were more discriminating. Not all Muslims were portrayed as dyed-in-the-wool villains, even if the overall impression was one of hostility. The image of the 'noble Moor' was an ancient one. In the eleventh-century *Poema del Cid*, for example, the faithful Avel-galvón is favourably contrasted with the treacherous Infantes of Carrión, as is Othello to Iago centuries later. A degree of respect for the 'other side' is also to be found in the *Parzival* and *Willehalm* of the thirteenth-century poet, Wolfram von Eschenbach, for 'they are all the creatures of God's Hand'.[12]

As for more recent fiction, it was with Sir Walter Scott, the father of the historical novel, that there appeared the prototype of the heroic Muslim adversary in the person of Saladin (ruler of Egypt, 1169–93), just as Scott set the fashion for the age of the Crusades as a favourite period for later generations of historical novelists with *The Talisman* (1825) and *Count Robert of Paris* (1832). *The Talisman* has found few admirers amongst discriminating critics, yet, apart from *Ivanhoe*, few amongst his novels have been more widely read. The setting is the Third Crusade of 1190 and the story pits Richard the Lion Heart against his no less chivalrous opponent, Saladin, while at the same time he is surrounded by treacherous or self-serving fellow Christians – King Philip Augustus of France, Duke Leopold of Austria, Conrad of Montferrat, etc. Richard himself is in no doubt as to the unequal distribution of virtue and vice in his great enterprise. Thus, he reflects on the Grand Master of the Temple:

> were it fair to take the Holy Land from the heathen Saladin, so full of all the virtues which may distinguish unchristened man, and give it to Giles Amaury, a worse pagan than himself – an idolator – a devil-worshipper – a necromancer – who practises crimes the most dark and unnatural, in the vaults and secret places of abomination and darkness?[13]

As for Saladin, when first encountered by the Scottish Knight of the Couchant Leopard, his appearance heralds generations of latter-day Hollywood Sheikhs:

> His features were small, well-formed, and delicate, though deeply embrowned by the Eastern sun, and terminated by a flowing and curled black beard, which seemed trimmed with peculiar care. The nose was straight and regular, the eyes keen, deep-set, black, and glowing, and his teeth equalled in beauty the ivory of his deserts. The person and propor-tions of the Saracen, in short. . . might have been compared to his sheeny and crescent-formed sabre, with its narrow and light, but bright keen Damascus blade. . . The Emir was in the very flower of his age, and might perhaps have been termed eminently beautiful, but for the narrowness of his forehead, and something of too much thinness and sharpness of feature. . .
>
> The manners of the Eastern warrior were grave, graceful and decorous; indicating, however, in some particulars the habitual restraint which men of warm and choleric tempers often set as a guard upon their native impetuosity of disposition, and at the same time a sense of his own dignity,

which seemed to impose a certain formality of behaviour in him who entertained it.[14]

Again and again, Saladin is held up as a model against which the Crusaders as a whole are displayed in a most unfavourable light. As Avrom Fleishman has pointed out, notwithstanding Scott's loving evocation of medieval times, there is explicit and sustained criticism of medieval mores and values in Scott's novels set in the Middle Ages, and this was to be true of much English-language historical fiction of the nineteenth and early twentieth centuries.[15] This was because medieval Europe was viewed, for the most part, as a superstitious, fanatical and priest-ridden society by Protestant Anglo-Saxon writers, who, in their eagerness to emphasise the greed, hypocrisy and obscurantism of the medieval Church, were not unwilling to implant, by way of contrast, the seeds of a more sympathetic interpretation of Islamic society. Thus, twelfth or thirteenth-century Crusaders, in so far as they represented the interests of a Church thirsting for power and dominion, were often presented less favourably than their Saracen foes. In a Spanish setting, Moorish Andalusia was portrayed as a relatively tolerant and open-minded society compared with that of the Christian North, while the sixteenth-century Ottoman Empire was similarly compared with contemporary Europe. In a number of works of historical fiction, Islamic society was held up as a mirror reflecting the flaws of contemporary Christian society. Islamic values and life-styles were not necessarily exonerated, but violence and cruelty in an exotic Middle Eastern setting seemed less revolting or more explicable than among Christians.

This tendency becomes more pronounced in twentieth-century historical fiction. It does not mean that Muslim societies cease to be represented as savage and fanatical, but a kind of balance is attained. Two very popular historical novels of the 1950s illustrate this point. In Mika Waltari's *The Wanderer* (1951), the Finnish hero (having in an earlier novel made his way across sixteenth-century Europe amid scenes of mounting horror which reach their climax in the burning of his wife as a witch) now makes his way to the Istanbul of Suleiman the Magnificent, the metropolis of an empire which embodies a degree of order, prosperity and internal peace, which is in marked contrast with what the hero encountered during his travels through Christendom. The Turks are certainly not portrayed as paragons of civilised behaviour, and by the time the novel draws to its close, its hero has fared no better in Turkey than in Europe, but the two societies are self-consciously compared very much to the disadvantage of

Christendom, whilst the Sultan and Grand Vizier are represented as far-sighted statesmen in a quite different class from contemporary European rulers.

Frank Yerby's *The Saracen Blade* (1952) is set in an earlier period, the Hohenstaufen kingdom of Sicily and the Mediterranean world of the early thirteenth century, but the contrast between Christendom and Islam is as great as in *The Wanderer*. Thus, towards the end of the novel, its hero, Pietro di Donati, finding himself in Egypt with Walter of Brienne on the Fifth Crusade of 1218, bitterly contemplates the paradoxes inherent in the whole crusading episode:

> He was forced into doing some thinking about Crusades, past, present, and future. . .In every case, the Saracens had had much the better of it; even in defeat they had been victorious. No Saracen leader had ever disgraced himself, no Saracen army had behaved to the conquered like the soldiers of the gentle Christ. From the very first, when they had left their homes to 'take back the Holy places from the unclean hands of the infidels', they in the first of the Crusades had marched out by the light of the pyres in which screamed the helpless Jews that they had murdered in their homelands as an earnest of their intent. And when these gentle Christians had won at last, they flocked to the Church of the Holy Sepulchre, and embraced each other and wept, thanking the merciful God for their victory. But they marched to the Church through streets choked with the bodies of their victims; on the corners they had to circle the carefully piled stacks of severed heads and hands, stepping over the bodies of infants whose heads had been smashed against posts.[16]

The 'noble Moor' may seem to be yet one more stereotype, but this idealisation of a non-European type, held up as a reproach to the vices of 'civilised' Europeans, has been ubiquitous in the centuries since the Renaissance, with the sage Chinese, the wise Hindu, the noble savage, the Redskin child of nature, or, in the case of H. Rider Haggard, the heroic Zulu contrasted with the greedy and perfidious White Man. Thus, in fiction the likes of Saladin and Suleiman the Magnificent serve as literary exemplars of princely justice and magnanimity in contrast to the more common and conventional stereotypes of Muslim bigotry and hyprocrisy.

Between these two extremes are to be found relatively humble characters who exude practical common sense, good humour, a capacity for survival and, on occasion, loyalty and courage. They are servants, tradesmen, retainers or outlaws - honest or otherwise, they are generally endearing rascals and a world apart from the heroes and villains alike. In novels with an imperial setting, they are often servants of Europeans (the Gunga Din type), and not infrequently their sharp wits and 'savvy' help to keep their masters, the real heroes of such tales, out of trouble. Sometimes they operate outside the law, but are redeemed in the reader's eyes by their audacity, loyalty or ingenuity. Such is Kamil in Kipling's 'The Ballad of East and West' and, best of all, Mahbub Ali in *Kim*. Two characters particularly noteworthy in this regard are the protagonists of James Justinian Morier's *The Adventures of Hajji Baba of Ispahan* and James Elroy Flecker's *Hassan*. Hajji Baba begins life as a barber in Isfahan and achieves precarious eminence as the Shah's Ambassador at the Court of St James. He has something of both Tom Jones and Sancho Panza about him. Hassan is a confectioner with a taste for versification in the Baghdad of Harun al-Rashid. Both embody lower class attitudes, aspirations and values. Both are thoroughly human and wholly admirable, in contrast to the cruelty and corruption of those above them. The epitome of such types who pass their lives in the streets and bazaars, the tea-houses and caravanserais, rather than in the durbar-halls or harems, is Mahbub Ali, the Pathan horse-dealer who plays a central role in Kipling's *Kim* (1901). Loyal Muslims in the service of the British were, naturally enough, stock figures in novels set in the outposts of the Empire, as in the case of recent works by John Masters and M.M. Kaye, but Mahbub Ali is different, his own person and no mere agent of the Raj.

A rather different motif often present in novels with an Islamic setting was the evocation of the traditional 'East' as a location for the romantic, the exotic and the fantastic. From the time of Scott, probably the majority of those who wrote Eastern fiction did so without any first hand knowledge of the peoples of whom they wrote, so that from the *The Talisman* to Hollywood spectaculars, it often seems as if Muslim protagonists are only distinguishable from their Christian adversaries by their dress or, in the case of the cinema, by their sinister accents and colour. Perhaps the work of escapist fiction with an Islamic setting which had the widest vogue among English readers of the early nineteenth century was *Lalla Rookh* (1817) by the Irish poet, Thomas Moore (1779–1852). Inspired by such diverse material as Sir William Jones's translations from the Persian and Alexander Dow's *History of Hindostan* (1778), the poem encapsulated much of the information then available to the educated Englishman regarding the culture of Muslim India and Iran. *Lalla Rookh* did for the English drawing-room of the first half of the nineteenth century what Edward Fitzgerald's *Rubaiyat of Omar Khayyam* (1859) was to do for the second, providing a gorgeous Orient far removed from the conventional ways of the bourgeois England of the Industrial Revolution.

The setting of *Lalla Rookh* is as charming as any tale from *The Thousand and One Nights*. Abdullah Khan, ruler of Bukhara, has resigned his throne to end his days as a holy mendicant in Mecca.

Travelling to his destination by way of India, he comes to the court of the Great Mogul, Aurangzeb, where he is lavishly entertained. Aurangzeb arranges with his guest that his daughter, the beautiful Lalla Rookh, shall marry Abdullah Khan's son. Splendid festivities are held to celebrate the forthcoming nuptials, and Lalla Rookh is dispatched with a great procession of retainers to meet the bridegroom in Kashmir. On the way, the entourage is joined by a handsome poet, Faramarz, who beguiles the princess with a series of stories. Moore selected these stories from such translations of Persian folklore and literature as were then available to him, of which the most striking is that of the 'Veiled Prophet of Khorasan'. The journey ends with the princess arriving at the beautiful Shalimar-Bagh, where, as she approaches the two thrones prepared for her and her husband-to-be, the latter advances to meet her and proves to be none other than the poet Faramarz himself.

Although Moore's poetry strikes the modern reader as insipid, *Lalla Rookh* was enormously admired in its day and provided a brilliant and colourful picture of those eastern Islamic lands which were, at that very time, first becoming familiar to Europeans. As the East India Company's hegemony was expanding to include the Mogul centres of Delhi and Agra, and as British travellers such as Bishop Heber were compiling journals describing the twilight of Mogul rule, it must have seemed as if the world of *Lalla Rookh* was about to reveal itself anew to a generation of Europeans who would soon be penetrating Kashmir, Kabul and even Bukhara itself. The publication of *Lalla Rookh* coincided with, and was largely inspired by, an expanding literature of books on India, both scholarly and popular, as well as a growing British familiarity with the subcontinent.

Much the same was true of Morier's *The Adventures of Hajji Baba of Ispahan*, published in 1824, at a time of growing Western, and especially British, familiarity with Iran as a result of frequent diplomatic missions to the court of Tehran and the publication of a number of books on that country, of which Sir John Malcolm's *History of Persia* (1815) was the most influential. Morier (1780–1849) did for Iran and Turkey what Moore did for Mogul India, but, unlike Moore, Morier had extensive firsthand experience of the countries about which he wrote. Of the nineteenth-century novelists who dealt with Islamic subject-matter, none was so inventive, good-humoured or so well-equipped as a result of personal observation as was Morier. His ancestors had been long established in Izmir (Smyrna) as merchants, and he acquired an extensive knowledge of both Turkey and Iran in the course of serving on various diplomatic missions. None of this altogether explains how he came to be such a perceptive observer of Middle Eastern, and especially Iranian, life. Indeed, so penetrating were his observations that when, towards the close of the nineteenth century, a Persian translation of *Hajji Baba* first appeared, Iranian readers apparently assumed that an authentic Iranian author, who had wonderfully captured the foibles of his countrymen, was responsible for the work. When it was discovered that the book was the work of a foreigner, it was regarded as a libel on the national character.

Morier wrote several novels with a Middle Eastern setting, but apart from *The Adventures of Hajji Baba of Ispahan*, which has been in print for the past century and a half without interruption, the rest sank quickly into oblivion, as did the Iranian novels of James Baillie Fraser (1783–1856).[17] Morier's novels fall into distinct categories: *Hajji Baba*, for example, is pure picaresque. *The Adventures of Hajji Baba in England*, however, also published in 1824, is a non-European's satirical view of European society in the tradition of Montesquieu's *Lettres Persanes* or Goldsmith's *Chinese Letters*. *Ayesha, the Maid of Kars* (1834) is an adventure story set in eastern Anatolia in the early nineteenth century and is concerned with Europeans rescuing a beautiful heroine from the clutches of a villainous Turkish pasha. A beautiful heroine is also central to the plot of *Zohrab the Hostage* (1832), a particularly interesting example of an early nineteenth-century historical novel, set in the period of the consolidation of the Qajar dynasty during the late eighteenth century. Unlike *Ayesha*, there are no Europeans in it, all the participants being Iranian. In form, it closely follows Scott's medieval novels and may well have been inspired by *Quentin Durward* (1823). Against a background of military expeditions, palace intrigues, escapes and pursuits, Morier describes life in Qajar Iran as it was immediately before his own residence there, based upon his own observations and conversations with contemporaries. In contrast to Moore or Scott, however, Morier's Middle Easterners emerge from his pages with a vitality which is unmistakably authentic.

For many today, the nineteenth-century cult of the exotic East, whether in the form of the novels of Morier or Fraser, or the poetry of Moore or Fitzgerald, is hard to stomach: the dust has long since settled on the 'Golden Road to Samarkand'. Reviewing a recent study of the Victorian passion for Hellenism in all its aspects (including the paintings of Alma-Tadema), Bernard Knox wrote in the *New York Review of Books* (11 June 1981):

> One reason for this insistence on fake classical themes (or the equally spurious medieval subjects of Burne-Jones and Rosetti) must have been the overpowering ugliness of the Victorian industrial landscape and the appalling conditions in which most people lived.

Herein too lay the charm of the exotic East: the evocative names of the cities, the tiled domes and minarets, the bazaars and the caravanserais, the pleasure gardens where the nightingales serenaded the roses in eternal springtime, the sultans and amirs, the poets and dervishes, and all the elements of romance which a Moore, a Fitzgerald or a Loti could conjure up so well.[18] Nor was the effort restricted to writers and painters: Rimsky-Korsakov's *Antar* and *Scheherazade*, Balakirev's *Islamey* and *Tamara*, Borodin's *Polovtsian Dances*, and Ippolitov-Ivanov's *Caucasian Sketches* are but a few of the numerous examples of attempts to convey the exotic East in sensuous sound as well as in sensuous imagery.

In some respects, James Elroy Flecker's play *Hassan: The Story of Hassan of Baghdad and How He Came to Make the Golden Journey to Samarkand* (1922) can be regarded as the summation of this tenacious tradition. Flecker (1884–1915), like Morier and Fraser, knew the Middle East at first hand: in his case, as a British consular official. Posthumously published and performed, *Hassan* contains all the predictable ingredients: Baghdad in the days of Harun al-Rashid, caliphs, viziers, executioners and star-crossed lovers. There is the local colour and the romance of *Lalla Rookh*, the juxtapositioned comedy and cruelty of *Hajji Baba*, and the same irony, as when Hassan the infatuated and naive confectioner tries to woo with an exquisite serenade the mercenary harlot, Yasmin. Moreover, *Hassan* contains in addition, in the person of the poet Ishak, yet another European perception of the exotic East, the mystical and the renunciatory, echoed in scores of Western renderings of Persian Sufi poetry. Forced to witness the deaths by torture of the faithful lovers, Pervaneh and Rafi, Hassan and Ishak resolve to leave forever the splendours and cruelties of Baghdad, and the latter says:

> You hear? The camels are being driven to the gate of the moon. At midnight starts the great summer caravan for the cities of the Far North East, divine Bokhara and happy Samarkand. It is a desert path as yellow as the bright sea-shore: therefore the Pilgrims call it the Golden Journey. . . I have broken my lute and will write no more *qasidahs* [panegyric odes] in praise of the generosity of kings. I will try the barren road, and listen for the voice of the emptiness of earth. And you shall walk beside me.[19]

The preceding pages identify at least three significant strands in the way Muslims have been represented in English-language fiction. First, there is the hostile and contemptuous stereotype, part of a tradition reaching back to the Middle Ages and the days of the Crusades. Secondly, there is a contrasting tradition in which the virtues of the 'noble Moor' exemplified by the figure of Saladin in *The Talisman*, contrast with the vices of unworthy Christians.

Thirdly, there is Islamic society as romantic and fantastic, as in the pages of *Lalla Rookh*, *Hajja Baba* and *Hassan*, part of a tradition in European letters going back to the earliest transmissions of *The Tales of the Thousand and One Nights*. A detailed investigation of a kind which has not been possible here could better document the interlocking pieces in this complex and colourful puzzle, while the overall argument could be strengthened by the inclusion of material derived from theatre, opera, cinema, television and comic-books. For, in considering the superficial and distorted coverage of the Middle East and of Middle Easterners by so much of the Western media today, it is not difficult to detect how pervasive still are the stereotypes derived from the historical confrontations of past centuries.[20] In such scenarios, pro-Western leaders (the last Shah, for example, or the late President Sadat) are cast in the roles of 'noble Moors', like actors fitted into costumes made for predecessors of quite different proportions; Iranian revolutionaries become reincarnations of those fanatical mobs which Gordon faced at Khartoum in so many boys' adventure-yarns, or Cavagnari in Kabul in M. M. Kaye's *The Far Pavilions*; and in Ayatullah Khumaini or Yasir Arafat, Marco Polo's 'Old Man of the Mountain' lives again, his dread Assassins reborn as present-day terrorists. There seems to be no limit to the West's capacity to misunderstand and to misrepresent the world of Islam, and both history and literature have been enlisted in that service.

Notes

1 Readers should note that although I have used throughout the chapter the adjectives Muslim and Islamic, in the literature under discussion they are more likely to encounter such terms as Muhammadan, Mahomedan and Musulman. My spelling of Muslim names is generally in accordance with popular usage.

2 See Edward W. Said, *Orientalism*, New York, 1978; and Maxime Robinson, *Europe and the Mystique of Islam*, London, 1987.

3 William of Tyre, *A History of Deeds Done Beyond the Sea*, translated by E. A. Babcock and A.C. Krey, New York, 1941, I, pp. 78 and 153.

4 Anon., *The Deeds of the Franks and Other Pilgrims to Jerusalem*, edited and translated by Rosalind Hill, Oxford,1962, p. 21.

5 For the ways in which Europeans in different periods have seen Muslims and Muslim civilisation, see Maxime Rodinson, 'The Western image and Western studies of Islam', in the *Legacy of Islam*, 2nd edn, ed. J. Schacht and C. E. Bosworth, Oxford, 1974, pp. 9–62; R. W. Southern, *Western Views of Islam in the Middle Ages*, Cambridge, Mass., 1962; J. Muldoon, *Popes, Lawyers, and Infidels*, Philadelphia, 1979; N. Daniel, *Islam and the West: The Making of an Image*, Edinburgh, 1960, and *Islam,Europe and Empire*, Edinburgh, 1966; D. Metlitzki, *The Matter of Araby in Medieval England*, New Haven,Conn., 1977; R. Schwoebel, *The Shadow of the Crescent: the Renaissance Image of*

the Turk (1453–1517), New York, 1969; and C. Chew, *The Crescent and the Rose: Islam and England during the Renaissance*, Oxford, 1937.

6 Daniel, *Islam and the West*, pp. 135–61.

7 For the Mediterranean as battleground for Christians and Muslims, see F. Braudel, *The Mediterranean and the Mediterranean World in the Age of Philip II*, 2 vols, New York, 1973.

8 A. Kinglake, *Eothen*, London, 1844, p. 26.

9 R. Kipling, 'Beyond the Pale', *Plain Tales from the Hills*, New York, 1888 p.173.

10 G. A. Henty, *With Clive in India*, London,1884, p. 255.

11 Henty, *With Clive*, p. 264.

12 Wolfram von Eschenbach, *Willehalm*, translated by M. E.. Gibbs and S. M. Johnson, Harmondsworth, 1984, p. 218.

13 Sir Walter Scott, *The Talisman*, London, 1825, p. 77.

14 Scott, *Talisman*, p. 25.

15 A. Fleishman, *The English Historical Novel: Walter Scott to Virginia Woolf*, Baltimore, 1971, pp. 54–61. But it should be noted that Saladin had long been a hero-figure in Christian literature. See, e.g., 'The presence of the Sultan Saladin in the Romance literatures', in *An Idea of History: Selected Essays of Americo Castro*, edited and translated by S. Gilman and E. L. King, Columbus, Ohio, 1977, pp. 241–69.

16 F. Yerby, *The Saracen Blade*, New York, 1952, pp. 230 – 1.

17 James Baillie Fraser's Middle Eastern novels were: *The Kuzzilbash: A Tale of Khorasan*, London, 1828; *The Persian Adventurer*, 3 vols, London 1830; *Tales of the Caravanserai*, London, 1833; *Alee Nemroo the Buchtiaree Adventurer: A Tale of Louristan*, 3 vols, London, 1842; *The Dark Falcon: A Tale of the Attreck*, 4 vols, London, 1844; and *The Khan's Tale*, London, 1850.

18 For Iran, see J. E. Heseltine, 'The Royame of Perse', in *The Legacy of Persia*, ed. A.J. Arberry, Cambridge, 1953, pp. 359 – 87.

19 J. E. Flecker, *Hassan*, New York, 1922, p. 157.

20 See, e.g., J. G. Shaheen, *The TV Arab*, Bowling Green, Ohio, 1984.

Reading list

Buchan, John, *Greenmantle*, London, 1916.

Conrad, Joseph, *An Outcast of the Islands*, London, 1896.

Flecker, James Elroy, *Hassan*, London, 1922.

Fraser, George MacDonald, *Flashman*, New York, 1969.

——, *Flashman in the Great Game*, New York, 1975.

Fraser, James Baillie, *The Kuzzilbash: A Tale of Khorasan*, London, 1828.

——, *The Persian Adventurer*, 3 vols, London, 1830.

Henty, George Alfred, *For Name and Fame, or Through the Afghan Passes*, London, 1886.

——, *In Greek Waters*, London, 1892.

——, *To Herat and Cabul*, London, 1892.

——, *With Kitchener in the Soudan*, London, 1903

——, *The Tiger of Mysore*, London, 1890.

Kaye, Mary Margaret, *The Far Pavilions*, New York, 1978.

——, *The Shadow of the Moon*, New York, 1979.

Kipling, Rudyard, *Kim*, London, 1901.

Lamb, Harold, *Omar Khayyam: A Life*, New York, 1934.

Moore, Thomas, *Lalla Rookh* (1817), New York, 1937.

Morier, James Justinian, *The Adventures of Hajji Baba of Ispahan* (1824), Oxford, 1923.

Oldenburg, Zoe, *The Heirs of the Kingdom*, New York, 1971.

Scott, Sir Walter, *The Talisman*, London, 1825.

Waltari, Mika, *The Wanderer*, New York, 1951.

Yerby, Frank, *The Saracen Blade*, New York, 1952.

——, *An Odor of Sanctity*, New York, 1965.

CHAPTER FOUR

The literature of the Raj

Robin Jared Lewis

British writing about India, usually referred to as 'Anglo-Indian'[1] literature, can be divided into three distinct periods, each with its own set of attitudes and assumptions. The first, roughly from 1800 to 1857 (the year of the Indian Mutiny), can be called the 'era of romance'. It yielded historical romances full of action, adventure and sentimentality. Important events in the history and development of British hegemony in India, such as the battle of Plassey and the Anglo-Mysore Wars, were the favoured settings. The issue of race, so crucial in later periods, plays a very small role at this time: India is new and fascinating, and the emphasis is on rich scenic detail rather than on racial or national superiority. Early Anglo-Indian novels, such as Sir Walter Scott's *The Surgeon's Daughter* (1827), W. B. Hockley's *Tales of the Zenana* (1827) and Colonel Meadows Taylor's *Tipoo Sultaun: A Tale of the Mysore War* (1840), introduced many of the stereotypes which later dominated the British imagination about India. Naked holy men and cruel 'Oriental' despots, fabulous jewels and rare spices, snakes and tigers, luxuriant jungles and snow-covered mountain peaks – all of these conceptions (and misconceptions) of India are the central subject matter in these early nineteenth-century writings.

The second era, from the Mutiny to the beginning of the First World War, may be termed the 'era of orthodoxy'. During this time, the social and political barriers between Indians and British seemed insurmountable and, thus, the fiction was characterised by an acute awareness of race. The historical novel remained a popular genre, but the violent events of 1857 and the resulting atmosphere of hostility and suspicion provided the impetus for a shift from romance to tragedy. It was also in this period that the so-called 'novel of mixed marriage' attained great popularity. Written primarily by women, many of these novels were didactic tracts masquerading as imaginative fiction, and they preached of the dangers of intimacy between rulers and ruled. Happy endings were rare.

Whereas writers of the earlier period had stressed India's newness and strangeness, their Victorian successors often aggressively asserted their knowledge of the country and their familiarity with its peoples and cultures. They offered to their English readers this 'knowledge' of an Oriental society: a knowledge which, in Edward Said's words, dealt with the society 'by making statements about it, authorizing views of it, describing it, by teaching it, settling it, ruling over it'.[2] Fiction played a vital role in propagating the central imperialist stereotypes of English masters and Indian subjects.

The one dominant figure in this period is, of course, Rudyard Kipling, whose works so powerfully shaped British perceptions of India that many English people had little idea where art ended and life began. Leonard Woolf, writing of his first days as a colonial administrator in Ceylon (Sri Lanka) around 1905, expressed this confusion:

> The white people were also in many ways astonishingly like characters in a Kipling story. I could never make up my mind whether Kipling had moulded his characters accurately in the image of Anglo-Indian society, or whether we were moulding our characters accurately in the image of a Kipling story[3]

The third and final period of Anglo-Indian writing can be called the 'era of doubt and disillusionment' because it was pervaded by a feeling of deep distress. After the upheavals of the First World War, politics came to the forefront as a theme. Race was still an issue, but it was now only one aspect of the larger question of India's freedom. Authors such as E. M. Forster and George Orwell used their works to raise fundamental questions about the moral and political legitimacy of the British raj. In Forster's great novel *A Passage to India*, he seems to have rediscovered the sense of wonder which characterised the earliest British writing on India, while at the same time rejecting the simplistic stereotypes relied upon by earlier writers as a staple of their narrative art. His descriptions of the Indian landscape are precise and evocative, and his Indian characters are drawn on a human not a mythical scale. Forster opposed British rule in India and hoped that his novel would help to hasten the advent of Indian independence.

The stereotypes in Anglo-Indian fiction must be seen as the result of imperial England's obsession with discovering and codifying certain essential 'truths' about the lands and peoples they ruled. As a way of asserting knowledge and control, stereotypes encouraged English readers to believe that India's 'mystery' and exoticism could be tamed, that Indians could be managed and made to bow to the rule of a 'superior' race. To accept, for instance, Sir Walter Scott's facile, prefabricated account of India's diverse races – 'the patient Hindoo, the warlike Rajapoot, the haughty Moslemah [Muslim], the savage and vindictive Malay'[4] – was to gain a sense of security. One could always expect Hindus to be patient, Rajputs to be warlike, Muslims to be haughty.

To understand better these stereotypes of India, it is necessary to examine the books read by most middle-class and upper-class Victorian children. The men and women who were sent out to India often encountered the country for the first time in adventure-novels like those of G. A. Henty, seminal works written for boys.

In the latter half of the nineteenth century, an entirely new genre of boys' literature appeared in England. This earnest and dogmatic writing was promoted by ruling elites (church, army, public schools, colonial services) anxious to alter the reading habits of male English adolescents. Before 1850, boys' fiction was dominated by the 'penny dreadful', so called because of its low price and emphasis on violent crime. But middle-class parents, along with schoolmasters and clergymen, were openly hostile to works that paid so little heed to their own values of hard work, self-discipline and social order. They wanted something morally elevating and socially useful, and, in 1857, they got just that in Thomas Hughes's *Tom Brown's Schooldays*, a fictionalised account of the author's own experience as a schoolboy under the legendary headmaster of Rugby, Dr Thomas Arnold. This book spawned a new type of boys' literature which was intended to instruct as well as entertain, and to this end relied upon stereotyped characters representing good and evil, order and chaos, strength and weakness. Britain had a vast overseas empire which required men utterly certain of who they were and what they stood for, and boys were psychologically trained for their future adult roles by learning to recognise instantly acceptable and unacceptable modes of behaviour.

Tom Brown's Schooldays is not usually thought of as a book about the Empire. There is little flag-waving in it, but the concept of awesome responsibility which Kipling, Newbolt and others so fervently advocated is already present in embryonic form. Tom Brown's adventures at Rugby School are presented as a dry-run for real life, and the closer one looks at Hughes's book, the more obvious it becomes that the school is meant to represent the Empire in miniature.

During his fourteen years (1828–42) as headmaster of Rugby, Dr

Arnold laid the foundations of a public school system which would provide a steady flow of imperial administrators and warriors. Before his time, the great public schools had been in a state of severe decline: some of them were little more than violent and disorderly way-stations for the pampered sons of rural gentry.[5] But after Arnold's reforms, the public schools were rejuvenated with a new sense of social purpose. He was the first to turn the curriculum away from Greek and Latin to more practical subjects (modern history, modern languages, mathematics), but his principal innovation was the prefect (or *praepostor)* system, whereby the youngest boys performed menial tasks for the older ones until they themselves were mature enough to be given command of the smaller boys. Thus, virtually every moment of a schoolboy's day offered an object lesson in how to wield power and responsibility within a carefully defined social hierarchy. Dr Arnold himself, the stern but just patriarch, represented the ideal authority figure. Significantly, Hughes describes Arnold's mission in exactly the same terms which were often used to justify British rule in India: '. . . he had found the school in a state of monstrous license and misrule, and was still employed in the necessary but unpopular work of setting up order with a strong hand'.[6] This is the rhetoric of benevolent paternalism, one of the cornerstones of Victorian empire-building, and it runs consistently throughout the novel.

If Dr Arnold is the properly benevolent ruler in *Tom Brown's Schooldays*, then the cowardly Flashman personifies the abuse of authority. He bullies the smaller and weaker boys, instead of protecting them in approved paternal fashion, and he eventually provokes Tom and his companion East to rebel against him in a chapter entitled 'The War of Independence'. Again, Hughes's language is shot through with metaphors borrowed from imperial rhetoric: Flashman and his allies are called 'the unlawful – the tyrants, who are responseible to nobody'.[7] In other words, Flashman is like the conventional stage villains of Anglo-Indian history, such as Tipu Sultan or Hyder Ali, whose cruel and arbitrary use of power was cited as ample justification for British rule. Bullying, whereby the strong dominate the weak through the application of brute force, becomes in Hughes's novel the moral equivalent of Oriental despotism. Thus, the noble schoolboy must shield the weak from injustice, whether it occurs in the dormitories of Rugby or on the plains of Hindustan.

In the thirty years or so after the publication of *Tom Brown's Schooldays*, the relationship between the public schools and the Empire grew steadily more intimate. By 1887, the year of Queen Victoria's Golden Jubilee, most public schools had special courses for those planning careers in the Army, Indian Civil Service or other colonial services. Schools like Haileybury (founded by the East India Company), the United Services College (which Kipling attended), Wellington and Marlborough were particularly favoured by parents who wished their sons to serve the Empire. One school, Cheltenham, even boasted a department of foreign languages where one could study Sanskrit and Hindustani.

This enthusiasm for Empire naturally generated a demand for more boys' literature along the lines of *Tom Brown's Schooldays*, but with explicitly imperial themes and settings. The result was a flood of historical writing for boys which depicted the history of the British Empire as a series of object lessons on how to win an empire. In the forefront of this genre was the indefatigable George Alfred Henty, whose more than eighty adventure novels (many of them set in India) shaped the historical consciousness of countless English schoolboys. Henty was an ardent imperialist, and he worked tirelessly to convince his readers that each and every one of them could play a role, no matter how small, in securing and ruling the Empire. Just as Tom Brown rises to the occasion on his very first day at Rugby by deflecting an enemy attack in the football match, so Henty's boy heroes inevitably respond to their imperial destiny, whether the opponents are Afghans, Sikhs, Mahrattas, Burmese, Ashantis, Zulus, Boers, French, Spaniards or Russians. Henty's novels are frankly formulaic: an obscure, unknown adolescent (sometimes an orphan) is thrust suddenly into a great moment in British imperial history (the siege of Khartoum, the battle of Delhi, the defeat of the Spanish Armada) and proves himself under great pressure. Historical personages, such as Clive or Lord Roberts, make brief appearances in order to lend an atmosphere of verisimilitude.

Most noticeable in Henty's young protagonists is their lack of individuality. As one critic has put it, the typical hero in Henty's novels 'had no real personality, but was, in fact, a kind of abstraction of pluck, physical endurance, and honour'.[8] Thus, a youthful reader could plug himself into the imperial myth and see his own future linked to that of the Empire.

Two stereotypes which frequently appear in Henty's works are those of youth and old age. His imperial heroes are invariably identified by their adolescent vigour and lack of hesitation, while the villains are often old men in positions of power and influence, who endanger the Empire through inaction, indecision and cowardice. In *To Herat and Cabul: A Story of the First Afghan War* (1901), the defeat of the British is blamed solely on a general scornfully depicted as 'imbecile', 'old and infirm, incapable of decision'.[9] And in Henty's novel of the Indian Mutiny, *In Times of Peril: A Tale of India* (1881), the commander of the British garrison at Meerut is termed 'an old man who had lost all energy'.[10] Henty is, in fact, what we today would call an 'ageist', and his ageism can be said to derive directly from *Tom Brown's Schooldays*, a book which created a virtual cult of youth. The idea that the rest of a man's life could never quite compare to the glory of his schooldays did not really fade until well into the twentieth century, when it was debunked by social critics like Lytton Strachey and Cyril Connolly, who characterised the typical public school graduate as frozen in 'permanent adolescence'.[11]

Racial stereotypes also figure prominently in Henty's works. He was a firm believer in the doctrine of Anglo-Saxon superiority and never hesitated to give his readers quick summary judgements of Indians: 'there are no better or more pleasant waiters in the world than the natives of Hindostan.'[12] Although Afghans and Sikhs are sometimes praised for their courage and toughness, all Indians are seen as inherently unable to rule their own live: 'Their [the Afghans'] weakness consists in their want of organization, their tribal jealousies, and their impatience of regular habits, and of the restraint necessary to render them good soldiers. But when led and organised by English officers there are no better soldiers in the world'.[13] Henty's version of Indian history is based on the crude premise that Britain's destiny is to rule, while India's destiny is to be ruled.

The hero in most Victorian boys' literature is an easily recognisable type. Certain qualities distinguish him – self-assurance, courage, a talent for leadership and organisation – and every young reader is prompted to admire and emulate him. He grows up by learning how to fit into his public school or the Army or Indian Civil Service, and he achieves personal fulfilment through loyalty to these institutions. Against him are ranged the enemies of order and progress – public school bullies like Flashman, rebellious Indian soldiers, tyrannical native princes, and they too are stereotypes which young audiences learnt to recognise.

Rudyard Kipling brought to Anglo-Indian literature two things it had lacked previously: complexity of viewpoint and real literary genius. His predecessors were, almost without exception, second-rate writers whose limited knowledge of India was all too apparent in their works. No other English writer has presented such a broad and varied imaginative portrait of India as has Kipling. From his sketches of high Anglo-Indian officials at play in the hill stations to his tales of rough-and-tumble bazaar life, Kipling offered his readers a vivid panorama of everyday life in a land most of them had never seen. Although his earliest Indian writings were intended primarily as light amusement for an Anglo-Indian audience, he soon became the single most important interpreter of India for those in England as well.

Kipling has always been a controversial figure. In some of his fiction on India, he glorified the rulers at the expense of the ruled. This is the Kipling most people are familiar with today – the belligerent imperialist, the Bard of the British Empire whose voice is often cruel, arrogant and contemptuous of Indians. But there is another Kipling as well, the one who wrote *Kim* and *The Jungle Books,* and his voice could be subtle and compassionate. Kipling's writing draws its power from the constant tension between the imperial prophet and the creative artist. Born in Bombay in 1865, Kipling was, like so many other Anglo-Indians, perpetually divided between two different identities. Growing up surrounded by Indian servants and their numerous songs and stories, he had to be reminded to speak English to his parents when brought to see them in the family drawing-room. The lilting rhythms of Hindustani and the rich sensual impressions of India from his early childhood never left him, and were later rendered with the utmost freshness and vitality in *Kim,* a book about a young orphan of English (actually Irish) parentage who has grown up as an Indian.

As was the custom amongst well-to-do Anglo-Indian families, Kipling was sent back to England for his schooling. But he returned to India in 1882 as a fledgling journalist and remained for seven years. During this time, he travelled extensively, gathering the raw material for his poems and stories by listening carefully to India's many voices and by observing its spectacular natural and human scenery. Describing this period of his life, Kipling wrote: 'Sometimes I wore dress-clothes and consorted with princes and politicals, drinking from crystal and eating from silver. Sometimes I lay out upon the ground and devoured what I could get from a plate made of leaves, and drank the running water, and slept under the same rug as my servant.'[14]

Out of this intense experience, Kipling fashioned for himself an ambiguous identity comprised essentially of English values and Indian instincts. The profound ambivalence at the heart of Kipling's works on India expressed the deep confusion felt by most Anglo-Indians about India. The British image of India has always been dual in nature: India is seen as beautiful and alluring, but also dark, dangerous and threatening. In many of Kipling's stories of India, this contradiction remains unresolved. One example is 'Without Benefit of Clergy' (1890), a finely crafted tale of inter-racial love in which the author's obvious sympathy for Holden and Ameera is at odds with the entirely conventional tragic ending. Another vivid illustration of

Kipling's ambivalence is his short novel 'The Man Who Would Be King' (1890), which tells of two charming rogues who set themselves up as kings in a remote mountain area. The story is an allegory of empire in which Kipling is questioning the process whereby the British have gained dominion over India. The author's mixed feelings of horror and respect towards his protagonists reflect his confusion about the raj itself: are these two swindlers-turned-imperialists 'the lawless' or 'the law-givers'? It is worth noting that the poet laureate of the Empire could be at the same time one of its sharpest critics.

Kim (1901) is undoubtedly Kipling's masterpiece. Here Kipling has at last ceased to propagandise, and the India which emerges from the pages of this deeply lyrical book is a land of variety and vitality. *Kim* is in the great English picaresque tradition of Fielding's *Tom Jones* and Dickens's *Pickwick Papers*. As in these earlier novels, the essential movement is from innocence to experience, from a benign but limited point of view to a true understanding of the larger world in all its complexity. Kim and his travelling companion, an elderly Tibetan lama, are surely two of the most engaging figures in Anglo-Indian fiction: the one youthful, energetic and infinitely adaptable, the other innocent of worldly things but instinctively wise in matters of the spirit. For the first time in Kipling's work, an Indian world-view is granted equal validity with Western ones, and he seems to be striving for a synthesis of East and West, a unitary world-view made up of the best that each culture has to offer.

Two questions echo insistently throughout the novel: 'Who is Kim?' and 'What is Kim?' Kipling was really addressing these questions to himself, for Kim is Kipling's alter ego, and the boy's search for an identity mirrors Kipling's own quest for self-definition. There can be little doubt that Kim's enthusiasm for India's sweep and variety is Kipling's too:

> Kim was in the seventh heaven of joy. The Grand Trunk [Road] at this point was built on an embankment to guard against winter floods from the foothills, so that one walked, as it were, a little above the country, along a stately corridor, seeing all India spread out to left and right. It was beautiful to behold the many-yoked grain and cotton waggons crawling over the country roads: one could hear their axles, complaining a mile away, coming nearer, till with shouts and yells and bad words they climbed up the steep incline and plunged onto the hard main road, carter reviling carter. It was equally beautiful to watch the people, little clumps of red and blue and pink and white and saffron, turning aside to go to their own villages, dispersing and growing small by twos and threes across the level plain. Kim felt these things, though he could not give tongue to his feelings, and so contented himself with buying peeled sugar-cane and spitting the pith generously about his path.[15]

Kim's epithet, 'Little Friend of All the World', represents that part of Kipling which wanted to replace a faith in England's imperial destiny with the all-embracing notion of a common human destiny. It is this deliberate movement away from the simplistic 'we/they', 'master/subject' dichotomy which makes Kim, as one Indian writer has put it, 'the finest story about India in English'.[16]

E. M. Forster's *A Passage to India* (1924) is the most eloquent expression of the grave doubts about the empire felt by many English people after the First World War. The courage and efficiency of many Anglo-Indians had already been fully chronicled in fiction; until *A Passage to India*, however, their darker qualities had not. Forster's novel rejected the traditional stereotypes which formed the basis of Anglo-Indian fiction and replaced them with characters of recognisably human proportions. It is this freshness of vision which has given the novel its high reputation.

The gallery of Ango-Indian characters in the novel is Forster's depiction of the failure of British rule in India: his insistence upon viewing political questions in terms of human relationships is presented here in its purest form. Forster's earlier novel, *Howards End*, had posed the question of how to 'connect the prose in us with the passion',[17] and *A Passage to India* can be seen as his final attempt to solve this riddle of human existence. The waning years of the raj provide a setting in which the divisions between British and Indians have become magnified almost beyond the point of no return. Forster expresses here, in no uncertain terms, his conviction that British rule in India has become above all a matter of shoddy and unsatisfactory connections between people. The Anglo-Indian community of Chandrapore is motivated by base fears and hypocrisies, and Forster refers to its inhabitants as 'the herd'.[18] In contrast to this mass of prejudiced and ignorant men and women, Forster presents two English characters who are clearly distinguished from 'the herd'. They stand for Forster's last, tenuous hope for human relations in a world of division and dispersion.

Cyril Fielding, the principal of the local government college, and Mrs Moore, an elderly Englishwoman visiting her son Ronny, who serves as Civil Magistrate, are the crucial English characters in the novel. They may be said to embody, respectively, 'the prose' and 'the passion' which are so important to Forster. Fielding is, to a certain extent, the author's mouthpiece and his ideas are more or less those of the humanitarian liberal, while Mrs Moore, a far more complicated and elusive character, is a sort of seer. Her strangely successful initial meeting in a mosque with Aziz, a local Muslim doctor and the principal Indian character, immediately sets her apart sharply from the Anglo-Indians. Her openness and honesty make Aziz happy and excited, and here for the first time in the novel we see Mrs Moore as one who transcends the 'dissociation of sensibility' between East and West:

> She had proved her sympathy by criticizing her fellow-country woman to him, but even earlier he had known. The flame that not even beauty can nourish was springing up, and though his words were querulous his heart began to glow secretly. Presently it burst into speech.
>
> 'You understand me, you know what others feel. Oh, if others resembled you!'
>
> Rather surprised, she replied: 'I don't think I understand people very well. I only know whether I like or dislike them.'
>
> 'Then you are an Oriental.'[19]

The Anglo-Indians most markedly do not resemble Mrs Moore, and their implacably racist feelings come to the fore when Aziz is accused of 'interfering with' a young Englishwoman, Adela Quested, during an expedition to the nearby Marabar Caves. An outraged official, Turton, harangues Fielding for his suggestion that Aziz might be innocent, and his outburst sets forth simply and brutally the theory of social distance so fundamental to British India:

> 'I have had twenty-five years' experience of this country' – he paused, and 'twenty-five years' seemed to fill the waiting-room with their staleness and ungenerosity – 'and during those twenty-five years I have never known anything but disaster result when English people and Indians attempt to be intimate socially. Intercourse yes. Courtesy, by all means. Intimacy – never, never.'[20]

This is the imperialist mentality in its most mannered and refined form. Other Anglo-Indians are capable of real cruelty and venom, as when Mrs Turton exclaims: 'Why, they ought to crawl from here to the caves on their hands and knees whenever an Englishwoman's in sight, they oughtn't to be spoken to, they ought to be spat at, they ought to be ground into the dust, we've been far too kind . . .'.[21] In times of crisis, the Anglo-Indian community withdraws even more tightly into itself. Fielding, who sides with Aziz and his Indian supporters in the dispute over what happened at the Marabar Caves, is forced to resign from the local club, the bastion of all that is secure and meaningful for Anglo-India. Fielding is ostracised for his independence, and becomes an outsider in his own community. And when Aziz's case is dismissed because Adela Quested cannot truthfully state to the court what really occurred, the Anglo-Indians again react with fear and rage, banishing her too for her failure to play the role assigned to her in their scenario of retribution. Clearly, there is no room in their hearts for kindness, a commodity Forster values highly. As Aziz says to Fielding: 'Mr Fielding, no one can ever realize how much kindness we Indians need, we do not even realise it ourselves.'[22]

The colossal tableau of India itself is the heart of the novel, and the utter folly of Britain's imperial pretensions becomes fully clear only in relation to the immensity and intangibility of a land which offers the greatest possible contrast with England. In Forster's earlier novels, personal relations dominate the fictional landscape: Italy or the English countryside seem congenial to the characters' sense of self-importance, but India's enormity makes human endeavour appear to be of miniscule significance. A discussion between Fielding and Adela Quested is, thus, rendered nearly meaningless in the Indian setting:

> When they agreed, 'I want to go on living a bit', or, 'I don't believe in God', the words were followed by a curious backwash as though the universe had displaced itself to fill up a tiny void, or as though they had seen their own gestures from an immense height – dwarfs talking, shaking hands and assuring each other that they stood on the same footing of insight.[23]

The theme of human insignificance is made even more obvious in Forster's vision of India's proximity to a world of chaos, in which 'the inarticulate world is closer at hand and readier to resume control as soon as men are tired'.[24] This 'inarticulate world' is symbolised in *A Passage to India* by the Marabar Caves, each of which is indistinguishable from the next. They contain the amorphous echo – an echo which reduces 'vileness' and 'poetry' to the same dull sound – which dispirits and defeats Mrs Moore and produces her negative vision of human existence. In Forster's novel, India functions as a paradigm of human existence. India's divisions – English/Indian, Hindu/Muslim, brahmin/ untouchable, civilisation/nature, men/women – are those of human-ity as well.

All of Forster's humanistic values, which emphasise connections rather than divisions between individuals, are epitomised by Fielding, whose creed is 'goodwill, plus culture and intelligence'.[25] When Aziz's bitterness over his treatment by Anglo-India causes him to reject even his closest friend, who had stood by him throughout the crisis, it is an expression of Forster's doubts as to the efficacy of his own liberal humanism. His previous idealism seems to have been reduced in *A Passage to India* to a gun-shy scepticism: personal relations, Forster now realises, must proceed gingerly, often in deference to the absolutisms of nationality, race and ideology.

For Forster, the greatest failing of the British in India was that they had isolated themselves from the people they presumed to rule, an isolation which promoted only disharmony in human affairs. Yet the joyous festival near the end of the book proclaims that while individuals may be small in the grand scheme of the universe, they nevertheless have meaning. This is the antithesis of the ominous message of the Marabar Caves, which asserts that 'Everything exists, nothing has value.'[26] In the end, both Fielding and Aziz realise that they cannot be friends while England perpetuates the unwanted rule of one race over another in India. The clear-headed realism of this final scene also declares that the echo of the Marabar Caves has been diminished, and points to an uncertain but hopeful future when Aziz and Fielding can met as equals in a free India. *A Passage to India* thus expresses a guarded optimism that meaningful human relationships can arise from the shambles of the past.

Far more angry and pessimistic than Forster was George Orwell, whose savagely ironic pieces on the raj were written in the early 1930s. Orwell's involvement with India was an intimate one: he had been born there in 1903, and, after fifteen years of schooling in England, returned to serve with the Indian Imperial Police in Burma. Orwell went to Burma seeking an exotic adventure. As a boy, he had eagerly read Kipling: now he hoped to escape from the dreariness of England to the lush landscapes of *Kim* and *The Jungle Books*. But it seems that he had little idea what was to be expected of him.

Throughout his training at Mandalay and his subsequent assignments in various backwaters of the Burmese jungle, Orwell was forced to play a role which he came to despise. He discovered that certain attitudes were expected of him by English and Burmese alike, and he began to realise how repellent to his own deepest instincts the persona of the imperial policeman really was. He leaves a clear account of this anguish in two powerful short pieces he wrote about his stay in Burma, 'A Hanging', and 'Shooting an Elephant'.[27]

Orwell returned from Burma in 1927, totally disgusted with himself for the part he had played in the Empire. Writing of his feelings at that time, he later said:

> For five years I had been part of an oppressive system and it had left me with a bad conscience. Innumerable remembered faces – faces of prisoners in the dock, of men waiting in the condemned cells, of subordinates I had bullied and aged peasants I had snubbed, of servants and coolies I had hit with my fist in moments of rage . . . haunted me intolerably. I was conscious of an immense weight of guilt that I had got to expiate.[28]

Burmese Days (1934) marks Orwell's attempt to work out this guilt through a novel which would expose the corruption of human relations under the raj. Without descending into outright polemicism, the book forcefully indicts imperialism by demonstrating that the unwanted rule of one race over another is morally indefensible. Orwell's condemnation of imperialism is unhesitating, but nowhere does he suggest that the blame can be set rightly in any one place. Every character, English and Burmese alike, is to some extent guilty of opening up the abyss between human beings. Orwell's duties as a policeman had taught him how useless it was to judge people according to race or social status, and when writing *Burmese Days* this lesson was fresh in his mind. Like E. M. Forster, Orwell chose to replace the usual stereotyped figures of Anglo-Indian fiction with characters of human proportions.

The story takes place in a small trading town in Upper Burma called Kyauktada. The opening description is of the insular European section of the town, huddled together in the midst of a terrain which humiliatingly dwarfs it:

> There was an English cemetery within a white wall half-way down the hill, and nearby a tiny tin-roofed church. Beyond that was the European Club, and when one looked at the Club – a dumpy three-storey wooden building – one looked at the real centre of the town. In any town in India the European Club is the spiritual citadel, the real seat of the British power, the Nirvana for which native officials and millionaires pine in vain. It was doubly so in this case, for it was the proud boast of Kyauktada Club that, almost alone of Clubs in Burma, it had never admitted an Oriental to membership.[29]

The Club is the physical centre of the novel – much of the story occurs there, and it symbolises everything dear to the English in Kyauktada. It is their fortress against the 'natives' outside, the embodiment of order in what they feel is a chaotic environment and the one place into which they can retreat from the threatening world which surrounds them. In the Club, the reader first meets the English community: Ellis, local representative of a timber firm and a vicious racist; Mr Lackersteen, anothe teak-firm agent, who lives in an alcoholic stupor; Westfield, the District Superintendent of Police; and MacGregor, the District Commissioner, whose interminable anecdotes are a staple of Club conversation. All bitter and complaining people, this gallery of defeated Englishmen is meant to represent the moral bankruptcy of imperialism. Their punishment for bearing the responsibilities of power is ironic: in the midst of their despair, they must 'keep a stiff upper lip', playing the role of pukka sahib to all Burmese with whom they come into contact. Only in the Club can they relax and vent their resentment by cursing the natives (especially the nationalists) and abusing the Club servants.

In contrast to all of this is Orwell's protagonist, John Flory, yet another agent of the timber industry. He, too, comes to the Club, but the role of superior white man is an uneasy one for him. Flory is a loner, the only Englishman in the book who has any personal dealings with non-Englishmen other than the servants. But these interracial relationships, with his mistress Ma Hla May, a Burmese, and with his closest friend, the Indian Dr Veraswami, are only purgative ones which enable him to go on living what he knows to be a lie. Flory's furtive liaison with Ma Hla May is his miserable attempt to combat the overwhelming loneliness of his everyday existence. And Flory's friendship with the Indian doctor, genuine though the affection is on both sides, really only provides a chance to vent his frustrations verbally to a man of some intelligence, as there is no one at the Club who even approaches that description. In their endless debates about the Empire, it is Dr Veraswami who defends the raj, parroting glibly the conventional platitudes of the 'noble white man' when confronted with Flory's weary cynicism:

> 'But truly, truly, Mr Flory, you must not speak so! Why is it that always you are abusing the pukka sahibs, ass you call them? They are the salt of the earth. Consider the great things they have done – consider the great administrators who have made British India what it is. Consider Clive, Warren Hastings, Dalhousie, Curzon. They were such men – I quote your immortal Shakespeare – ass, take them for all in all, we shall not look upon their like again!'
> 'Well, do you want to look upon their like again? I don't.'[30]

Orwell's deliberate effort to escape the usual stereotypes of Anglo-Indian fiction is evident in this reversal of roles, with the ruler expressing anti-imperialist opinions and the subject reciting the dreary litany of British India's superheroes.

Flory is a complex and tragic figure, and Orwell conveys fully the despair of this sensitive man trapped in a role he abhors: 'You are a creature of the despotism, a pukka sahib, tied tighter than a monk or a savage by an unbreakable system of tabus.'[31] At the end of the book, Flory is a man totally alone: the British have cast him out for his sins against racial solidarity, and the Burmese remain on the other side of that mysterious barrier which somehow permits disembodied physical intimacy while forbidding relationships of any authentic substance.

Orwell's acerbic vision of the raj reflects the intense disenchantment about the Empire felt by many English people in the 1930s. The end of England's dominion in India seemed near, and Anglo-Indian writers who were Orwell's contemporaries often adopted an elegiac tone about the raj, as in Edward J. Thompson's *A Farewell to India* (1931).

There was very little Anglo-Indian writing of consequence from

1935 until Indian independence in 1947, but in the 1950s and 1960s a new generation of writers, such as John Masters, Paul Scott, J. G. Farrell and M. M. Kaye, sparked a revival of interest in the now-gone days of British India. The best of these is Paul Scott, whose massive four-volume work *The Raj Quartet* (1966–75) is the one unquestionable masterpiece of post-1947 English fiction on the raj.

The first novel in *The Raj Quartet*, *The Jewel in the Crown*, is so similar to *A Passage to India* in its basic details that it almost seems Scott was rewriting Forster's novel, setting it in 1942 instead of 1912. Both books have at their centre a mysterious incident in which a white woman is said to have been violated by Indians; the settings in which these incidents take place (the Marabar Caves and the Bibighar Gardens) assume great symbolic importance; and both victims have troubled relationships with narrow and unfeeling Anglo-Indian officials named Ronald (Ronny Heaslop and Ronald Merrick). In addition, both Adela Quested and Daphne Manners refuse to accept the prejudices of the Anglo-Indian community, which first embraces them as heroines and then ostracises them when they will not play their assigned role. Despite these many parallels, there is a vital difference in the tone of the two books. Forster's Anglo-Indians are certainly ill at ease in India and often feel threatened by the unfamiliar surroundings, but their counterparts in *The Raj Quartet* have sunk into permanent doubt and depression. Living mostly in the past, they are connected to the present only by their consciousness of being participants in the melancholy final act of an immense tragedy. As one of Scott's characters dramatically puts it, 'It's time we were gone. Every last wise, stupid, cruel, fond or foolish one of us.'[32] Similarly, the vaguely menacing landscape of Forster's India has become in Scott's novel oppressive and claustrophobic:

> This sense of danger, of the sea-level rising, swamping the plains, threatening the hills, this sense of imminent inundation, was one to which people were now not unaccustomed and although the outbreak of war in Europe had momentarily suggested the sudden erection of a rocky headland upon which to stand fast, the headland was far away, in England, and India was very close and all about.[33]

And the English Club, that beleaguered but sturdy fortress of Anglo-Indian solidarity in *A Passage to India*, is now described by Scott as 'the *Titanic*, with all the lights blazing and the bands playing, heading into the dark, with no one on the bridge'.[34]

Scott's vision of the raj is a tragic one, and the essence of that tragedy is that the embrace between England and India has become so intimate that their identities have merged and can no longer be distinguished from one another. *The Raj Quartet* is filled with characters who are neither wholly English nor wholly Indian; to one extent or another, they have absorbed something fundamental in the alien culture and been utterly changed by it. The most memorable of these is Hari Kumar (Harry Coomer), whose Indian origins and English upbringing are a source of constant torment to him. He is, to use Conrad's term, *homo duplex* (double man), cruelly caught between two cultures, neither of which is truly his own. Kumar's dual identity is exactly what Ronald Merrick cannot accept, for Merrick's simplistic imperialist mentality recognises only two human types – 'master and man' – and, as he says at one point, 'only two basic human emotions, contempt and envy'.[35]

Although Scott frequently presents the raj in an unfavourable light, he is unabashed in his admiration for the imperial British work-ethic, which he characterises as 'an extraordinary talent for running things and making them work'.[36] We sympathise with his Anglo-Indian characters through their struggles to find in their work a meaning for their lives in India. The two basic questions which pervade Anglo-Indian literature from its beginnings are 'Who are we?', and 'What are we doing here?' Scott believed that the answer to the second question would suffice for the first as well. Work gives his characters a sense of purpose and enables them to resist sporadic attacks of acute existential distress. The tragic tone of *The Raj Quartet* indicates Scott's feeling that in the final days of the raj, Anglo-Indians have lost their identity because there is no more work to do. As Susan Layton asks her sister in bewilderment, 'Why are we finished, Sarah? Why don't we matter?'[37]

The unique virtue of Scott's work is his innate understanding of the essential 'doubleness' of Anglo-India, which he has symbolised in the Layton sisters. These two women, whose lives are the focus of all but the first volume of *The Raj Quartet*, represent two opposing tendencies within the Anglo-Indian psyche: Sarah Layton never ceases to examine her family's tradition of service to the Empire and its meaning for her own life, while her sister Susan appears mesmerised by what Scott calls 'the powerful and terrible enchantment of inherited identity'.[38] In the figure of Susan, who seems to have lost control over her own fate as she floats from one marriage to the next, Scott offers a striking human metaphor for Anglo-India's drift towards self-destruction. Possessed of a keen sense of history, Scott depicts all of the characters in *The Raj Quartet* as victims of overwhelming historical forces, so that the personal tragedies of Susan Layton, Teddy Bingham, Ronald Merrick, Hari Kumar, Daphne Manners and Ahmed Kasim become part of the greater tragedy of the raj. The demise of the raj is a tragedy for Scott because in its origins he discerns a noble idea, that of service and responsibility to other human beings. But this idea has gone terribly sour in the period of which he writes. In the twilight of British rule in India and the muddle which accompanies it, Scott can no longer discover any moral imperatives in a situation which has progressed beyond good and evil.

Notes

1 Throughout this chapter I have used the term 'Anglo-Indian' to denote British people living and working in India. And I have used the term 'Anglo-Indian literature' (or fiction) to indicate British writing about India.

2 E. W. Said, *Orientalism*, New York, 1978, p. 3.

3 L. Woolf, *Growing: An Autobiography of the Years 1904–1911*, London, 1961, p. 46.

4 Sir Walter Scott, *The Surgeon's Daughter* (1827), Edinburgh, 1871, p. 10.

5 In three separate incidents at Eton, Winchester and Rugby the army had to be called in to suppress student uprisings.

6 T. Hughes, *Tom Brown's Schooldays* (1857), New York, 1910. p. 126.

7 Hughes, *Tom Brown's Schooldays*, p. 168.

8 M. Naidis, 'G. A. Henty's Idea of India', *Victorian Studies*, VIII (1), September 1964, p. 51.

9 G. A. Henty, *To Herat and Cabul: A Story of the First Afghan War*, New York, 1901, p. vi.

10 G. A. Henty, *In Times of Peril: A Tale of India*, New York, 1881, p. 26.

11 C. Connolly, *Enemies of Promise* (1938), New York, 1948, p. 263.

12 Henty, *In Times of Peril*, p. 14.

13 G. A. Henty, *For Name and Fame or, Through Afghan Passes*, New York, 1885, pp. iii–iv.

14 R. Kipling, 'The Man Who Would Be King' (1890), New York, 1975, pp. 4–5.

15 R. Kipling, *Kim* (1901), New York, 1974, pp. 65–6.

16 See N. C. Chaudhuri, 'The finest story about India in English', *Encounter*, VIII, April 1957, 47–53.

17 E. M. Forster, *Howards End* (1910), New York, 1921, p. 186.

18 E. M. Forster, *A Passage to India*, New York, 1924, p. 62.

19 Forster, *Passage*, p. 23.

20 Forster, *Passage*, p. 164.

21 Forster, *Passage*, p. 216.

22 Forster, *Passage*, pp.116–17.

23 Forster, *Passage*, p. 264.

24 Forster, *Passage*, p. 114.

25 Forster, *Passage*, p. 62.

26 Forster, *Passage*, p. 149.

27 G. Orwell, 'A Hanging', and 'Shooting an Elephant', *The Orwell Reader*, New York, 1956.

28 G. Orwell, *The Road to Wigan Pier* (1937), New York, 1961, pp. 127–8.

29 G. Orwell, *Burmese Days* (1934), New York, 1962, pp. 17–18.

30 Orwell, *Burmese Days*, p. 38.

31 Orwell, *Burmese Days*, p. 38.
32 P. Scott, *The Raj Quartet* (1966–75), New York, 1978, II, *The Day of the Scorpion*, p. 405.
33 Scott, *Quartet*, III, *The Towers of Silence*, p. 25.
34 Scott, *Quartet*, I, *The Jewel in the Crown*, p. 376.
35 Scott, *Quartet*, IV, *A Division of Spoils*, p. 313.
36 Scott, *Quartet*, II, *The Day of the Scorpion*, p. 3.
37 Scott, *Quartet*, II, *The Day of the Scorpion*, p. 343.
38 Scott, *Quartet*, IV, *A Division of Spoils*, p. 132.

Reading list

Ackerly, Joe R., *Hindoo Holiday*, New York, 1932.
Anstey, F. (Thomas Anstey Guthrie), *Baboo Jabberjee, BA*, London, 1897.
Farrell, James G., *The Siege of Krishnapur*, New York, 1973.
Forster, E. M., *A Passage to India* (1924), New York, 1952.
Henty, George Alfred, *In Times of Peril: A Tale of India*, New York, 1881.
Henty, George Alfred, *For Name and Fame, or Through Afghan Passes*, New York, 1885.
Jhabvala, Ruth Prawer, *Heat and Dust*, New York, 1975.
Kaye, Mary Margaret, *The Shadow of the Moon* (1957), New York, 1979.
Kaye, Mary Margaret, *The Far Pavilions*, New York, 1978.
Kipling, Rudyard, *Plain Tales from the Hills*, Calcutta, 1888.
Kipling, Rudyard, 'The Man Who Would Be King' (1890), New York, 1975.
Kipling, Rudyard, *Kim* (1901), New York, 1974.
Masters, John, *Bhowani Junction*, New York, 1954.
Orwell, George (Eric Blair) 'A Hanging' (1931) and 'Shooting an Elephant' (1936) in *The Orwell Reader*, New York, 1956.
Orwell, George (Eric Blair), *Burmese Days* (1934) New York, 1962.
Perrin, Alice, *Idolatry*, London, 1909.
Scott, Paul, *The Raj Quartet* (1966–75), New York, 1978.
Scott, Paul, *Staying On*, New York, 1977.
Scott, Sir Walter, *The Surgeon's Daughter* (1827), Edinburgh, 1971.
Sherwood, Mary Martha, *Little Henry and His Bearer*, London, 1814.
Steel, Flora Annie, *Indian Scene: Collected Short Stories* (1893–1923), Freeport, NY, 1971.
Steel, Flora Annie, *On the Face of the Waters*, London, 1896.
Taylor, Philip Meadows, *Confessions of a Thug*, London, 1839.
Thompson, Edward John, *A Farewell to India*, London, 1931.

CHAPTER FIVE

Imagining India:

English-language fiction set in post-independence India

Ainslie T. Embree

'I'm in love with the country', the young Rudyard Kipling exulted soon after his arrival in India: 'I find heat and smells and oils and spices, and puffs of temple incense, and sweat and darkness, and dirt and lust and cruelty, and above all, things wonderful and fascinating innumerable.'[1] This response to India was transmuted by Kipling's extraordinary creativity as a poet and novelist into imagery which has strongly coloured subsequent Western perceptions of India. All the familiar images and stereotypes are subsumed in his catalogue (including Indian religion, which he would have linked in some fashion to each of the items), from heat to lust to things truly wonderful, such as the lama's faith in *Kim*.

Western novelists who use contemporary India – that is, India since independence – as a setting for their novels, have, with very few exceptions, neither denied Kipling's vision of India nor created a replacement. The great majority of such novels are by British or American authors, as in the past, but a new element, in sharp contrast to earlier periods, is that Indian writers now produce far more novels in English about India than do Western writers. These Indian novelists compel consideration in an examination of novels written in English. It is an arresting fact that for them, as for Western novelists, there is a durability and power in the old interpretations of India which have often been dismissed as stereotypes based on a distorted perception of Indian reality.

That Indian writers share the foreigner's vision of India is illustrated in a novel by Khushwant Singh which was widely popular both in India and the West. *Train to Pakistan* (entitled *Mano Majra* in the American edition) is probably the most dramatic and realistic of all the novels about Partition. The brutalities of the time are summarised and blame apportioned:

D

Muslims said that Hindus had planned and started the killing. According to the Hindus, Muslims were to blame. The fact is, both sides killed. Both shot and stabbed and speared and clubbed. Both tortured. Both raped.

In the end, Iqbal Singh, who had just returned to India after a long stay in England, and who had been trying to stop the bloodshed and violence, concluded that the root of the trouble is India itself:

India is constipated with a lot of humbug. Take religion. For the Hindu, it means little besides caste and cow-protection. For the Muslim, circumcision and kosher meat . . . Take philosophy . . . it is just a muddle-headedness masquerading as mysticism . . . And Yoga, particularly Yoga, that excellent earner of dollars . . . Have perfect control over the senses. Make women come until they cry 'Enough!' and you can say 'next please', without opening your eyes . . . We are of the mysterious East. No proof, just faith. No reason, just faith.

After this tirade, Iqbal, not quite sure what he meant, in the symbolic gesture of his Western self, 'poured himself another whiskey'.

The most popular Western novelists who use India as a setting – E. M. Forster, Paul Scott, M. M. Kaye, John Masters – write about pre-independence India, and their focus is on conflicts which have their origins in Western political domination. For this reason, with the exception of Scott's *Staying On*, their work will not be discussed in this chapter. Nor will translations from Indian languages into English, since the original versions are intended for quite different audiences than those written in English by Indian authors.

The West would not have been so receptive of Kipling's vision of India if it had not been based on material long present in the Western imagination. In a witty book entitled *Imagining America*, Peter Conrad describes how famous British travel writers – Mrs Trollope, Dickens, Oscar Wilde and the rest – knew what they were going to see in America because 'America' was a construct of the European imagination, and before coming they had, like Columbus, 'imagined America'. India has had much the same experience of being 'imagined' by writers for whom it was a necessary creation, the screen on which they projected their fears and their desires.

That the old images of India have retained their hold upon Western imagination in the world of post-independence India is suggested by an article distributed by an airline to introduce travellers to India. Its authors record how, on their first visit, 'a series of fragmented images' swept them into the 'immense bittersweet cauldron of Indian life'. They had come with a preconceived notion of a Gandhian, non-violent society; instead they found 'an aggressive, mystical, cruel and always fascinating reality'. Although almost certainly accidental, the similarity of the language of the travel writers to that of Kipling is remarkable.

That Europeans 'imagined America' does not mean that their reporting was false, or that the America they described did not exist. What they were presenting was what they had perceived, and while one can argue that Trollope and Dickens did not see the 'real' America, nevertheless, America fitted their perceptions. So it is with Western novelists, who, even when their setting is contemporary India, seem to be responding to the old and persistent foreigner's image. It may not be the India which Indians themselves would like to have presented, but it is the India which, in fact, presents itself to foreigners. Furthermore, since contemporary Indian novelists, writing in English, use the same themes as Western writers, it would seem that the stereotypes are rooted in reality; the themes and imagery are only stereotypes when they are secondhand experience. Novelists who set their narratives in contempary India may not have escaped the seductive pull of the India of the imagination and the dream, but they do not have ready at hand the legerdemain of colour film or, in the novelist's own medium, the mythic world of M. M. Kaye's *The Far Pavilions*. They are bound, more so than the historical novelist, by a physical reality known to the reader.

India is almost always more than a stage setting; it dominates the novels which use it as a setting and a sense of place imposes itself. This sense of place can become, of course, the tedium of the picturesque, but sensitive novelists respond to the power of the Indian landscape and the pervasive strength of the culture. Gore Vidal's *Kalki* is an interesting example of this. The novel centres on the career of the holy man, a guru who may or may not be a charlatan, and whose inspiration is India.

Vidal's India is carelessly drawn: his description of the road from the airport, for example, is ludicrously inaccurate, but in the end a sense of the reality of India overcomes the factual errors, giving plausibility to the bizarre story. An obvious contrast is R. K. Narayan's *The Guide*, where the reluctant – and self-made – holy man is placed in a wholly authentic Indian setting. The books are different in every way, but the theme is a persistent one in fiction about India: the nature of holiness.

Even mediocre novels take on momentary importance because of the pervasive power of India. A useful example is Elwyn Chamberlain's *Gates of Fire*, which is a badly structured story of lust, violence and religious delirium set in contemporary India in luxury hotels and on the beaches of Goa. On one level, such novels perpetrate the most deplorable stereotypes, and yet the main themes of contemporary Western novels about India emerge: the foreigner in search of himself;

the ambiguity of good and evil revealed in an Indian context; the paradoxes of spirituality. One is reminded of moments in two of the greatest novels with Indian settings: when the young Kim in the train considers 'his own identity, a thing he had never done before, till his head swam. He was one insignificant person in all this roaring whirl of India'; and when Mrs Moore in *A Passage to India*, hears the sound of India – and of life – in the cave: 'Everything exists, nothing has value.'

No less than their predecessors, novelists use contemporary India as the arena in which their characters seek a meaning for their lives in the roaring whirl of the country; and the questions they address to India continue to receive enigmatic and ambiguous answers. Seeming to deny common sense, the echo in the cave hints at profundities which, on closer examination, are the stereotypes of the East–West confrontation and of the seeker after Oriental wisdom.

In a number of striking novels, David Rubin, an American writer, has translated the metaphor of East–West confrontation into disturbing imagery of alienation and redemption. In *The Greater Darkness*, which is subtitled, quite simply, 'A Novel of India', the leading roles are played by those most ubiquitous of modern Westerners in India, an academic on a sabbatical and his wife. The title is taken from a verse of the *Upanishads*: 'All who worship what is not truth enter into blind darkness; those who delight in truth enter, as it were, into greater darkness.' Those who, like Bill, the husband, are insensitive to India, survive; his wife, Carol, responds to it and is killed in a riot at a great Hindu festival. As she died, 'pity stirred her heart, giddy with the swing of the rickshaw under the tamarinds, the inescapable rhythm of drums under the sitar, the undercurrents of the Jumna frantic with debris and garlands; all found its shape in motion, sound and colour'. Through the darkness of death, India had led her to the deliverance she sought.

Perhaps the most ambitious novel in terms of structure and imagery, and one of the best set in post-independence India, is Rubin's *Cassio and the Life Divine*. The protagonist, Cassio, is an American who, in the fashion of the sixties, is cadging his way through India, when he finds himself involved with a swami. Cassio is searching for an American girl, Susanna, who is an amalgam of spirituality, sensuality, world weariness and *naïveté*, and she confronts India, with all its baffling contradictions. 'What is transcendent reality?', Elinor, Susanna's sister, asks the swami. His answer is that reality is not 'the dirty old man who set up Eden'. This mocking insight is immediately called into question by that most banal of Indian stereotypes, the statement that 'All is One, everything and everyone is truly God.' 'The one', the swami declares, 'in its highest triplicate nature is consciousness, existence and bliss.' When Susanna claims that she understood 'a little' of the swami's exposition, Elinor's comment is 'Really, pet! Why, you couldn't pass freshman mathematics at Finch.'

If the overarching theme of Rubin's novel links it with the tradition of fiction based in India, its irony and humour, even more than its thematic complexity, set it apart, for an odd characteristic of the genre is its lack of humour. Only Paul Scott's *Staying On*, to be noted in more detail later, matches *Cassio* for a humour which derives from a compassionate understanding of the poignancy and despair of the moment when one realises that there are no answers and no security in India, nor can these be found in a return to an equally mythical homeland. In *Cassio*, when the man from the American Consulate, seeking to belittle the swami, says that criminals sometimes seek safety in joining religious groups like the swami's ashram, the swami's reply is, 'Let us hope they find it. Safety, after all, is Anglo-Saxon (corrupted) for salvation.' In the end, when he is through with the 'spook racket', the term he gives to the Westerner's spiritual quest in India, Cassio knows that 'the future lies behind me with the past', and that 'I don't have to go anywhere as long as I let the road go under me.'

The same sense of the future collapsing into the past as the result of India is conveyed with vivid power and with great humour in Paul Scott's *Staying On*. While it did not enjoy the celebrity of the novels which make up *The Raj Quartet*, it is a more remarkable artistic achievement. Lucy and Tusker Smalley, an English couple who have stayed on in India after 1947, would seem to have nothing in common with the picaresque Cassio; but their future also disappears with the past. Because they are old and tired, they are forced, as Cassio is not, to recognise the meaning of their failure: they were mediocrities in a mediocre society.

Lucy, as a tipsy, tired, old woman, is sitting in a darkened bathroom in an Indian hill station after the death of her husband, thinking of India and of their place in it. They had stayed on and discovered, or finally admitted to themselves, that they had no place either in the past or future of India or England. Lucy remembers trying to keep up appearances in a society where little else mattered, and how in order to save money, they would stand around after parties, hoping to get a lift home. 'I remember one party when we seemed to be absolutely stranded. Perhaps it was symbolic. I mean everyone else gone and just Tusker and me, peering into the dark waiting for transport that never turned up.' And in the end, she cries out to the dead Tusker, 'How can you make me stay here by myself, while you yourself go home?'

Two other novels of high quality: *A New Dominion*, by an established writer, Ruth Prawer Jhabvala, and *Neglected Lives*, a first novel by Stephen Alter, explore the theme of staying on in a land that is not one's own, of seeking a meaning that may not exist either there or elsewhere. In both novels, with the discovery that the India they have imagined does not exist, the realisation of their own isolation from both the past and the future comes to the characters.

Jhabvala's *A New Dominion* (called *Travellers* in the American edition) is, in the terminology of Rubin's *Cassio*, about the 'spook racket', the guru business, and the search for an imagined India by Westerners. The novel has been criticised for perpetuating stereotypes – the lecherous holy man, the gullible young foreign girl, the nymphomaniac princess – but the characters are self-consciously playing these roles, not out of hypocrisy, but because they are the only ones they know. They have an inner emptiness which, in the end, leaves them in despair.

At the beginning of *A New Dominion*, Raymond, an Englishman, has arrived in Delhi. The familiar theme of Western-language fiction set in modern India is established at the very beginning. Raymond is uncomfortable sitting on the floor, and a new Indian acquaintance asks, rather oddly, if he has not brought any furniture with him. His answer is that 'he had brought nothing because he wanted to stay quite free and also he didn't know how long he was going to stay'. Meanwhile, with matching symbolism, the young Indian visitor is looking at Raymond's clothes: 'He fingered the material with approval and desire.'

The search for holiness, for a guru, for India, leads to Benares, where the lives of young foreigners interweave with the dirt, cruelty, lust and holiness of their imagined India. The final scenes of the novel take place in another symbol of Jhabvala's India – a moth-eaten palace of a former maharaja. One of the swami's young devotees dies of disease and malnutrition; and her friend, Lee, who had been subjected to a brutal semi-rape by the swami as part of his spiritual therapy, cries out against him and India:

> I was full of bitterness and rage. It was he who brought us here to this room. I detested him and not only him but everything connected with him, all the roads that led us to him – literally those roads: the trains and buses we had travelled on, the makeshift places where we had slept, crowded in together with the deformed, diseased people . . . squatting in filthy places that no one was low enough to clean so that excrement festered in the heat, feeding up flies. Those very flies that were now settling on Margaret's dead face.

Here is the recurrent theme: the self-deluded spiritual quest, the enigmatic holy man, the desire to return home. The conclusion of the book does not make clear if Lee returns to America or to the swami; all that she knows is the future is not hers to choose.

Indian, and some Western, critics have argued that Jhabvala's social vision is circumscribed by a limited knowledge of India, and that her novels are confined to the upper and middle classes of contemporary Delhi. But this world is no less authentic than the 'real' India, village India, so beloved by people ignorant of it. As Professor Brajraj Singh, one of Jhabvala's most discerning critics, has pointed out, the limitations of the India she portrays are the limitations of the Indians and the Westerners, and both are mediocre: 'The Westerners, in turning away from India, are doing so because they hoped to find India different from the West, but find instead that India contains the worst features of the West.'[2]

In Alter's *Neglected Lives*, the people in search of India and of themselves are Anglo-Indians, the descendants of mixed Indian and British marriages. In the days of British rule, they were accepted by neither community, but they identified themselves as British and had a special role in such occupations as the railways. During the Second World War, they achieved a certain status in British eyes for their loyalty and dependability. With the coming of independence, this world turned upside down. They lost their links with the old rulers, and they were aliens everywhere. An Anglo-Indian boy, Lionel, has to leave Lucknow because he has had an affair with a Hindu girl. A retired brigadier, also an Anglo-Indian, sums up the situation in a letter inviting Lionel to visit him in the hills:

> I don't know which it is worse to get caught with, white, Muslim, or Hindu. For us, all three are a problem. Nobody wants his daughter in bed with someone until it's proper, and especially not with an Anglo-Indian . . . . The Indians will kill you if they get a chance. It's their country now. They can do as they please.

Behind the familiar phrases is the implication that, without the restraining Western power, Indians will choose lawlessness and anarchy.

India as seen through the memories of the brigadier and his wife, and also of Lionel, and the Anglo-Indian girl he marries is, as Lionel says at one point, a sterile, dying world because in the contemptuous phrase the English used, he is only 'a bloody half and half'. One set of memories comes from a friend of Lionel's who is not Anglo-Indian. This is Salim, a Muslim, who is as alienated from the new India as are the Anglo-Indians. It is a measure of Alter's achievement that from these unlikely actors a vision emerges of the reality of India which is as powerful as that of Rubin's Cassio or Jhabvala's people.

The effect of India on the personal lives of estranged Westerners is treated with considerably less success, but nonetheless in an interesting manner, in *The Cats of Benares* by Geraldine Halls. The familiar stereotypes are present in such startling profusion that at first one suspects the novel is a parody of its genre. A scene at the beginning of the novel is typical. A Western woman walking in Benares is confronted by lepers who 'thrust their crumbling fingers in her face and it seemed to her that all the misery and importunity of India would seize her and pull her down'. One of the central themes of the book is, on one level, similar to that of Jhabvala's *A New Dominion*, where Raymond, the new arrival in search of the meaning of India, falls under the spell of Gopi, 'a graceful boy' who was an unsuccessful student at a third-rate college. In *The Cats of Benares*, the Westerner is Giles, who liked India because he could relax in its 'climate of unrestrained individualism and permitted excesses'. Cynical where Raymond is believing, he takes Krishnan, also an unsuccessful student, as his lover, even though he calls him 'a rotten little whore'. Krishnan is more of an actor in his drama than Gopi was in his, and, in a rage with the life-style made possible by Westerners but which he cannot sustain, he causes an accident while driving Giles's car. This tears apart the lives of the other characters. Krishnan and Gopi, in their emptiness and inanity, stand for the India that Westerners come to know, but, in a curious way, they are less mediocre than the Westerners, and more in control of their destiny. *The Cats of Benares* is not a very good novel but there is one scene which is startling in its summation of the response to India by Westerners in many novels: Giles cuddled Krishnan's face in his hands and 'poured down into his upturned face a look of expectant and unaffectionate lust'.

Few Western writers have attempted to communicate their vision of modern India wholly through Indian eyes, and those who have attempted to do so have not been particularly successful. An example is Evelyn Harter's *Bosom of the Family*. The theme is a familiar one in Indian fiction and cinema: the conflict between love and marriage. Mohan, the young brahmin, goes to the USA and falls in love with an unsuitable girl – in this case, an Indian Christian. As the dust-jacket correctly puts it, the novel 'is rich with the sounds and smells and colour of life' of India, but it is not true that it is 'tense with the conflict of honourable tradition and new values'. The tension is more described than felt, and the novel becomes a kind of tour of Indian life.

A much more ambitious attempt by a Western novelist to see

India through Indian eyes is Stanley Wolpert's *Nine Hours to Rama.* Erik Erikson, in *Gandhi's Truth*, speaks of how witnesses and recorders of an event make it 'their own', by the act of reviewing it; the event Wolpert sought to make his own is the most dramatic moment in the history of modern India, the assassination of Mahatma Gandhi. The novel provides a plausible reconstruction of the motivation of the assassins and of the apparent failure of the authorities to protect Gandhi, but, as in so many novels about India, the setting becomes obtrusive and didactic, and the characters recede, bleached of their colour by the author's fascination with India.

Novelists who are undeniably Indian by birth and cultural heritage, but who write in English, provide an interesting comparison with non-Indians. The role of English in India is the product of a unique historical experience which has, perhaps, no analogy in the history of any other imperial domination. In India, English is the language in which Indians communicate, very often not only with the British and the rest of the world but also with each other. That it was used by the rulers to communicate with the ruled was of secondary importance. The result is that a segment of Indians – the small English-knowing group – now communicate easily with the English-speaking world. While novels about India have been written in other Western languages, fiction set in contemporary India is overwhelmingly written in English. Many of the novelists are British or American, but most of the novels written in English are by Indian authors.

Writing in English by Indians has received considerable attention under the designation 'Indo-Anglian' writing. Reasonable arguments have been made for treating it as a genre separate from English fiction, but there seems little reason not to consider fiction written in English both by Westerners and Indians under a single rubric. While Indian writers bring the different perspective and knowledge of the insider, they are within the same literary tradition as Western writers. Not only do they share a common critical approach with Western writers in their education and intellectual background but also Indian writers in English are writing for a Western as well as an Indian audience. They, too, have to communicate the complexity and variety of India to a reading public unfamiliar with it, in the same way as does the Western writer. They have to stop, as it were, and explain what otherwise could be communicated by indirection or allusion if, say, an American were writing about the USA for an American audience. Raymond Chandler never explicates (except in the most indirect way) his Californian settings for his audience;

Mulk Raj Anand comments continually on his regional backgrounds, even in such early novels as *Coolie.*

What this means is that for Indian novelists writing in English, India and Indian culture are as obtrusive and dominant as in novels written by Westerners. The point can be illustrated by reference to the work of two novelists covering approximately the same time period. One is Anthony Powell's multi-volumed *A Dance to the Music of Time,* where the background is, of course, vividly England, but it is the characters and their passions which are always centre stage. In Paul Scott's series, *The Raj Quartet,* it is India which dominates, not the people. Paul Scott is always identified as a novelist who writes about India; this appears to be the primary referent for his readers. It would be odd to refer to *A Dance to the Music of Time* as interesting because it is about England.

The need to explicate the background flaws a remarkable novel by Attia Hossain entitled *Sunlight on a Broken Column.* While it is set in the period immediately before Partition, it draws its meaning from that event. The locale is a very special one and unfamiliar even to many Indian readers, an upper-class Muslim family in Lucknow, and the asides and expansions the author felt were necessary for her readers mar the delicate sensitivity of the portrayal of generational relationships.

Kamala Markandaya is another example of a novelist who is Indian, but who lives abroad and clearly addresses herself to a Western audience. She chose a phrase from an English poem for the title of her novel of Indian peasant life, *Nectar in a Sieve.* In the nature of things, no actual 'insider' could write a novel of that world where work seems, indeed, to be without hope, and where the bareness of life seems to deny all communication with the outside world. While Markandaya is remarkably successful in conveying a sense of India, one is never certain that it is not as much an 'imagined India' as that of Western writers. This is also true of Rama Mehta's *Inside the Haveli.* Although perceptive and informative, it is not different from a novel which might have been written by a Western woman who had similar experience of a Rajasthan household, with all the complexities of relationships engendered by a great extended family. It fails as a novel because the reader is left with the sense that her purpose is essentially didactic: to give information about a special Indian locale.

In English novels by Indian writers, as in those by Western writers, the themes of confrontation of value and culture systems, of individuals alienated from their own society and of the search for the reality of India, are dominant. Most Indian novelists do not, of course, use

Western characters as their actors, and the confrontation is not between India and the West so much as between generations, between tradition and modernity, and very frequently between men and women. These conflicts are often set against the great events of the post-independence period: the trauma of Partition and the resulting upheaval of the flight of refugees; Hindu–Muslim communal tension; the China war; or the Bangladesh war. Less common are political novels, which is somewhat surprising in so political a society. An exception is the work of Nayantara Sahgal, who weaves the knowledge of well-informed and perceptive comment on post-independence politics with the experience of a modern woman moving in the vibrant world of Delhi and the Punjab, with all its cross-currents of caste, religious prejudice and corruption. *The Day in Shadow* is the story of a young Hindu woman who defies convention in her private life to accept a divorce and live with a Christian, but it is also a novel of Indian politics. The political theme is more implicit in her *Storm in Chandigarh*, where the factional struggles of politicians are counterposed with the conflicts and tensions within the marriages of two young couples.

Some of the best-known Indian novelists writing in English have not set novels in contemporary India, or they have depicted a society where the time of events is irrelevant. This is true of Bhabani Bhattacharya's novels, as well as those of Raja Rao. R. K. Narayan's novels reflect more closely the changing world of new India because the conflicts and tensions which shape the lives of his characters are rooted in Malgudi, which is at once the India of the past as well as of the present and the future. Of all novelists, Indian or Western, Narayan's work is the most free from the seeming stereotypes of suffering, cruelty and saintliness, but behind his humane urbanity and the lightness of his narrative lie many of those same aspects of India which have fascinated Westerners. The heat and smells, the lust and cruelty of the foreigners' vision, are not exotica but the stuff of ordinary life, and they are responsive to ordinary people. In *The English Teacher*, the narrator, beginning a new life in independent India, hangs up the necklace of flowers with which he had been garlanded. This is a commonplace act in Indian life, but 'the atmosphere became surcharged with strange spiritual forces. Their delicate aroma filled every particle of the air . . . oblivion crept over me like a cloud. The past, present, and the future welded into one.' In *The Man-Eater of Malgudi*, there are only a few clues which suggest that the action is taking place in independent India, but the man-eater, the violent irascible taxidermist who is proud that he is a scientific man, is surely meant to represent the new forces breaking into the traditional world. He is also, as the narrator's small son perceives, one of the demons of mythology. When he is found dead with a smashed skull, circumstantial evidence points to the narrator as the murderer. Then it is discovered that the taxidermist had smashed his skull when he slapped a mosquito too hard. 'Every demon', someone observes, 'while by nature indestructible, carries within him, unknown to himself a tiny seed of self-destruction.' The conflict between the old world and the new is resolved by an appeal to another level of experience. This level is not 'spiritual' or 'supernatural'; it is part of the known world.

In *Clear Light of Day*, Anita Desai, a writer of great sensitivity, portrays a middle-class family caught in the turmoil of Delhi in the days after Partition, torn between old loyalties and the new freedom. One of the protagonists, Bim, at the end of the novel turns to *The Four Quartets* for meaning and solace, and reads the line that, ironically, is Eliot's reading of Indian religion: 'Time the destroyer is time the preserver'. As so often, India returns to India via the West. And then in a passage which recalls Rubin's Cassio and Jhabvala's Lee in their search for meaning, Bim saw 'with her inner eye how her own house and its particular history linked and contained her as well as her family with all their separate histories . . . That soil contained all time, past and future, in it.'

Three other English novels by Indians can be briefly noted to demonstrate the continuity of themes between Indian and Western novelists, but with special emphases and insights. Chaman Nahal's *The English Queens* is a rarity, a comic novel about India. The queens of the title are from groups which pride themselves, in various ways, on their English language and their Western ways; all the groups have been represented in the novels already discussed. One of the queens was a teacher of English in a college; 'she was sorry she had not been able to land an Englishman as a husband'. Another was the wife of a brigadier, 'known as Chopper to his friends.' Caroline Oaks was an Anglo-Indian, a caricature of the Anglo-Indians in Alter's novel, but a recognisable caricature. Another is a European woman married to an Indian; she had 'drifted into writing; she now turned out charming novels about the Indians, which were devoured in all the fashion capitals of the world'. This is probably a thinly disguised reference to Jhabvala. Shrimati Mathur, a judge's wife, devoted herself to social welfare, most notably the organisation known as 'Rape While Awake'; this injunction was addressed to Indian husbands who had intercourse with their wives while they were asleep – the organisation wanted men to wake their wives first. The sixth of the queens belonged to a family which had amassed immense wealth overnight: 'She had the remarkable knack of making her English more mellifluous by suffixing "ji" to any word or sentence she spoke. Papaji, Mamaji.'

In Shiv Kumar's novella, *The Bone's Prayer*, a young philosopher, Suresh, moves between India and the USA as a teacher of philosophy. His quest is for 'nothing short of total sharing, absolute truthfulness', and his human relationships collapse under the burden of this commitment. When his love affair with an Indian girl ends he attempts suicide; then in the USA his affair with an American also ends disastrously, and this time he is successful in killing himself. Neither India nor the West could give him the absolutes he craved.

The third novel, *The Naked Triangle*, is called 'an autobiographical novel' by its author, Balwant Gargi. All characters are actual persons, and their real names are used; many of the episodes appear actually to have happened, more or less as described. Why then is the book a novel and not an autobiography? Because, according to the author, he wanted to share 'the magic of sex, the truth of desire, of creation, of my nightmares and their dark taste'. So the story is one of betrayals and disloyalties: 'the power and torture of sex, its ecstacy, its destructive nature . . . how geniuses are blinded by it and how they lust to be destroyed by their women'. The wheel has come full circle: the Indian writer in the closing decades of the twentieth century imagines life in terms very close to those in which Kipling – and a succession of Western writers – had imagined India.

'The most consistent demand of contemporary history', according to Mircea Eliade, the historian of religion, is 'the fact that the West is committed (one might be tempted to say "condemned") to a confrontation with the cultural values of the others'. Of all 'others', India is the most evasive, the most intransigent in yielding its meaning. That novels about India written in English provide images of confrontation rather than of resolution is not surprising. If novels mirror society through individuals, then one can expect the images of contemporary India which emerge from novels to lack definition, to be contradictory, even to appear to be stereotypes echoed from other novels. 'The rule is simple', remarks the heroine in Shourie Daniels's remarkable novel, *The Salt Doll*, the story of a Hindu–Christian marriage and of the interaction of Indians and Westerners, 'anything complex can be reduced to a simple axiom: Any remark made about India, any part of India, of any Indian living abroad, requires the contrary to be stated.' Novelists, more than other writers, have succeeded in this fashion in confronting the West with India, and India with itself.

Notes

1 Quoted in Lord Birkenhead, *Rudyard Kipling*, London, 1978, p. 63.
2 Brajraj Singh, private communication.

Reading list

Alter, Stephen, *Neglected Lives,*, New York, 1978.
Chamberlain, Elwyn, *Gates of Fire*, New York, 1978.
Daniels, Shourie, *The Salt Doll*, New Delhi, 1978.
Desai, Anita, *Clear Light of Day*, New York, 1980.
Gargi, Balwant, *The Naked Triangle*, Delhi, 1979.
Halls, Geraldine, *The Cats of Benares*, New York, 1967.
Harter, Evelyn, *Bosom of the Family*, Delhi, 1979.
Hossain, Attia, *Sunlight on a Broken Column*, London, 1961.
Jhabvala, Ruth Prawer, *Esmond in India*, New York, 1958.
Jhabvala, Ruth Prawer, *The Householder*, New York, 1960.
Jhabvala, Ruth Prawer, *Getting Reading for Battle*, London, 1962.
Jhabvala, Ruth Prawer, *A Backward Place*, New York, 1965.
Jhabvala. Ruth Prawer, *A New Dominion*, London, 1972.
Joshi, Arun, *The Foreigner*, Bombay, 1968.
Joshi, Arun, *The Strange Case of Billy Biswas*, Bombay, 1971.
Joshi, Arun, *The Apprentice*, Bombay, 1974.
Keating, Henry, *Inspector Ghote's Good Crusade*, London, 1966.
Kumar, Shiv K., *The Bone's Prayer*, New Delhi, 1980.
Markandaya, Kamala, *Possession*, New York, 1960.
Markandaya, Kamala, *Nectar in a Sieve*, New Delhi, 1978.
Nahal, Chaman, *Azadi*, New Delhi, 1979.
Nahal, Chaman, *The English Queens*, New Delhi, 1979.
Narayan, R. K., *The English Teacher*, New York, 1946.
Narayan, R. K., *The Guide*, New York, 1958.
Narayan, R. K., *The Financial Expert*, New York, 1959.
Narayan, R. K., *The Man-Eater of Malgudi*, New York, 1961.
Narayan, R. K., *The Vendor of Sweets*, London, 1967.
Rajan, Balchandra, *The Dark Dancer*, New York, 1958.
Rajan, Balchandra, *Too Long in the West*, London, 1961.
Rao, Raja, *The Serpent and the Rope*, New York, 1963.
Rubin, David, *The Greater Darkness*, New York, 1963.
Rubin, David, *Cassio and the Life Divine*, New York, 1965.
Rubin, David, *Enough of this Love Making*, New York, 1970.
Sahgal, Nayantara, *A Time to be Happy*, New York, 1958.
Sahgal, Nayantara, *The Day in Shadow*, New Delhi, 1976.
Scott, Paul, *Staying On*, New York, 1977.
Singh, Kushwant, *Mano Majra* (Train to Pakistan), New York, 1950.
Vidal, Gore, *Kalki*, New York, 1979.
Wolpert, Stanley, *Nine Hours to Rama*, New York, 1962.

CHAPTER SIX

The Himalayas in fact and fiction

Luree Miller

Nowhere in the world are the peaks higher, the air thinner or the passes more treacherous than in the Himalayas, on the southern rim of Central Asia. Sparsely populated and largely unmapped, this stupendous range of mountains is 1,600 miles long. Shaped like the curve of a closed eyelid, it separates the hot, populous peninsula of India from the cold, barren plateau of Tibet. The awesome, remote and inaccessible Himalayas inevitably became for Western writers an idealised setting for novels of magic, romance and high adventure, and for travellers' tales that read like fiction. For this part of the world remained virtually unknown to Westerners, except for a handful of explorers, mountaineers, soldiers and spies, until after the Second World War. Then Russia, China, Europe, the USA and India began to pour huge amounts of aid and thousands of technicians and administrators into the Himalayan border states.

The British, because they ruled India for two hundred years, were vaguely aware that there were some ridiculously small, ferociously independent, semi-autonomous kingdoms, with improbable names like Chitral, Dir, Gilgit, Hunza and Swat, tucked away in inaccessible valleys beyond snowbound passes. Yet, how credible could a state like Hunza be if, in the 1880s, it received annually from Britain two rolls of satin, and paid one and one half ounces of gold yearly in tribute to China? Even in the great age of Victorian travel, the dangers for most people of trekking to any such mountain fastness far outweighed the possible pleasures. The Victorians read in the popular *Book of Nonsense* by the geographically minded Edward Lear that 'There was an Old Man of Cashmere', and even an improbable Akond of Swat. (Actually he was the Wali of Swat, but who cared?) More to the point, Lear wrote: 'Who, or why, or which, or *what*, Is the Akond of Swat?'[1]

So Western novelists had free rein. They could read the accounts of actual travellers, and incorporate authentic details for a modicum of verisimilitude, and their readers could believe what they liked. For about a hundred years, from 1838, when Michael Guinn published *Nourmahal, An Oriental Romance,* set in Kashmir, until 1939, when Rumer Godden departed from the usual romance/adventure/thriller novel to consider seriously the clash of Eastern and Western cultures in her small masterpiece, *Black Narcissus.* Western writers generally held to familiar plots with high-spirited delight. In that ethnocentric age, the British found the landscape and the peoples of the Himalayas equally fascinating. These polyglot peoples seemed to them marvellously colourful. Tibetan Buddhists predominated from Ladakh to Bhutan, with Muslims in Kashmir and Hindus in Nepal, though all of these mountain inhabitants clung to animistic rituals and beliefs which blended into and often overpowered the standard doctrines of their recognised religions. The resulting cultural complexities troubled pre-Second World War writers not at all. They catered to a taste often characterised as a peculiar British 'longing for the East', which required a Western hero, vivid against an exotic background, who reaches an apotheosis of individualism in a dramatic setting.

The French priest, Abbé Huc, had provided a wealth of fantastic material in his delightful *Travels in Tartary, Tibet and China During the Years 1844–5–6,* and it became a classic book of travel as well as a standard reference for modern readers. But the British, like most people, were excited by narratives of their own exploits: how they came to the mountains, the tribes they encountered, the battles they fought and the passes won all became the historical background of this colonial fiction.

Antithetical to the Western idea of progress and conquest, the Indian view of the Himalayas was ahistorical. To the Indians, these mountains are timeless and holy, sanctified in Hindu mythology, religion, literature and art, the inaccessible seat of the great god Siva, his consort Parvati and other Hindu gods. They are the source of all the major life-giving rivers of India and have been the object of pilgrimages by devout Hindus for thousands of years. The ascetic holy man, the sannyasi, who retreated to the Himalayas and remained unmoving and impervious to winter rigours at high altitudes, became a stock figure in Western fiction. Putting a sannyasi on a mountainside in a novel signified remoteness, exotic rites and possible resistance to progress by the natives. In deference to Indian sensibilities, some Western mountaineers stopped short of scaling those summits which were abodes of the gods; such self-restraint became a standard inclusion of novelists to prove their protagonist's sensibilities.

[86]

Nineteenth-century British readers' interest in accounts of their explorers and empire-builders is evidenced by the number of travel articles, and reviews of scores of travel books. The line between fact and fantasy, always tenuous in non-fiction writing, was more often than not blurred by an excessively romantic outlook, for who could resist a bit of embellishment for the dash of it all? A writer in the prestigious British journal *The Academy* of 31 July 1880 illustrates the prevalent tone in his review of *The River of Golden Sand: The Narrative of a Journey through China and Eastern Tibet to Burma* by Captain William Gill, RE. A novelist might envy the reviewer's firm establishment of mood and character: 'Captain Gill's attention was first directed to China by the chance remark of a friend whom he met in Trafalgar Square in May, 1876, and though at the time he did not pay much heed to it, the result was that in June he began to make arrangements for a journey. . .'. [2]

Chances were, readers guessed, that Captain Gill, with a distinctive British air of insouciance, was in fact off on a secret mission. The best-selling English travel writer Isabella Bird Bishop (who had several of her books reissued in the 1960s and 1970s by university presses) recounted, in *Among the Tibetans* (1894), her accidental meeting with a Major Sawyer, who proposed she accompany him on a surveying expedition, implying that her presence would deflect suspicion from the true purpose of his journey. Travel writers then, and now, often cast themselves as central characters in their books – innocent bystanders who played an unwitting part in larger events, the significance of which became apparent to them only at the end of their journeys.

Fiction writers could not fail to see the possibilities in such accounts. Half a dozen books appeared in the 1880s and 1890s bearing titles like *Dual Lives* (1893) by P. J. Chillington, a mystery set in the Himalayan hills, and *The Secrets of the Lamas* (1889) by a Traveller.

Thus, the accumulated literature had established the Himalayas as a splendid setting for tales of adventure incorporating secrecy, disguise, and magic when, in 1901, Kipling's *Kim* appeared as the first major novel of political espionage. The awesome burden of Empire is laid on young Kim's shoulders when his mentor, the Muslim horsetrader and spy, Mahbub Ali, tells him: 'Lurgan Sahib has a shop among the European shops. All Simla knows it. Ask there . . . Men say he does magic . . . Go up the hill and ask. Here begins the Great Game.'[3]

All Kipling readers were familiar with that ringing phrase: the Great Game. They knew the object of the 'Game' was to checkmate

Russia and, if need be, China. In that famous, fabulous, hill-station shop of Lurgan Sahib (based on the actual shopowner and secret agent, Alexander Jacob) Kim learns the spy's 'magic'.

Kim is ambiguous about the destiny thrust upon him, and his own natural affinity for Indian life infuses every page. Kim's devoted friend the lama, on the other hand, is a flat character, a simple, child-like figure, the fictional forerunner of all good Buddist monks. With his 'ivory-yellow face, serene and untroubled', set 'towards the beck-oning Hills',[4] the lama embodies the spiritual aspect of the East: a single-minded figure utterly apolitical, seeking total detachment. Together in perfect harmony, Kim and the lama traverse the plains and climb the hills in as joyous a book as has been written about the subcontinent. Like the wonderfully characterised old woman from the Himalayan valley of Kulu, Kim and the lama 'love the bustle and stir of the open road'.[5]

The enduring popularity of *Kim* has been attributed to the moder-nity of his identity crisis, his search for self and his conflict with authority. But the development of a large and increasingly popular body of political espionage novels suggests that it is this element of the novel which continues to appeal most to readers. Kim is an insid-er. He operates in two major cultures, Anglo-Saxon and Indian, though the Indian side really can be counted as three: Muslim, Hindu and Buddhist. He speaks the languages and knows the customs of all of them. When, as readers, we travel with him, though we run risks, his special knowledge saves us from being duped and made fools of – the fear of all travellers in foreign lands. As the world becomes more complex and we are battered by more international news than we can make sense of, we all are, like it or not, travellers trying not to be taken in. Hence the satisfaction of identifying with secret agents: they know what we can only guess.

Kipling based Kim's two other companions – the Muslim, Mahbub Ali, and the Hindu, Babu Mookerjee – on actual Indian agents. They were trained in the arts of scientific exploration and disguise by the Indian Government at a hill station near Simla, so that they might reconnoitre areas which had become too dangerous for British offi-cers. After the Gurkha War of 1814–15, when Nepal invaded Tibet, travel beyond the frontiers carried greater risks. So the unprecedented step was taken of selecting men indigenous to the hills as surveyors. This remarkable group, called 'pundits', was able to travel quite incredible distances beyond the frontiers, survive rigourous hardships and return to British India with considerable information about the lie of the land in all of the Himalayan border states beyond the rule of the Raj.

'Till the summer of 1904, if one had been asked what was the most mysterious spot on the earth's surface, the reply would have been Lhasa', wrote John Buchan, an expert practitioner of the spy novel, in *The Last Secrets* (1924). 'It was a place on which no Englishman had cast an eye for a hundred years. . . '.⁶ Buchan referred to the Younghusband Expedition, a British military force, which marched from India to Lhasa in 1904 to settle rights of trade and access with the Tibetans, an action Buchan felt would open the frontiers permanently. But Tibet's xenophobia was not to be altered by one military foray. Subsequently, Westerners were apprehended at the borders with even greater diligence.

However, nothing challenges the adventurous spirit more than official secrecy and restrictions: 'What decided me to go to Lhasa was, above all, the absurd prohibition which closes Tibet',⁷ wrote Madame Alexandra David-Neel. Flouting prohibitions and besting officialdom immediately bestows on personal travel books such as David-Neel's the elements of plot: conflict and resolution. 'I had sworn that a woman would pass the Tibetan frontier and I would',⁸ she wrote. In 1926, after being turned back three times, this fifty-six-year-old scholar of Oriental cultures made her extraordinary journey of over 2,000 miles from China, the first European woman to enter the forbidden city of Lhasa.

Although she was French, David-Neel wrote about her travels first in English: *My Journey to Lhasa* (1927), followed by *Tibetan Journey* (1936). She had fabulous adventures, encountered improbable peoples and met the requirements of every bold hero: by her great daring, courage and keen wits she eluded detection to reach her goal. On her journeys she was accompanied by her adopted Tibetan son, Yongden, the requisite faithful companion.

With less literary skill, Yongden wrote *Mipam: The Lama of the Five Wisdoms* (1938), the first fictional attempt by a Tibetan to depict true Tibetan life. In their travels together, David-Neel and Yongden sat around innumerable campfires on the cold Tibetan plateau laboriously noting down the verses of the great epic poem of Central Asia, *Gesar of Ling*. Their translations into French and English introduced that ancient poem to the Western world.⁹

From 1900 to 1920, women fiction writers outnumbered men in their use of Himalayan settings for novels of war and romance. None was as popular as Ethel M. Dell, who had never been to India. But, Dell blithely noted, the magic of the East was everywhere. Reviewers called Dell's work 'tosh', but at her death *The Times* ranked her as one of the four or five most popular novelists in the English-speaking world. Generations of Ethel Dell readers, even after the Second World

War, picked up highly romanticised notions about India and hill-station life from her books. Dog-eared copies still lie about in local lending libraries and English country inns.

By the 1920s, a few new twists were clearly needed. Talbot Mundy disguised his secret service agent as a Brahmin, which was a bit of a trick, in *Om, the Secret of Abhor Valley* (1924), and he introduced two new characters: a beautiful American heroine and an Indian hero, Chullender Ghose of the Indian Central Intelligence Division. But it was 'Ganpat', the pseudonym of Martin Louis Gompertz, a former captain in an Indian infantry regiment, who utilised Himalayan settings most successfully to write pure fantasy. 'Ganpat' knew his territory; his details were completely accurate. Eleven of his twelve novels were set high in the Himalayas and involved smuggled treasure, Tibetan lamas, princesses – the standard fare. But in *The Speakers in Silence* (1929) 'Ganpat' endows a 'lost race' with the ability to employ audiogenic sounds. A sizeable body of science fiction takes off from Himalayan peaks.

A yearning for paradise, for a real but remote contemporary world where values are clearer, life is simpler and good triumphs over obvious evil is the essence of escape literature, as these works were. And the less one knows of history, the more one believes in the possibility of finding such a paradise on earth. In his novel *Lost Horizon* (1933), James Hilton created a paradise so irresistible that its name, Shangri-La, became a synonym for utopia. In it the hero, Conway, is 'whisked away to trans-Himalayan solitudes'.[10] His flight on a hijacked plane may be the first fictional use of an all-too-frequent contemporary reality. *Lost Horizon* is in the tradition of nostalgic utopian literature: a criticism of society as it is and a defence of older, better values, which the hero finds preserved at the lamasery where he is taken.

Hilton had put a new hero in the Himalayas: all before him had been robust soldier-adventurers, but Conway was an Oxford man who preferred 'feelings sheathed in thoughts'. The American caught on the same hijacked plane is a 'Middle West Rotary' type, who bumbles about asking for the *Herald Tribune*. In a nice swipe at such a crude interloper, Hilton writes that 'Shangri-La has files only of the London *Times*'.[11] For those who had never heard of the Himalayas (probably most Americans), Shangri-La was their only point of reference and it would colour their thoughts, whatever else they read,.

Lost Horizon is in a category by itself, its only direct successor being Lionel Davidson's zany updated version, *The Rose of Tibet* (1977), written thirty years later. Davidson uses many of the same devices as Hilton: a third person narrator tells a fantastic but 'true' story about a man whose extraordinary adventure in a beautiful hidden valley in the Himalayas renders him unfit to live in ordinary Western society after he has been exposed to the exquisite pleasures of that enchanted place. In keeping with the tastes of the 1960s for more middle-class heroes, Davidson does not designate his protagonist, Houston, a member of the elite as Hilton's Conway was. Rather, Houston is an almost down-and-out artist–teacher without prospects. He goes on his journey for lack of anything better to do, and to escape his tangled affairs in London. The beautiful Tibetan princess whom he rescues from the ruthless Chinese is delectable and sexually eager, in contrast to Conway's love who 'calms the throb of desire to a murmur that is no less pleasant when left unanswered'.[12] Depending on one's tastes, either book can be read as a wonderful romp through the magical mountains of Asia. Hilton's has a good deal more literary merit and is a classic of its kind, but Davidson writes superbly and keeps the reader riveted with his breathless prose. *The Rose of Tibet* is not utopian literature but pure adventure.

A claim implicit in all these novels is that the British talent for adventure is the genius of their race. Nothing proves that character is destiny better than the triumph of an individual endeavour. Mountain climbers, particularly those who attempt the most formidable mountains in the world, offer stunning proof of this superiority. A mystique surrounds these daring men and women who climb the Himalayas. Inevitably, novels followed popular non-fiction accounts of climbing expeditions. Those set in the Himalayas, notably Wilfred Noyce's *The Gods Are Angry* (1957), and James Ramsey Ullman's *And Not to Yield* (1970), are like other mountaineering books: the mountains are the challengers, the hero/climber is torn between his overwhelming desire to climb them and the obligations attendant on his love for a woman/family/friends. The climber cannot resist the call of the mountains: he must be up and away. However mystical he may feel in the face of awesome nature, he uses the language of the soldier–adventurer: he attacks the mountains, forces the pass, bridges the chasm, makes the ice face yield to his pick and conquers the summit. The mystery and romance associated with the Himalayas is somewhat diffused by a great deal of technical information. These novels reflect the evolution of mountaineering techniques and equipment, but not much change in 'macho' attitudes.

The only exception in this genre is non-fiction: Arlene Blum's *Annapurna: A Woman's Place* (1980), a candid, thoughtful account of the all-woman's climbing team which put the first Americans on that 26,540 ft peak.

But travel literature in general does not alter significantly from the 1920s to the present. Travellers persist in viewing the landscape as exotic and themselves as intrepid wayfarers, and the journals continue to be written as high adventure. George Schaller, Director of Conservation for the New York Zoological Society, reports on wild animals in Nepal in *Stones of Silence: Journeys in the Himalayas* (1980); Edward W. Cronin, Jr on the flora and fauna in *The Arun: A Natural History of the World's Deepest Valley* (1979); and Peter Matthiessen on himself in *The Snow Leopard* (1978). Matthiessen, a novelist, accompanied Schaller and states that his was an inner journey, a pilgrimage. *The Snow Leopard* went into several printings and reinforced the idea of the Himalayan region as perfect terrain for a mystical quest. But Matthiessen's philosophical ramblings are cliche-ridden: his is a quick search for a quick fix and devoid of that original, exact observation which elevates the two former books to a permanent place in Himalayan travel literature. Andrew Harvey's *A Journey in Ladakh* (1983) is, like Matthiessen's, a spiritual quest. But Harvey, a young novelist and poet who was a Shakespearean scholar at Oxford, has a deeper understanding of the region once called Little Tibet. His journey is a humble quest spiced with humour as well as descriptions of Tibetan Buddhism practised in a magical setting.

The possibility of a Westerner opting for a permanent place in Himalayan life was exceptional and not treated in fiction until Rumer Godden wrote *Black Narcissus* (1939). Her novel is about five Anglican nuns who attempt to establish a school and hospital in a remote Himalayan village. Godden, an English writer born in 1907, spent the first thirteen years of her life in Bengal. For many years she returned to the subcontinent, pulled, she says, by a deep love for the sights, the sounds, the smells and above all the people of a culture so different from her own. Few writers express so well that dual loyalty which complicates the lives of people living in countries not their own, but which they find congenial, as she does. Rumer Godden, Han Suyin and John Masters all share this personal experience, which may account for the fact that they rank as the best and most widely read writers of recent times who have used the Himalayas as a backdrop for their serious novels. *Black Narcissus* does not allude to any of the political issues which have animated other Himalayan novels. Godden's nuns attempt to meet the hills people at the level of their greatest concern: namely, religion. Nothing is portrayed as fantastic. Godden describes the fierce beauty of the hills and their almost supernatural effect on the nuns, but attributes it to the power of nature, the isolation and the effects of living in an alien culture.

After the Second World War Godden took up the same theme of

conflict of values and lack of understanding between East and West in *Kingfishers Catch Fire* (1953). This beautifully written book draws more sympathetically on a wider range of indigenous characters than do her previous works. Her protagonist, Sophie, is a widow with two small children who tries to live a simple life of poverty away from the other Europeans in Kashmir. In her vanity, Sophie idealises the simple life and claims to understand the peasant. Genuinely poor by European standards, she is to the Kashmiris fabulously rich. The ripple effect of her obtuseness activates a casual violence from Kashmiri children, as well as adults, which is incomprehensible to Sophie and the other Westerners. It is the violence necessary for survival in a precarious existence. Ultimately, Sophie understands:

> In those lonely solitary weeks a hardihood had crept into her, a hardening that she knew was honest; it linked her with the people and brought her into her proper place with them. There was no pretence; each was what he was, each kept to what he did.[13]

Godden demystified this romantic Himalayan setting and placed in it a modern adventurer, philosophical, apolitical, lacking all those swashbuckling characteristics which continued to flourish in an increasing number of Himalayan spy novels. What she does perpetuate is Kipling's belief that East and West can never meet but should learn to understand and respect each other, each keeping its own place.

Another novel examining this problem was the best-selling *The Mountain is Young*, written in the 1950s by Han Suyin, the pseudonym of Elizabeth Cromer, a Eurasian born in China and educated in the West. She wrote about Nepal, a remote kingdom then so little known that she may be said to have introduced it to a wide audience. Here Buddhism and Hinduism meet and neither triumphs. What does triumph in *The Mountain is Young* is sex, at times elevated to religious ecstasy. Anne, a frigid Westerner, comes to life in sensuous Kathmandu through a passionate love affair with a very dark half-Indian, half Nepali engineer, an interracial liaison which attracted almost as much criticism of the novel as did the sexually explicit scenes. Dr Han condemned Western imperialism and Nepalese backwardness in about equal amounts, but in the end came down on the side of progress, if delivered in dams and hospitals by the 'right people' – meaning those who are sensitive to Eastern cultures. Not that she gives a blanket approval to everything Oriental: her villain is an unscrupulous Tibetan lama, the opposite of Hilton's High Lama and the generally benign monks appearing in other novels.

The 1950s saw Nepal transformed from an isolated kingdom,

where no wheeled vehicles were allowed, to a fiercely courted recipient of foreign aid from the USSR, China, Britain and the USA. Han Suyin's novel was peopled by thinly disguised real characters involved in this new version of the 'Great Game', building roads, dams, hospitals and airstrips. This new strategy to gain influence in Asia through huge amounts of aid, requiring vast personnel, made the 'Great Game' more democratic. But the greater number of players made it less romantic.

Despite this influx of all nationalities, the old gung-ho heroes slogged on alone, crossing frontiers in pursuit of elusive information vital to Western defence in these updated novels of the 'Great Game': F. Van Wyck Mason, *Himalayan Assignment* (1952); Berkely Mather, *The Pass Beyond Kashmir* (1960); William H. Murray, *Appointment in Tibet* (1959), Simon Harvester, *The Chinese Hammer* (1961); Jon Cleary, *The Pulse of Danger* (1966); Stanley Wolpert, *The Expedition* (1968); and John Masters, *The Himalayan Concerto* (1976).

The American writer, Mason, a Harvard man who planned a career in the foreign service, wrote instead more than sixty novels, many concerned with international intrigue. In *Himalayan Assignment,* one of his Colonel North novels, Mason pays the traditional tribute to actual Himalayan explorers, the often-mentioned Colonel Francis Younghusband, Sven Hedin and others, and includes his own countryman, the explorer Roy Chapman Andrews. Cold War politics are explained in hefty chunks of prose: Central and South Asia must be saved from communism and the locale of the 'Game', familiar to the British, must be made clear to the Americans. There is a mercenary, one of the new villains who offer their Western expertise to the highest bidder, in this case the USSR. While these explanations slow the story down a little, all the expected characters offer enough surprise, horror and suspense to make it a 'good read'.

In the British writer Berkely Mather's *The Pass Beyond Kashmir,* the villain explains to the captured hero just why the Chinese want control of the disputed border area of the western Himalayas: they need oil from the Persian Gulf, incredible as that may seem. Nobody in the West can conceive of the Chinese plan to tunnel through the Himalayan ranges a hundred miles at a stretch because, he says, 'they are still thinking in terms of Kipling's *Kim* and the 'Great Game', when Russia, not China, was 'the bogeyman to be watched'.[14]

Since the Chinese marched into Tibet in 1950 and the Dalai Lama fled to India in 1959, Tibetans have become more sympathetic characters in fiction. They are the dispossessed, the underdogs, ill-equipped and outnumbered, fighting against the conquerors. William Murray put his hero briefly in Tibetan disguise in *Appointment in Tibet* and has him state fiercely: 'the European who thinks of the Asiatic as 'expendable', in that same moment loses equality and becomes the Asiatic's inferior'.[15]

But Murray is still looking to the USSR as the chief enemy, while Simon Harvester, in *The Chinese Hammer*, agrees with Berkley Mather that China is the greater threat. 'I don't like what the Chinese are doing to these people',[16] says the hero, referring to Chinese domination of Tibet. Like Mather, Harvester writes a knowledgeable, compelling and fast-moving novel. His Tibetan beauty is aristocratic, speaks English as did Hilton's in Shangri-La, and, in a slight variation, marries the hero's best friend.

Still, the Westerner is always the hero fighting for his country, the future of which depends on the power politics played out in Asia. He was British before the Second World War, occasionally American after it. None develops this honourable protagonist more fully than John Masters. Born in India, Masters was educated at Sandhurst and served in the British Army. His chronicle of the Savage family is interwoven with the history of British India, beginning in the seventeenth century, when the first Savage, Jason, in *Coromandel!* (1955) travels from South India to the Himalayas in search of his Golden Fleece. Masters is a superb storyteller and his tales are old-fashioned adventures set in a sea of imperialism. From the Masters canon, readers gain a richly detailed, sympathetic picture of the subcontinent.

Only with his *Himalayan Concerto* (1976) does Masters's spellbinding technique sag a bit under the load of unfamiliar information necessary to the plot. In it, Rodney Bateman, a musician, seeks inspiration for his concerto, which is a metaphor for the delicately balanced political situation on the roof of the world. Across the whole sweep of the mountains, international intrigues develop like musical themes, interdependent, one growing out of another, reaching a crescendo, disappearing, then reappearing in variations on the theme. The politician, like the musician, must see his work *in toto* in order to understand this complexity and interdependence.

The rest of the world does not realise that the future depends on preventing a major collision of the great powers in this distant theatre of war. Bateman, marooned with spies like himself, says to them:

> Look, we are . . . representatives of humanity, or, if you prefer, we represent the people of India and China and Russia and Kashmir, as well as their governments. And the governments of India and China, at least, are bent on courses which will cause the deaths of thousands of their own people besides Pakistanis, Bengalis, and probably Russians and others.[17]

Then, in a sudden metamorphosis, the reluctant spy changes to an eager publicist. Because governments acting in secret only exacerbate unstable political conditions, and no one power alone can dominate the other, secret information is of limited use; it is quickly dated, ultimately irrelevant. The spy becomes an anachronism. In concert with the other agents, Bateman devises a revolutionary plan 'to stop this madness'.[18]

Masters wrote *Himalayan Concerto* after the Sino-Indian War of 1962 and after India had absorbed the small, semi-independent state of Sikkim in 1975.

A certain melancholy, absent from his other works, creeps into this tale, unsettling to readers and robbing them of the joy of escape associated with Himalayan adventure. From now on, it will take authors, like Simon Harvester and Berkley Mather, who are firmly committed to the simple, unshakeable belief that might and right go hand in hand, and that the West can win, to create dauntless heroes who continue to risk their necks in clandestine activities.

For Jon Cleary, an Australian prize-winning novelist, it is already all over for the West in Asia. The problem now is how we can remain neutral. In *The Pulse of Danger* (1966), Cleary places a British and an American couple in Bhutan, where they are caught up in the Indian – Chinese conflict. The standard chase, up mountains and down, takes place. Cleary's hero condemns the Chinese for their brutal aggression in Tibet, but unlike Masters's musician, he feels both powerless and uninvolved.

As a sort of last gasp of Western involvement, Stanley Wolpert sends an international group of self-seekers after the yeti, or abominable snowman, in *The Expedition* (1968). Wolpert, a professor of history, is the author of several novels and non-fiction works on India. As one of the new breed of travelling American scholars who are as at home on the streets of London, Bombay and Hong Kong as they are in the libraries of New Haven and Berkeley, Wolpert is able to show off his sophistication, but his novel is a sad, cynical adventure. His denouement reveals that the expedition has been duped – used, conned – the traveller's deepest dread. They had been sent, his anti-hero shouts, 'to save mankind from some lunatic's dream of what another lunatic might have been dreaming about . . . someday you intelligence men will blow us all to kingdom come!'[19] His sense of raging impotence is uncharacteristic of the true adventurer.

That spirit of gaiety and panache, possessed by earlier Western travellers, which seemed to be drying up in the 1960s and 1970s, happily and appropriately appeared again in the writings of two Indians; Ved Mehta and Dom Moraes, both expatriates. After coming down from Oxford, they took a 'bummy holiday' together in India and Nepal. Their separate accounts varied so fundamentally and caused enough comment and confusion that Ved Mehta wrote a defence of literary license, 'Introduction, Bummy Holiday Revisited', in his revised edition of *Walking the Streets of India* (1971). Moraes and Mehta were simply carrying on a fine tradition of hyberbole employed by imaginative travellers from time immemorial.

A more serious view, quite naturally, is taken by the people who lived there all along. Two excellent books written for English-language readers are Tsewang Pemba's *Idols on the Path* (1966) and Bhabini Bhattacharya's *Shadow From Ladakh* (1966). Tsewang Pemba is sensitive to the Western idea of Tibetan primitiveness, shaped to a large extent by the works discussed in this essay. His hero, Rinzin, is a refugee like himself. Describing him, Pemba notes: 'Everywhere in books written by foreigners he discovered a Tibet which he hated and which embarrassed him, a mysterious forbidden country, with monks living up to hundreds of years in fabulous Shangri-Las'.[20]

Now that China has opened Tibet to a limited number of tourists, it is no longer quite the same mysterious forbidden country it once was. And, once inside Tibet, it was inevitable that adventurous travellers would spread out beyond the limits of Lhasa and the areas officially open to foreigners. Vikram Seth, an Indian fluent in Chinese, headed home from Nanjing University in China to Delhi by hitchhiking across Tibet. His *From Heaven Lake: Travels Through Sinkian and Tibet* (1983) brings fresh information about an essentially medieval country reeling under the impact of forced modernisation.

Before a road linked Lhasa to China and Nepal, Robert B. Ekvall published in both French and English his Tibetan novel, *Tents Against the Sky* (1954). Born in 1898 in China of missionary parents, Ekvall himself lived and worked in the far northern regions of Tibet. Later he became a social anthropologist. His novel, slowed by a wealth of information, does not move as swiftly as Tsewang Pemba's, but it has been reissued in paperback and is more readily available to readers interested in a detailed account of nomadic Tibetan life.

Bhabini Bhattacharya's *Shadow from Ladakh* is one of the first English-language novels in which India alone is held responsible for its Himalayan frontier. There are no European or American characters or allusions to Western events. Bhattacharya's tone is gentle and understanding; his great charm is in telling a serious story with such marvellous humour. With a few deft strokes, he paints a picture of modern India struggling against traditional beliefs. The Chinese invasion of Ladakh and into the Eastern Himalayas along the McMahon line forces the four main characters to come to terms with each other

[97]

and their consciences. Very little of the action of the novel takes place in the Himalayas – this is not a political espionage adventure story – but the mountains are omnipresent: 'The ultimate fate of mankind will be decided on the Himalayan snows.' The mountains are no longer an impregnable barrier against invasion but an actual battleground. As one character says: 'Each mountain pass changing hands could be a pistol pointed at the heart of India. High altitude airstrips and high altitude planes make bombing missions possible and who knows if and when the enemy will have a nuclear bomb!'[21] The war with the Chinese compelled a hitherto relatively isolated India to relinquish its old dreams of solidarity with its Asian brothers.

The period when Westerners were overcome by the importance of their place in the landscape also is over – or is stretching thin. The cruel fact is that Tibetan civilisation as it has evolved for the past thousand years has been destroyed by the Chinese. Secret Tibet no longer exists. Sikkim has been swallowed up by India and its American queen has gone home. Where yak trains used to climb over the Natu La Pass, vigilant Chinese and Indian soldiers now watch each other. But the air is still thin and cold in the high Himalayas. Peaks remain unclimbed, valleys unexplored and legends die hard. Nuclear threats notwithstanding, it will be a long time before Shangri-La is annihilated and the magic goes out of the mountains.

Notes

1 See E. Lear, 'Laughable Lyrics' (1877), in *The Complete Nonsense of Edward Lear*, New York, 1951, p. 257.

2 *The Academy*, 18, 31 July 1880, p. 75.

3 R. Kipling, *Kim* (1901), New York, 1962, p. 66.

4 Kipling, *Kim*, p. 252.

5 Kipling, *Kim* , p. 81.

6 J. Buchan, *The Last Secrets*, Boston, 1924, p. 17.

7 A. David-Neel, *My Journey to Lhasa*, New York, 1927, p. xii.

8 David-Neel, *My Journey*, p. 9.

9 A. David-Neel and The Lama Yongden, *The Superhuman Life of Gesar of Ling*, New York, 1934, 1948.

10 J. Hilton, *Lost Horizon* (1933), New York, 1936, p. 126.

11 Hilton, *Lost Horizon*, p. 128.

12 Hilton, *Lost Horizon*, p. 225.

13 R. Godden, *Kingfishers Catch Fire* (1953), New York, 1975, p. 128.

14 B. Mather, *The Pass Beyond Kashmir*, New York, 1960, p. 227.

15 W. Murray, *Appointment in Tibet*, New York, 1959, p. 244.

16 S. Harvester, *The Chinese Hammer*, New York, 1961, p. 175.

17 J. Masters, *Himalayan Concerto*, New York, 1976, pp. 369–70.

18 Masters, *Concerto*, p. 370.

19 S. Wolpert, *The Expedition*, Boston, 1968, p. 331.

20 Tsewang Pemba, *Idols on the Path*, New York, 1966, p. 68.
21 Bhabini Bhattacharya, *Shadow from Ladakh*, New York, 1966, p. 214.

Reading list

Bedier, Julie (ed.), *High Road in Tartary: An Abridged Revision of Abbé Huc's Travels in Tartary, Tibet and China During the Years 1944–5–6*, New York, 1948.

Bhattacharya, Bhabini, *Shadow from Ladakh*, New York, 1966.

Blum, Arlene, *Annapurna: A Woman's Place*, New York, 1980.

Cleary, Jon, *The Pulse of Danger*, London, 1966.

Cronin, Edward N., *The Arun: A Natural History of the World's Deepest Valley*, Boston, 1979.

David-Neel, Alexandra, *My Journey to Lhasa* (1927), Boston, 1983.

Davidson, Lionel, *The Rose of Tibet*, London, 1977.

Godden, Rumer, *Black Narcissus*, Boston, 1939.

——, *Kingfishers Catch Fire* (1953), New York, 1975.

Han Suyin, *The Mountain is Young*, London, 1973.

Harvester, Simon, *The Chinese Hammer*, New York, 1961.

Harvey, Andrew, *A Journey to Ladakh*, Boston, 1983.

Hilton, James, *Lost Horizon*, New York, 1933.

Kipling, Rudyard, *Kim*, New York, 1901.

Mason, Van Wyck, F., *Himalayan Assignment*, New York, 1952.

Masters, John, *Coromandel!*, New York, 1955.

——, *The Himalayan Concerto*, New York, 1976.

Mather, Berkley, *The Pass Beyond Kashmir*, New York, 1960.

Matthiessen, Peter, *The Snow Leopard*, New York, 1978.

Mehta, Ved, *Walking the Streets of India*, New York, 1971.

Moraes, Dom, 'The Himalayan Kingdoms', in *From East and West: A Collection of Essays*, Delhi, 1971.

Noyce, Wilfred, *The Gods Are Angry*, Cleveland, 1957.

Pemba, Tsewang, *Idols on the Path*, London, 1966.

Schaller, George B., *Stones of Silence: Journeys in the Himalayas*, New York, 1980.

Seth, Vikram, *From Heaven Lake: Travels Through Sinkian and Tibet*, 1983.

Ullman, James Ramsey, *And Not to Yield*, New York, 1970.

Wolpert, Stanley, *The Expedition*, Boston, 1968.

CHAPTER SEVEN

Chinese fictions in the twentieth century

Jonathan D. Spence

China, which once seemed to promise endless wealth to a new breed of sea-borne Western adventurers, now provides endless ground for armchair speculation instead. We do not understand China and so we constantly invent it; and what we think we know is constantly disproved. The collapse of the last dynasty in 1911, the cycles of warlordism that followed, the baffling communism (seemingly springing from the USSR and yet often fiercely antagonistic to it) and the equally baffling barrage of statements about the need for Western technology have now criss-crossed with older 'memories' of the Great Wall, silk paintings, concubines, gowned sages and simple, sturdy peasants, but have not replaced them. By and large the intricacies of Chinese politics, the complexities of intellectual debate, the shifts in domestic economic structures have all remained in the domain of scholarship, and there has been little ability to present them to a wide Western audience; nor, indeed, does that audience necessarily *want* such information, China's opacity is what draws people, along with the remoteness and the size.

Thus, Chinese fictions flourish in many guises. As an introduction to these it is better to consider broad genres rather than to follow certain attitudes which allegedly reveal 'patterns' of Western hostility or admiration. Such 'patterns' are, in fact, simplifications. China has remained multi-layered in our consciousness, and old themes are constantly refurbished, never rejected with any finality. It is the genres that may help to illuminate our own history, and the subtleties of nuance within them. Six are apparent: first, fictions which deal with the Chinese inside China; secondly, those in which Westerners within China are the focus; thirdly, the world of overseas Chinese; fourthly, the uses made of China as a focus for political statements; fifthly, the fictional value of scholars of China; and finally, the possibilities of what might be called 'internal' Chinas, in which the country itself begins to fade into another mode of discourse.

The Chinese in China

The challenge of describing the Chinese in their own land, in a fictional form, has naturally attracted many writers. In such fictions the difficulties of language, locale and historical background could be glossed over when they were not understood, and, though such simplifications have not been common among the more effective writers, it remains true that an avoidance of the real complexity of life in Chinese society – whether rural or urban – has always been at the heart of these fictional re-patternings.

The genre of 'Chinese in China' has many subthemes; here we will consider three in particular in terms of popular reception. The first is that of life on the Chinese land, and there is no doubt that Pearl Buck ruled this field, with *The Good Earth* (1931) and the series of other novels which followed under the general title of *A House Divided*. Pearl Buck had lived a long time in China and had access to all kinds of information. Her husband, John Lossing Buck, was perhaps the most important Western analyst of China's rural social conditions who worked in this century; his researchers visited rural communities in every province to gather information which was also available to Pearl Buck. The power of her evocations comes from her concentration on the elemental forces of the struggles for survival on the land, with famine, drought, flood and pestilence as the darkening backdrop behind the puny yet moving lives of her peasant protagonists. As a cross-cutting theme, she reflects on the new demands on age-long family values, and attraction to the land, which Western incursion had introduced. She sees this as erosion rather than imperialism, as a slow shifting in the subsoil that had once seemed to give a secure foundation to the buildings perched above.

Pearl Buck used a curious and rather stilted language for her tales, a modified form of the style found in the King James's Version of the Bible, which brought both sonority and a sense of detachment to her presentation of rural life. One sees that whether she is dealing with the triumphs or the despairs of her peasant protagonist Wang Lung, her own tone does not vary, and her mood remains superior even if her emotional involvement is genuine. However, the ending of *The Good Earth* has great force, as Wang Lung confronts death clinging to old values that he is sure his sons are about to betray:

'It is the end of a family – when they begin to sell the land', he said bro-
kenly. 'Out of the land we came and into we must go – and if you will hold
your land you can live – no one can rob you of land —'.

And the old man let his scanty tears dry upon his cheeks and they made
salty stains there. And he stooped and took up a handful of the soil and he
held it and he muttered,

'If you sell the land it is the end.'

And his two sons held him, one on either side, each holding his arm, and
he held tight in his hand the warm loose earth. And they soothed him and
they said over and over, the elder son and the second son,

'Rest assured, our father, rest assured. The land is not to be sold.'

But over the old man's head they looked at each other and smiled.[1]

Though her language now seems arch and her plots contrived, there
is no denying the centrality in Chinese history of the themes she presented, and her influence in the Western world – as far as that can be
gauged through sales which exceeded four million – was greater than
any other writer about China of the 1930s and 1940s.[2]

If Buck evoked a modern Chinese world with 'timeless' components,
Robert van Gulik evoked a lost China with 'modern' overtones. His
successful 'Judge Dee' mystery stories, which are representative of a
second aspect of this genre, were originally rooted in the social and
legal history of the T'ang dynasty between the seventh and tenth
centuries AD, and though overtly belonging in the 'mystery story'
genre, they are crammed with imaginatively reconstructed historical
nuances, and with the social and economic detail only available to a
widely read scholar of pre-modern China who had lived long in the
Far East. Judge Dee stands for logic, decency and compassion, and
the bleak backdrop to his investigations, along with the vanished
elegance of the old society, give an authentic sense of paradox to his
stories.

There is little humour in Pearl Buck's work; in van Gulik's there is
often a wry smile, occasionally a hilarious if ironical moment. It was
left to Ernest Bramah Smith (writing as Ernest Bramah), to develop
the third aspect of this genre, that of humorous works, and to give
the most consistently funny evaluation of China's past. Why are his
'Kai Lung' stories so magically, effervescently, hilarious, even after
repeated readings? Because Kai Lung, utterly without control over his
destiny, submits with grave and impeccable demeanour to the worst
blows that fate can hand out, while entertaining his audiences (Kai
Lung is an itinerant story-teller) at the same time. There are certainly
old stocks-in-trade to the jokestar that Bramah uses constantly, such
as the 'translated through' Chinese name or chapter title – for example, 'The concave witted Li Loe's insatiable craving serves a meritori-
ous end and two (who shall be nameless) are led towards a snare' –

and he plays with the rhythms of Chinese speech when translated literally into English. (This had led, in the nineteenth century, to the odd linguistic hybrid known as 'pidgin' English.) The joy of Bramah's portrayals of Kai Lung comes from the predictability of catastrophe, the consistency of Kai Lung's responses and his genuinely intelligent awareness of his own vulnerability. It is as if Candide and the good soldier Schweik had been united. One might take an example from almost anywhere in the corpus of Kai Lung's adventures, but one short passage from *Kai Lung Unrolls His Mat* (1928) will suffice. Here we can see how Bramah, while celebrating with us Kai Lung's recent outwitting of a gang of fiendish bandits, manages at the same time to give a pervasive and sardonically negative overview of trade and manners in traditional Chinese society:

> Nothing could exceed the honourable distinction with which Kai Lung was greeted by all classes of those dwelling about Chi-U after the destruction of the rebel host. The lean and expectatious were never weary of professing their readiness to consume an unspecified abundance of rice spirit to the accompaniment of a hope that the story-teller's sinews would be thereby strengthened, and no matter how urgent might be the business on which he was engaged rich merchants did not disdain to stop him repeatedly as he went about the Ways to enjoy the gladness of shaking hands with themselves before him. Some of the actually charitable expressed a willingness, in view of the obviously threadbare state of the one with whom they conversed, to supply him with the needs of life at an appreciably lower rate than was usually imposed on strangers, and on Kai Lung displaying the empty folds of his deficient sleeve, a special edict of the Chi-U Confraternity of Impost Adjusters was issued, permitting him to pass round his collecting bowl at any time without being liable to any humiliating regulations.[3]

Evocation, humour and mystery all, of course, subsume the world of children's books about China which have been steadily successful. Though there is no room to go into the entire genre of children's literature on China here, one can at least say that at their best, as in *Ping* or *The Young Boy who Swallowed the Sea*, they present a tenacious, ingenious and generous world of Chinese children, even while both illustrations and sketched in background underline an essential strangeness, and otherness that sets them permanently apart.

Westerners in China

One of the central difficulties with any fictions about the Chinese in China has been this 'otherness', the difficulty of giving the Western reader a preliminary set of references to get his or her bearings in this new world. Therefore, most commonly, and in most other widely

[103]

selling books, there has been at least a Western narrator, and normally a steady patterning of Western characters, to interlard the narrative and allow the author to introduce predictable (and thus stress-reducing) lines of dialogue, and to construct situations with which the reader can more easily identify. Often the Eurasian plays a useful role too, suggesting past co-minglings which arouse the reader's anticipation of more of the same, while allowing Western values to be seen in an attractive Chinese dress.

One link between the Chinese in China genre and that of the Westerners in China, can, of course, come from the Western observer in total isolation within the Chinese scene. For this to be credible, the Western character must speak good Chinese and the situation leading to the isolation must be skilfully contrived. Surely the masterpiece of this genre is John Hersey's *A Single Pebble* (1956). Here, the narrator, a young American engineer out of language school, travelling through the Yangtze gorges on a Chinese junk with Chinese owner and crew at some indeterminate time in the 1920s, is left with his technical expertise in abeyance, unable to 'fix' anything in the world he has temporarily entered, since methods and materials are drawn from the past and sanctified by that past. 'Pebble', the leader of the coolies who pull the junk upstream against the swift Yangtze current, both reaches us in human terms and yet is acceptable as a symbol for China's enduring values; he is mortal, limitlessly intelligent and fatally stubborn, imaginative and obtuse. His battle with the river fixes the narrator's attention and our own, and his values become, briefly, ours:

> I had never heard old Pebble sing such a haunting melody. I saw that he was in a kind of ecstasy. His face shone in a grimace of hard work and happiness. I remembered my doubts about his credo of 'simplicity', which he had recited to me in our first evening on the river, and I remembered my distress that such a sturdy young man did not avow personal goals of wealth, love, honour, and fame. Now I saw from his face that this was his life's goal: this instant of work, this moment's line of song, this accord with his poor fellow men, this brief spurt of useful loyalty to the cranky, skinny, half-mad owner of the junk on which he had shipped, and above all this fleeting triumph over the Great River.
>
> At last the junk raised its head, shivered, and shot suddenly forward into the still water of the pond above the rapids.
>
> When it was over, and the junk was pulled up to the loading platform, Old Pebble was streaming sweat, but he looked very happy.
>
> I walked down to the river's edge to see what he would say. He jumped ashore and bent down to the river and scooped up double handfuls of the brown water and washed his face, sloshing and snorting like a small boy. I moved near to him. He looked up. All he said was, 'Ayah, this river is a turtle.'[4]

In *A Single Pebble*, though the Western narrator is unobtrusive, his few interjections are fatal to the life and happiness of junk and crew; the Promethean element thus rears its head above the Chinese apparent realities, and it is ambiguous, as it must be. The narrator, seeing the paths hacked into the naked rock, paths worn smooth by the feet and plaited tow-ropes of millenia of workers, has the wit to 'wonder whether a dam was the right thing with which to start closing the gap', but we know that this moment of doubt will not stop him from doing the job he has been sent to do.[5] In the many other books of Westerners in China the Western impact is more graphically presented, though analysis of its moral effect is often submerged in the dense flow of plot and character. In a tightly focused plot, like that found in Theodore White's *The Mountain Road* (1958), the corrosive power of the West has come with the GIs of the Second World War; in Richard McKenna's *The Sand Pebbles* (1962) it is the roving gunboat crew on the Yangtze; in Colonel John Thomason's stories of the 1920s or 1930s – published as *And a Few Marines* (1943) – it is the marines in Peking. The characters of all these authors have more awareness of China than one might have found in Henty or other books of the British heyday, though, as a rule, it is the Chinese who are there as a backdrop for the protagonists rather than being the protagonists themselves. The same feeling persists, more strongly, as one reads the best-selling blockbusters of recent years, such as James Clavell's *Taipan* (1966) and Robert Elegant's *Dynasty* (1977); though both Clavell and Elegant have done their homework, place their characters in historically quite persuasive settings and cleverly use Hong Kong as a meeting place between Chinese and Westerners' values, they cannot begin to present their Chinese characters' emotions in ways that carry any conviction.

Overseas Chinese

As well as Chinese in China and Westerners in China, any account of the fictions of China must include the Chinese overseas. In this realm one gets a different heightening of effect, as the displaced Chinese bring to their new environment their own colouration, and present familiar acts in startling lights. It is in this genre that we find the most famous of all the fictionalised Chinese, the only ones to have become household words to Western audiences, thanks to cheap paperbacks, radio, film and television. Surely their enduring power comes from their isolation from their own environment. It is in our world that we can savour *their* strangeness; thus they cannot threat-en us but only entertain, however awesome their intelligence or strength. Here we are at home with the exiles Fu Manchu, Charlie Chan and Kung Fu. Even if they develop powerful stereotypes, we should not be too alarmed, for each stereotype counteracts the next: Fu Manchu's diabolical cunning is no stronger than Charlie Chan's suaver intelligence, or more overwhelming than Kung Fu's physical courage and imperturbability.

The overseas Chinese do not bloom only in the fictional worlds of Britain or the USA. They are equally visible in South-East Asia, indeed it is in that milieu that Chinese characteristics have most recently struck English novelists, perhaps because they enjoyed the subtlety of effect to be gained by contrasting Chinese behaviour with Malay (for example) rather than with the more obviously different patterns of Western settlers. The displaced Chinese woman is removed from the realm of sexual stereotype and has new dimensions in the person of Teena Chang, the dominating figure in Paul Scott's *The Chinese Love Pavilion* (1960).

Teena's strength derives from her intelligence as well as from her beauty, and both are intensified by her dual ancestry, her mother having been Chinese and her father of Dutch–French descent. Teena lives in two moods, and charms her men with both:

> In her European mood she would undress in front of you, even demand help with the buttons at the back of her frock; but in her Chinese mood she would lower the oil-lamp and then lead you to the mattress, there with exquisite meekness to undress you first with hands that communicated a touching impression of shyness. Only when you lay in comfort would she attend to herself, undressing behind the screen or, if commanded, kneel submissively with her back towards you and allow you to help her.[6]

She uses either mood, according to her own whim, and with either she can charm the officers of the Japanese occupying army, the British officers who succeed them, and the communist Chinese guerrillas in the jungle who snipe at both the others. She retains her hope and her dignity by not only being Chinese but also by idealising that Chineseness as she adopts the added fictional persona of 'Madam Ho' – loosely translated as 'admirable' or 'very fine'. Scott makes this relationship clear in a snatch of dialogue between the narrator/protagonist, briefly Teena Chang's lover, and Teena herself:

> 'You're not full Chinese are you?'
> She drew back her head to look at me and placed one finger on my nose. 'My mother was Chinese. My father was French but his mother was Dutch.'
> 'Then you're not Chang. You're Dupont or something like that.'
> 'My mother was Chang. She wasn't Dupont or anything like that.

[106]

Sometimes I feel I should like to be full Chinese and know a lot about China. It is when this happens that I feel like Madam Ho. Why are we talking about me again?'[7]

Paul Scott's South-East Asian world is more constricted than the immense panorama of India he created in his *Raj Quartet,* and at times he grows a little solemn; his Chinese character, with her overlays of cultural complexity, can be delightfully contrasted with James G. Farrell's Singapore Chinese caught, along with the British, in the city as the years of inadequate preparation and inept defence bring them all to their knees before the Japanese armies in 1942. In Farrell's *The Singapore Grip* (1978) Mr Wu, formerly of 'Number 5, Pursuiting Squadron' in the Kuomintang airforce, now helps the British by driving in his elderly Buick to help the volunteer forces extinguish the flames of the Japanese incendiary bombs; while the zesty Vera Chiang, perhaps the fruit of a union between a faded Russian émigré aristocrat and a Chinese woman in Harbin (or perhaps, not, we are never sure when Vera is telling the truth), finds peace and security in Singapore with a group of strapping young Chinese girls hired to perform calisthenics – in a state of undress – before the fading eyes of an elderly British tycoon. Vera Chiang's past is linked realistically enough to the wartime worlds of Shanghai, from which she fled because of her possible association with Chinese communists there, and to her desperate search for an exit visa from Singapore lest she be captured by the Japanese. At the same time, the values of her traditional upbringing are mocked by Farrell along with the fatuous restraints of her would-be lover, the Englishman Matthew. The scene preceding their final conjunction, in which the mockery is tinged with a certain gentleness, is as funny in its way as an Ernest Bramah setting for Kai Lung:

And yet before the rivers joined, one river flowing into the other, the other flowing into the one, there was still some way to go. Vera, who had carefully educated herself in the arts of love, did not believe that this sacred art, whose purpose was to unite her not only with her lover but with the earth and the firmament, too, should take place in the Western manner which to her resembled nothing so much as a pair of drunken rickshaw coolies colliding briefly at some foggy crossroads at the dead of night. But in order to do things properly it was clear that she would have to give Matthew a hasty but basic education in what was expected of him. For one thing, a common terminology had to be established; Matthew's grasp of such matters had proven even more elementary than she had feared. Indeed, he seemed thoroughly bewildered as he stood there naked and blinking, for he had taken off his spectacles and put them down on the pile of books by the bed. So Vera set to work giving names to various parts, first pointing them out where applicable on Matthew, then on her own pretty person.[8]

[107]

Behind the drama of Scott's presentation, or the humour of Farrell's, lies the very real problem of the ambiguity of situations felt by the overseas Chinese: the financial and sexual insecurity both of men and women; the attracting and counter-attracting between adopted culture and original 'native place'. In this vein one should not ignore the overseas Chinese writers themselves, who search through their own fictions (rather than through the eyes of Western interpreters) to recapture meanings they have lost. The paradox is doubled for them, because if they wish to inform Western readers of their predicament then, of course, they must use Western language, Western modes of thought, even Western styles of presentation. They might choose the conventional novel, as was so effectively done by Han Suyin in *A Many Splendoured Thing* (1952), or the memoir form she chose for *And the Rain My Drink* and subsequent works. Or they might choose the conventional short story, as was done by Ch'en Jo-hsi in *The Execution of Mayor Yin and Other Stories* (1978), her account of her return to China and of her failure to rediscover there any values she believed she had lost (in her case though she had lived a long time in the USA she wrote in Chinese and the works were then translated into English). Or one might adapt a new genre, such as the mixed memoir–fiction–history form developed by Maxine Hong Kingston in *Woman Warrior* (1976). Here a girlhood in Stockton, California among Chinese parents is the base from which a prolonged emotional search is launched for the meaning of that Chineseness from which she feels estranged, and yet towards which she is also pulled. Maxine Kingston could not complete her search in that book, and resumed it in her next, *Chinamen* (1980). Here the myths and echoes seem to grow fainter, the distances from her own relatives longer, the oddities of behaviour more pronounced. And she wonders about her 'own' country, China, now.

China as a focus for a political statement

China could also serve as an ethos, a backdrop against which to formulate a political statement drawn from another culture. It was thus that Daniel Defoe used China in his *Further Adventures of Robinson Crusoe*, written early in the eighteenth century, to make known his feelings about corrupt bureaucracies and extravagant habits; and it was thus, not so many years later, that Voltaire used the China that he had been studying from Jesuit historical sources as the setting for a play about freedom from tyranny, the *Orphelin de la Chine*. The two most significant examples from the twentieth century were probably those by André Malraux in his two novels *The Conquerors*

(*Les Conquerants*, 1927) and *Man's Fate* (*La Condition Humaine*, 1933), and by Bertolt Brecht in *The Good Woman of Setzuan* (*Der Gute Mensch von Sezuan*, 1938–40). In Malraux's *The Conquerors*, it is the city of Canton in 1925 which is the backdrop for revolutionary heroism, as the Communist Party there seeks solidarity for the striking workers in the British Colony of Hong Kong. But the Chinese who live in Canton serve only to frame the plot run by Westerners: the Chinese are either faceless – noises in the street, a rumble in the distance, an unnamed corpse – or else stand for polarities: such as Hong, the terrorist intent on his kill; or Chen-Dai, a faintly reactionary Gandhi figure, whose conniving caution might imperil the revolution as much as Hong's reckless violence. Malraux may claim that Chen-Dai is 'finer, older, subtler', than the Europeans; or that Hong is representative of a new Chinese world 'with the new idea of a death which involves nothing, neither compensation nor atonement; but it is the consistently cool narrator, the (historically accurate) Borodin, the soon-to-be-murdered Klein, and above all the agent Garine who invoke our attention.9 Garine dominates, and he is the only one to whom Malraux allows the company of women.

Malraux used the China of 1927 as the backdrop for his other novel of China, *Man's Fate*, and again the time and place were brilliantly chosen. In 1927 the crisis within China came to a head as the nationalist armies under Chiang Kai-shek sought to consolidate their hold over the great international treatyport city of Shanghai, while the Chinese Communist Party tried to develop the worker's movement there as a prelude to a wider revolutionary upsurge inland. At the same time the international arm of the Soviet Communist Party, the Comintern, sought to dissuade the Chinese communists from over-violent actions which would alienate the nationalists irredeemably and the powerful financial interests of Shanghai – Western European, American and Japanese – watched the conflict anxiously, determined to protect their enormous investments in the area. Brilliant and moving though Malraux's story is, and full of insights into the Chinese civil war and the conflicts among the various forces in the Shanghai equation, one can, nevertheless, once again gauge his essential distancing from the Chinese as people by the fact that his plot can yield to this simple summary: the Chinese characters have to die so that the Westerners can work out their fate. Thus, it is the young revolutionary Ch'en, and Himmelreich's Chinese wife and child, along with the other underground workers and street-fighters, who die in the most random of purposeless fashions; it is Ferral, old Gisors, May, Kator and Clappique who are given the luxury of dialogue which enables them to decide the meaning of their actions and chart their courses of action in a way that arouses the interest and attention of the Western reader.

Brecht, unlike Malraux, had never been in China, and so his China is even more an abstraction, but Brecht shared Malraux's concern about the development of Fascism and sought within Marxism for solutions to the tyrannies which surrounded him. In *The Good Woman of Setzuan* the details of daily small-town Chinese life are lovingly and cleverly drawn, in an environment from which any 'Western' elements have been removed as if to emphasise yet further the universalities of the human predicament. (It is worth remembering that when he first wrote the play Brecht believed that Setzuan – in fact one of China's largest provinces, approximately the size of France, with a population of nearly forty million – was a medium-sized town. It was the name and echoes he needed, not the place. Later he amended the script to fit geographical reality.) The 'good Woman' of the play is Shen Te, a name which could be translated in English as 'Divine Goodness': a prostitute with a heart of gold, she is the only one in her city to recognise three visiting gods and offer them shelter. The gods reward her with money, and with the injunction to 'do good' in her community. The play swings between high comedy and tragedy as Shen Te, trying to do their bidding, arouses all the hostility and greed of her community, and finally has to shelter from their wrath by inventing an *alter ego* as callous and mercenary as they. 'Your injunction', she tells the gods at the end of the play, 'To be good and yet to live/Was a thunderbolt:/It has torn me in two.'[10] The vision that Shen Te shares with Brecht is that of a world where humour and courage can be a match for evil forces, but only just, and mankind lives always on the edge of both fear and despair. As Shen Te tells the audience, after saving an unemployed pilot from suicide:

> In our country
> The evenings should never be sombre
> High bridges over rivers
> The grey hour between night and morning
> And the long, long winter:
> Such things are dangerous
> For with all the misery,
> A very little is enough
> And men throw away an unbearable life.[11]

When people choose apathy rather than action, then life can only grow worse; but that, alas, is the course which both the workers and the bourgeoisie so commonly adopt.

Though Brecht knew little about China, there could be few more apt categorisations of Szechuan, riven by war-lord factionalism in the

1920s and early 1930s, before becoming the anti-Japanese wartime base of Chiang Kai-Shek during the Second World War. 'Help', cries Shen Te, in the last word of the play, as the gods leave her for the last time, and the curtain falls. Her cry rings out with historical accuracy as well as emotional truth.

Scholars of China

Fictions growing out of the pretence that a given protagonist is a scholar of China allow the author a different range of licence. Some of these are indeed scholarly, that is they allow the author to parade more erudition than the fictional form normally allows; others serve to illuminate some quirk of character that the protagonist manifests in his domestic setting; yet others intellectually transform the protagonist as the quest for knowledge of China is pursued.

Perhaps the most dignified and favourable picture of that process of learning is offered by Hermann Hesse in *Magister Ludi* or *The Glass Bead Game (Das Glasperlenspiel*, 1943). In this fine, intricate novel concerning individual growth, the meaning of education and the nature of service and friendship within a community, the Chinese influence is profound, a narrowing from Hesse's previously rather generalised interests in elements of Eastern religions and philosophy. The image of Chinese culture chosen by Hesse is that of order and metaphysical peace, that calm centre believed to lie at the centre of a world in flux, which some Chinese scholars (and their Western admirers) have indeed found either in *The Book of Changes* (the Confucian classic the *I-ching*) or in the enigmatic works of the Taoist thinker Chuang-tzu. Hesse's hero Joseph Knecht, in his long quest for enlightenment which brings him to heights of fame as the master of the glass bead game in Castalia – a 'game' of leadership which encompasses all levels of art, literature, music and logic – is drawn first to the study of classical Chinese language, then into the company of the only teacher who can help him, a teacher known simply as Elder Brother. Knecht is enchanted by this mild and scholarly eccentric, with his quiet garden called the Bamboo Grove; in describing his enchantment, Hesse summarised the spell of old China:

> Afterwards Joseph Knecht described the months he lived in the Bamboo Grove as an unusually happy time. He also frequently referred to it as the 'beginning of my awakening' – and in fact from that period on the image of 'awakening' turns up more and more often in his remarks, with a meaning similar to although not quite the same as that he had formerly attributed to the image of vocation. It could be assumed that the 'awakening' signified

knowledge of himself and of the place he occupied within the Castalian and the general human order of things; but it seems to us that the accent increasingly shifts toward self-knowledge in the sense that from the 'beginning of his awakening' Knecht came closer and closer to a sense of his special, unique position and destiny, while at the same time the concepts and categories of the traditional hierarchy of the world and of the special Castalian hierarchy became for him more and more relative matters.[12]

This vision might have seemed purely utopian, and the hours that Elder Brother and Joseph Knecht spend staring into the clear, limpid waters of the little goldfish pond as escapism of the naivest kind, rather like the vision of China presented in 1901 by Goldsworthy Lowes Dickinson in his equally fictional *Letters from John Chinaman*, where Confucian delicacy is presented as being a full answer in, and of, itself. But Hesse, ultimately, will not permit that. At the novel's end Knecht dies in the chill waters of the mountain lake, seeking to race one of his own disciples in the sunset waters. 'Stunned', writes Hesse of the disciple who has seen Knecht drown, 'he sat down in the sunlight and stared into the water, whose cool blue–green now blinked at him strangely empty, alien and evil.'[13]

In *Magister Ludi*, as in other of Hesse's novels, the air of rarified Chinese culture in which his protagonists bask is tinted with homosexual yearnings. In her novel *In a Dark Wood* (1977), Marina Warner develops this theme with ingenuity, by having her protagonist be a reclusive Jesuit sinologist, drawn back in time through texts describing the early Jesuit missions in China. He finds a startling erotic content in one set of rare texts which propel him – through an initially bashful love for a young male musician – into a harsher world of homosexual violence where he meets his death. *In a Dark Wood* (the title taken, perhaps with some hubris, from the opening of Dante's *Inferno*) is unique in the thoroughness with which it suggests the intimacy of the links which bind together the researcher, the Chinese world of the past, the historical figures being researched and the written texts left for decipherment by that figure; Warner also forces the reader and her protagonist to confront (and be subdued by) a contemporary reality from which there is no escape. One element of his reality, in the early 1970s, is the disclosure that Central Intelligence Agency funds had been pumped into various areas of the European non-communist liberal left. Marina Warner is being discreetly clever here, for the realisation that such funding was being provided to magazines dealing apparently independently with modern China did, indeed, have a powerful effect on Chinese studies overseas.

There is nothing discreet, chaste or high-minded about the finest and wildest of all fictions that centre on a student of China, Elias

Cannetti's *Auto-da-Fe* (originally written in German, the first English-language edition being in 1946). Professor Peter Kien lives for Chinese scholarship; he brooks no company; his spacious apartment, windows boarded to gain precious wall space, is one continuous flow of shelved books and texts. To an admiring outside world, which rarely sees him, he is an awesome figure: 'The papers which he had hitherto published, few in number, yet each one the starting point for a hundred others, had gained for him the reputation of being the greatest living authority on sinology.'[14] Immersed in the study of his texts, Kien is fatally jolted out of his routine by a small boy who engages him in conversation in front of a bookshop window, and astounds him: 'the child was interested in China. He read against his father's will. The stories of the difficulties of the Chinese alphabet fascinated instead of frightening him.'[15] When Kien reaches home, furious with himself for having given the child permission to take a look at his library, he drops a copy of Mencius; the housekeeper, summoned to dust the book, catches his eye by her apparent love of books and by her meek deportment. From this crazed parody of a Chinese scholastic environment all disasters flow: Kien marries the housekeeper to gain a permanent guardian for his books, but ends up losing first equanimity, then apartment and books, and finally his own life as reality, unbearable outside the study, convulses him with evidence of the terrors offered by the human race. At the novel's end Kien, briefly reunited with his books, and with his loathsome wife sent packing, can only fasten his world of books forever to him by one final act of immolation, the *auto-da-fe* of the old inquisition, in which he burns not just the books and not just the heretic, but himself as lapsed scholar too, on a pyre of the very books he loved.

Internal Chinas

Freest of all from China, but also creating fine literature which claims dependence on it, are those who made the quest to China purely internal. Theirs is an adventure of the mind which would, surely, have been different had another country been chosen, and yet eludes proof of that supposition. One is tempted to guess that their literary achievements have proved the most enduring because they are the least burdened with facts which might deflect them from their vision; they are content if they can give their readers a glimpse of their private worlds. At their best, these writers present a contradiction: they give piercing insights into Chinese culture from which they are divorced, and they illuminate with sudden radiance elements of China's history which they have barely studied.

Take James Merrill's 'Willowware Cup' in this book *Braving the Elements* (1973) and the echoes of trade, emigration and technology which it touches so lightly and yet so memorably:

> Mass hysteria, wave after breaking wave
> Blueblooded Cantonese upon these shores
> Left the gene pool Lux-opaque and smoking
> With dimestore mutants. One turned up today.
> Plum in bloom, pagoda, blue birds, plume of willow
> Almost the replica of a prewar pattern –
> The same boat bearing the gnat-sized lovers away,
> The old bridge now bent double where her father signals
> Feebly, as from flypaper, minding less and less.
> Two small retainers with lanterns light him home.
> Is that a scroll he carries? He must by now be immensely
> Wise, and have given up earthly attachments, and all that.

A similar magic can be observed in Franz Kafka's story *The Great Wall of China* (left in almost complete draft form at the time of Kafka's death in 1924), from which one can draw passages that speak with more immediacy of China's giant bureaucracy, and of the quest for interior meaning within such a structure, than anything else written:

> So vast is our land that no fable could do justice to its vastness, the heavens can scarcely span it – and Peking is only a dot in it, and the imperial palace less than a dot. The Emperor as such, on the other hand, is mighty throughout all the hierarchies of the world; admitted. But the existent Emperor, a man like us, lies much like us on a couch which is of generous proportions, perhaps, and yet very possibly may be quite narrow and short. Like us he sometimes stretches himself and when he is very tired yawns with his delicately cut mouth. But how should we know anything about that – thousands of miles away in the south – almost on the borders of the Tibetan Highlands? And besides, any tidings, even if they did reach us, would arrive far too late, would have become obsolete long before they reached us.
>
> The Emperor is always surrounded by a brilliant and yet ambiguous throng of nobles and courtiers – malice and enmity in the guise of servants and friends – who form a counter-weight to the Imperial power and perpetually labour to unseat the ruler from his place with poisoned arrows. The Empire is immortal, but the Emperor himself totters and falls from his throne, yes, whole dynasties sink in the end and breathe their last in one death-rattle. Of these struggles and suffering the people will never know; like tardy arrivals, like strangers in a city, they stand at the end of some densely thronged side street peacefully munching the food they have brought with them, while far away in front, in the market square at the heart of the city, the execution of their ruler is proceeding.[16]

In Victor Segalen's novel *Rene Leys* (published posthumously, 1922), one is drawn into an inner palace of the mind which is also the Forbidden City of the dying Manchu court before the revolution of

1911, into labyrinths of lies which are the streets of a vanished Peking, into webs of words which are the patternings of Chinese calligraphy. Here, as with the Kublai Khan of Italo Calvino's *Invisible Cities* (1972), or the central figures of Samuel Beckett's *Waiting for Godot* (1957), Estragon and Vladimir (whose nicknames 'Gogo' and 'Didi', given by Beckett, are the exact Chinese sounds for 'elder and younger brother,') we reach the edges of the subject and have to stop, teetering at the endless views the imagination alone provides.

1981

Notes

1 Pearl S. Buck, *The Good Earth*, New York, 1931, pp. 374–5.
2 Her work has been recently analysed by M. Hunt, 'Pearl Buck – popular expert on China, 1931–1969', *Modern China*, III(1), 1977, 33–64.
3 Ernest Bramah, *Kai Lung Unrolls His Mat*, New York, 1928, p. 195.
4 John Hersey, *A Single Pebble*, New York, 1956, pp. 82–3.
5 Hersey, *A Single Pebble*, p. 139.
6 Paul Scott, *The Chinese Love Pavilion*, London, 1960, p. 10.
7 Scott, *The Chinese Love Pavilion*, p. 113.
8 James G. Farrell, *The Singapore Grip*, London, 1978, p. 381.
9 André Malraux, *The Conquerors* (1927), Boston, 1956, pp. 70, 91.
10 Bertolt Brecht, *The Good Woman of Setzuan* (1938–40), quoted from E. Bentley, *Parables for the Theatre: Two Plays by Bertolt Brecht*, revised English versions, Minneapolis, 1963, p. 40.
11 Brecht, *The Good Woman of Setzuan*, pp. 434–5.
12 Hermann Hesse, *The Glass Bead Game* (Magister Ludi) 1943), New York, 1969, p. 132.
13 Hesse, *The Glass Bead Game*, p. 425.
14 Elias Canetti, *Auto-da-Fe*, New York, 1946, p. 18.
15 Canetti, *Auto-da-Fe*, p. 13.
16 Franz Kafka, *The Great Wall of China* (1924), New York, 1946, pp. 164–5.

Reading list

Bramah (Smith), Ernest, *Kai Lung Unrolls His Mat*, New York, 1928.
Brecht, Bertolt, *The Good Woman of Setzuan* (1938–40) in E. Bentley (ed.), *Seven Plays by Bertolt Brecht*, New York, 1961.
Buck Pearl S., *The Good Earth*, New York, 1931.
——, *A House Divided*, New York, 1935.
Calvino, Italo, *Invisible Cities*, New York, 1974.
Canetti, Elias, *Auto-da-Fe*, translated by C. V. Wedgwood, New York, 1946.
Ch'en, Jo-hsi (Ruoxi), *The Execution of Mayor Yin and Other Stories*, Bloomington, Indiana, 1978.

Clavell, James, *Taipan*, New York, 1966.

Dickinson, Goldsworthy Lowes, *Letters from John Chinaman* (1901), London, 1946.

Elegant, Robert, *Dynasty*, New York, 1977.

Farrell, James G., *The Singapore Grip*, London, 1978.

Flack, Marjorie and Wiese, Kurt, *Ping*, New York, 1933.

Gulik, Robert van, *Celebrated Cases of Judge Dee*, New York, 1976.

Han Suyin, *A Many Splendoured Thing*, Boston, 1952.

——, *And the Rain My Drink*, London, 1956.

Hersey, John, *A Single Pebble*, New York, 1956.

Hesse, Hermann, *The Glass Bead Game* (Magister Ludi), (1943), New York, 1969.

Kafka, Franz, *The Great Wall of China*, translated by Willa and Edwin Muir, New York, 1946.

Kingston, Maxine Hong, *Woman Warrior*, New York, 1976.

McKenna, Richard, *The Sand Pebble*, New York, 1962.

Malraux, André, *The Conquerors* (1927), New York, 1976.

——, *Man's Fate*, New York, 1936.

Merrill, James, *Braving the Elements*, New York, 1973.

Scott, Paul, *The Chinese Love Pavilion*, London, 1960.

Segalen, Victor, *Rene Leys* (1922), Chicago, 1974.

Warner, Marina, *In a Dark Wood*, New York, 1977.

White, Theodore, *The Mountain Road*, New York, 1958.

CHAPTER EIGHT

Hong Kong: fragrant harbour, city of sin and death

C. Mary Turnbull

Hong Kong, 'Fragrant Harbour' of the Chinese, has always exerted a fascination for Westerners as an outpost of empire, a minute enclave enveloped by the vastness of China, an exotic entrepot pulsating with life and adventure, yet paradoxically a speck of normality on the brink of a forbidding continent.

In the colony's early days, mid-nineteenth-century Western writing portrayed the small European community overawed by the closeness of China, as in William Thomas Mercer's *Under the Peak: Or Jottings in Verse Written During a Lengthened Residence in the Colony of Hong Kong* (London, 1869). This anthology, which was more serious than the title suggests, portrayed a community surrounded by natural beauty but vulnerable to the hazards of climate, ill-health and sudden death, with so few living in the town, while so many lay dead in the cemetery.

Albert Smith in *To China and Back: Being a Diary Kept Out and Home* (London, 1859, reprinted Hong Kong, 1974) reported the bickering and backbiting among colonial society, which was confirmed by James Dalziel's, *Chronicles of a Crown Colony* (Hong Kong, 1907). Dalziel's well-told short stories poked gentle fun at Hong Kong society, which was narrow, clique-ridden, preoccupied with status and money. 'Nowhere East is the colour line so strictly drawn as in Hong Kong', and Western rule mixed uneasily with Chinese custom.

'Dolly' (Leonard D'Oliver), in *Paul the Pretender: Romance of Hong Kong* (Shanghai, 1912) chronicled the empty lives and loves of young Europeans in Hong Kong at the turn of the century. His earlier *Tales of Hong Kong in Verse and Story* (Hong Kong, 1902) were a collection of slight sentimental romances and frivolous verse, but they also showed the inconsistency between Western Christians' claims of fraternity and the aloof contempt they exhibited towards the Chinese.

[117]

While Hong Kong was not Conrad country, at the turn of the century it had would-be Conrads who catered to the popular demand for stories of the sea and distant ports. Most successful was William Carlton Dawe, with *Yellow and White* (London and Boston, 1895), a collection of stories about love and danger in the Far East; and *Kakemonos: Tales of the Far East* (London and New York, 1897), yarns of the sea, of robbery, barratry and opium smuggling. Dawe's Asian men were generally ugly, corrupt and evil, their womenfolk beautiful, passionate, tantalising yet forbidden. Romance between the races was joyous but doomed, tragedy adding spice and piquancy to bitter-sweet fantasies.

But it was not always so. In the sentimental stories of the anonymous 'D.R.C.', *Lui Sing and Other Stories* (Yokohama, 1908), which ran into several editions, the Hong Kong Eurasian heroine of the title story was every Westerner's dream of the golden-hearted courtesan, and in another 'D.R.C.' story an American governess eloped with a charismatic Anglo-Chinese merchant of Macao and lived there happily ever after.

In contrast to their alluring Chinese or Eurasian sisters, shallow English girls in late nineteenth-century Hong Kong fiction frittered away their lives in flirtations, balls and parties, like the heroine of 'Caught on the Rebound', one of the stories in *Not So Black as They Painted Her: And Other Stories* (Hong Kong, 1895) by 'Lulu'.

However dangerous Hong Kong might be for those who succumbed to its temptations, the colony represented order and safety in contrast to the troubled hinterland, which most Englishmen at the time regarded as a benighted continent of cruelty and misery, where corrupt mandarins meted out barbaric punishments, and heathens drowned girl babies at birth.

Most contemporary Hong Kong fiction reinforced these impressions. William Dawe's, *The Mandarin* (London, 1900), which was hailed by London critics as 'sparkling adventure', was an improbable story about an infatuated mandarin's pursuit of an English missionary's daughter. The background came closer to life than most novels of the time, contrasting China with Hong Kong, 'its shipping peaceful symbol of the might of my race . . . nothing in the world is so dear to the patriot as a glimpse of his flag flying in a foreign land'. As Dawe had written in an earlier story. 'In the Far East all roads lead to Hong Kong'.

All roads for the Englishman perhaps, but not for Chinese political dissidents. Charles J. Halcombe, a maritime customs official who knew more of China than Dawe and had more concern for its people, presented a harsher view. His autobiographical *The Mystic Flower-*

ing Land: A Personal Narrative (London, 1896) described the harbour in the early 1890s aglitter with electric lighting and already a picturesque wonderland by night, but a place where the police protected the rich efficiently but bore heavily on the poor and weak. After surviving many adventures, Halcombe married a Chinese girl who had saved his life, and he wove his own experiences into *Called Out, or The Chung Wang's Daughter: An Anglo-Chinese Romance* (Hong Kong, 1894). In *Children of Far Cathay: A Social and Political Novel* (Hong Kong and London, 1906), which was the most ambitious Hong Kong novel of the period, Halcombe's Chinese hero, fleeing from the corrupt decadence of the Manchu Empire's twilight years, joined the revolutionary leader, Dr Sun Yat-sen, in Hong Kong. But Hong Kong offered no asylum for rebels, and Halcombe painted a grim scene of spies, informers and police surveillance; of the 'stiff-necked taipans who set the fashion on shore', and harsh unfeeling officialdom handing over dissidents to the Chinese imperial authorities for public execution in Kowloon City.

Despite these criticisms, Halcombe was confident of the blessings of Western culture and Christianity, but was exceptional in believing that Sun Yat-sen's brave new republic would bring friendship with Britain. Most Westerners feared that China was awakening from her slumber as a 'Yellow Peril' which would overrun and destroy the white man's world. In popular imagination Hong Kong represented the front line against this peril.

The most powerful stimulus to this feeling were the novels of Sax Rohmer (Englishman Arthur Henry Sarsfield Ward), with his creation, the evil genius Dr Fu Manchu. For millions of Westerners the dangerous, inscrutable, clever and menacing Fu Manchu personified the 'Chinaman abroad' as the 'archangel of evil,' 'the Yellow Peril incarnate in one man,' backed by the powerful international Si-Fan organisation, 'a menace to Europe and to America greater than that of the plague'.

Sax Rohmer's flair for mystery made the Fu Manchu books an instantaneous success. Altogether there were thirteen, ranging from *The Mystery of Dr Fu Manchu* (London, 1913), through his scheme to take over the American presidency, his plot to seize world domination for himself out of Western civilisation's self-destruction in the Second World War, to his final efforts to restore the lost grandeur of China in *Emperor Fu Manchu* (London and Greenwich, 1959).

The Fu Manchu phenomenon reached its peak in the 1930s, by which time the novels were translated into French, German, Spanish, Italian, Dutch, Portuguese, Greek, Swedish, Czech, Polish, Hungarian, even into Japanese and Arabic. They were adapted as radio serial plays and Hollywood films, when the character was immortalised by Boris Karloff, prince of horror movie actors, and the Chinese Embassy in Washington was driven to protest about this caricature as damaging to the image of the Chinese people.

The confrontation of communism and imperialism and the upheavals of civil war in the real China of the mid-1920s spilled over in riots and strikes in Hong Kong itself. On the flimsy basis of a few days in strike-bound Hong Kong in August 1925, André Malraux transposed his own anti-colonial experience of French Indo-China to southern China in *Les Conquerants* (Paris, 1927) translated as *The Conquerors* (London and New York, 1929). In this powerful and compelling first novel, which was hailed in France as 'a new vision', a Swiss adventurer worked with the Comintern agent, Michael Borodin, to mastermind the Canton revolt.

A sense of end of empire and of Britain as 'a crowded land whose people had gone to the ends of the earth and are now blind to what had driven them there,' appeared also in *The Port of Fragrance* (London, 1930) by Putnam Weale (Bertram Lenox Simpson), author of many fictional and non-fictional works about China and the Far East. As in Malraux's *The Conquerors*, the setting was the 1925 Canton–Hong Kong strike era, but the novel focused on the lives and emotions of European women living unhappily in idle comfort in Hong Kong while their husbands and lovers tackled problems and dangers in the shadowy background of a China in turmoil.

But for most of the English-reading public in the 1920s, Hong Kong took its place among the exotic far-away lands which appealed to Europeans as part of their reaction against the grim days of the First World War.

The Painted Veil (London and New York, 1924), written following a visit to Hong Kong and China by that paragon of story-tellers, Somerset Maugham, suited the escapist mood of the time. The reading public loved Maugham's stories of passion and scandal simmering beneath the surface of supposedly sedate European communities in the East. Notoriety boosted success when Hong Kong officials protested at the thinly disguised veneer of fiction and the leading characters portrayed won a libel action against Maugham. Hollywood brought the story to the screen ten years later starring Greta Garbo. But the novel went further than a clandestine love affair, when the rather shallow English heroine Kitty, who 'had never heard of the Chinese spoken of as anything but decadent, dirty and unspeakable', was dragged from the superficial familiarity of the colony into the real China. 'It was as though the corner of a curtain were lifted for a moment and she caught a glimpse of a world rich with a colour and significance she had not dreamt of.'

Equally acid in her commentary on the English suburban attitudes of pre-war colonial life was Stella Benson, who enjoyed a much smaller readership than Maugham but who had a more intimate experience of Hong Kong. She first visited the colony for a few months as a young teacher in 1920, and after several years in China returned to spend eighteen months in Hong Kong in 1930–31 as the wife of a British customs official. Stella Benson's youthful impressions of the colony were of 'that grave and misty tilted city, it makes no claims to a spirit of equality. It is a solid lump of England: from waterside to peak-tip the little funicular carries Anglo-Saxon civilization up and down.' (*The Little World*, London 1925 and New York, 1926). The same combination of neat 'Englishness' and racial arrogance emerged in a sequence in Benson's most remarkable novel, *The Poor Man* (London, 1923), in which the hero – or anti-hero – spent a disastrous interlude as a Hong Kong teacher.

Mundos (London, 1935), Stella Benson's last and unfinished novel, set in an imaginary tropical outpost of empire, painted a withering picture of colonialism as she observed it in Hong Kong: the well-meaning, often misplaced pomposity of officialdom, the bureaucratic remoteness from ordinary people, the hard masculine colonial scene in which society wives fluttered in their own little world of charity bazaars, oblivious to the ills and sufferings around them. 'There are no women in Hong Kong, only ladies' (*Some Letters of Stella Benson*, 1928 – 1933, edited by Cecil Clarabut, Hong Kong, 1978).

In the last years of her short life, Stella Benson's efforts were largely channelled into a campaign against child prostitution, which appeared only fleetingly in her novels, in the person of Lilla Liu, the prostitute 'from the organised slave markets of Hong Kong' (*Mundos*). For the most part Benson's literary talents on this subject lie buried in reports to the League of Nations. Never a 'popular' writer, Benson's work appealed to a devoted but limited circle of admirers, and her zeal for social reform made more enemies than friends.

These sceptics included Emily Hahn, an American writer and journalist, who brought a fresh and lively eye to bear on the colony on the eve of the Pacific war, and who had the unique experience of living at large in Japanese-occupied Hong Kong while most of her compatriots were in internment camps. Coming to Hong Kong after enjoying several years in cosmopolitan Shanghai, Emily Hahn was taken aback by the racial snobbery of the colony's Europeans, who excluded Asians from living in the fashionable Peak district and regarded the war raging over the border as 'a far-off manifestation of the natives'. But she was even more struck by the conservatism of the Hong Kong Chinese, who had been cut off from the progressive ideas of post-revolutionary China and clung to outdated customs and traditions.

A witty, candid waspish iconoclast, Hahn's stories of her experiences in wartime Hong Kong attracted considerable interest when she was repatriated to the USA in the latter years of the Second World War. They appeared in the form of *China to Me: Partial Autobiography* (New York, 1944); in articles and sketches published mainly in *The New Yorker* and reissued as *Hong Kong Holiday* (New York, 1946); and in fictional form in *Miss Jill* (New York, 1947). This was a no-nonsense view of an English prostitute, who left the sophistication of pre-war Shanghai to ply her trade in Hong Kong and encountered its small-town peacetime snobbery, followed by the topsy-turvy social values of a wartime internment camp.

James Allan Ford's *The Brave White Flag* (London, 1961) presented a contrasting but grimly authentic view of the fall of Hong Kong. This eyewitness, semi-documentary, soldier's novel about the campaign, 'its glories and muddles', was dedicated to the memory of his brother, Captain Douglas Ford, who also fought in Hong Kong's defence and was executed by the Japanese, being awarded the George Cross posthumously for refusing to break under torture.

Anthony Esler's *Bastion* (London, 1980), written nearly twenty years later, about an American merchant seaman caught in the battle for Hong Kong, was more of a straightforward adventure story. *Hiroshima Joe* (London, 1985) by Martin Booth, who had spent his childhood in Hong Kong, explored the wartime experience further from the battle through to prison camp in Japan.

The resurgence of Hong Kong after the Second World War and the upheaval in China culminating in the 'Liberation' in 1949, which sent refugees streaming across the border, inspired a new breed of writers: people who lived and worked in Hong Kong, often drawn to it by a mixture of affection and exasperation but also by the challenge to unravel its complexity. Notable among these were Han Suyin, a Western-trained Eurasian woman doctor; and Austin Coates, a young English official.

Westerners were excited and shocked by Han Suyin's autobiographical *A Many Splendoured Thing* (London and Boston, 1952), a best-seller and popular movie in its day, which was a frank account of her love affair with a well-known English journalist, Ian Morrison, correspondent for *The Times*. But the book had lasting significance in trying to come to terms not only with the disparity between China and Hong Kong, and between Chinese and Westerners inside the colony, but also with the conflicts and uncertainties among the Hong Kong Chinese themselves. Many were torn between revulsion at the violence of the Chinese revolution and pride in its ideals: 'sympathetic yet aloof in Hong Kong, watching events from that semi-detached observation tower', as the last act of the civil war drama played itself out, with 'China unseen but always felt'. 'The melting pot of the Orient they called Hong Kong. Indeed no, the place where everyone met and many stayed apart, divided by hedges of prejudice and hearsay.' This was Hong Kong in 1949 with its burgeoning population, influx of destitute refugees and Shanghai millionaires, poverty jostling affluence, lost heritages and war boom fortunes, 'a refugee camp, harbour of many ships, haven of people out from China, a squatters' colony, fun fair, bazaar and boom town'. Hong Kong was bursting with life and so different from the ghost town liberated only four years before, yet itself under threat at the heart of a Far East and South-East Asia in turmoil.

Austin Coates, who was appointed to the Hong Kong Civil Service in that same year of 1949, immediately fell under the colony's spell and tried to interpret it. With a keen sense of the absurd, Coates affectionately mocked the administration of which he was part, which was sometimes well-meaning, sometimes corrupt but invariably misunderstood. *The Road* (New York, 1959) portrayed the tragic–comic impact of European officialdom on Chinese country-folk, when a Governor's plans to build a road for the benefit of villagers on a remote island opened up a Pandora's box of ambition, speculation and bewilderment. It disrupted village life, rocked the English district officer's marriage and brought two young peasant lovers to suicide.

The Road was an intelligent novel, but Coates's autobiographical sketches and stories were more gripping. The final chapters of *Invitation to an Eastern Feast* (New York, 1955) described the author's introduction to Hong Kong's Chinese society. One long episode in *Personal and Oriental* (New York, 1957) presented a humorous but sad and sympathetic account of the impact of the communist victory on the mainland on an individual Chinese family, and the tug of loyalties between China, Hong Kong and Taiwan. Above all, *Myself a Mandarin* (London, 1968 and New York, 1969) brought to life Coates's own experience as a magistrate in the untouched rural New Territories of the 1950s. This now vanished world was 'not exactly China, not exactly Hong Kong . . . old in its ways of thought, unchanged by the Chinese politics of fifty years or by the Hong Kong sophistication of a century.

This sense of paradox also emerged from Preston Schoyer's last novel *The Typhoon's Eye* (New York, 1959). Schoyer, who taught in China in the 1930s, served there during the Second World War and married a Chinese girl, established himself as a professional writer on his return to the USA with an acclaimed first novel based on his China experience. He spent eight years in the colony from 1959, helping to set up the Chinese University of Hong Kong. In this last novel Schoyer's visiting middle-aged American heroine compared Hong Kong to the eye of a typhoon as 'a place of peace and calm round which whirl the turbulences of a changing Asia'. To which her long-term resident American friend replied:

> 'It's all wrong and yet it's exactly right, since at sea the typhoon's eye is anything but serene – huge waves banging aimlessly into each other, and the air's oppressive, and all around you is the scream and howl of the storm. It can be a nightmare sort of place. And so can Hong Kong, under this nice, serene exterior. There's a hidden intrigue here and a hidden cruelty, a dog-eat-dog attitude, and a terrific potential for open violence.'

As his guest found out for herself.

Richard Mason's evocative *The World of Suzie Wong* (London, 1957), published about the same time, dealt with a different aspect of Hong Kong life. For Western readers – male readers at least – the delectable Suzie Wong, warm, sympathetic, born to please men, conjured up the allure of Hong Kong's red light district. This became even more glamorous on the cinema screen, casting an air of innocent enchantment over the harsh neon-lit sordidness of the city's entertainment world.

Less widely read, but more true to life, was Donald Moore's *The Striking Wind* (London, 1959), in which an English schoolmaster, a drifting mediocrity, was seduced from a humdrum marriage by the elegant charms of an expensive call girl.

Alexander Cordell (George Alexander Graber,) an English civil servant who spent his childhood in China and some years in post-war Hong Kong, tried more ambitiously to describe inter-racial romance through the eyes of the Chinese girl. *The Sinews of Love* (London, 1965), in which a Tanka boat girl falls in love with an Englishman, portrayed the hard life of the boat people and particularly of girls virtually sold into marriage or concubinage in Hong Kong, where 'money is the sinews of love, as of war'. A well-meaning novel written with integrity and a good sense of story, it was not totally convincing in differentiating men and women, Chinese and Europeans.

For a constant stream of refugees, Hong Kong provided a haven from the upheavals of life in China. 'Go south, go south, go south' was the message of Po Nan-king's *The River Flows East* (Hong Kong,

1957)[1] a semi-autobiographical account of a young man's struggle to escape to freedom in the mid-1950s. Lois Mitchison's compelling novel, *Gillian Lo* (London, 1964), came to terms with the culture shock experienced by her British-born Eurasian heroine, who went to China in 1948 with her Chinese bridegroom and was released into a bewildering Hong Kong after years of persecution and indoctrination during the first decade after the Liberation.

Like any cosmopolitan international port and tourist centre, Hong Kong has always had its share of vice and crime. Statistically the crime rate is still lower than that of most ports of comparable size, but statistics make dull reading, and novelists shake a heady cocktail of detectives, gangsters, hit men, drug pushers, pimps, prostitutes, secret agents and sharp businessmen.

James Boswell captured the aura of shady opportunism in *The Blue Pheasant* (London, 1958), featuring crooked Chinese and Englishmen in the Hong Kong of the 1950s, where 'the flotsam which drifts in the wake of war and revolution provides a rich haul for the quick, the ruthless and the cunning'.

Gavin Black (Oswald Wynd) in *The Eyes Around Me* (New York, 1964, and London, 1966) used Hong Kong as one of a number of exotic Oriental backgrounds in which a businessman, working out of Singapore, wrestled with crooked dealing.

In *The Bengali Inheritance* (London and New York, 1975) Owen Sela wove his exciting novel round the search for treasure which disappeared with the aircrash death of the wartime Indian nationalist leader Subhas Chandra Bose. An accountant by profession, Sela recaptured the uneasy days of the early 1970s in Hong Kong with the first campaign against official corruption.

In Peter Driscoll's well constructed and sustained thriller, *Pangolin* (London and New York, 1979), a seedy British journalist conspired with a failed businessman, an American deserter and a Chinese ne'er-do-well in a near perfect crime to kidnap a CIA agent. The quartet led the Hong Kong establishment a merry dance in the shabby ambivalent half-world of Hong Kong's misfits before they were caught up and destroyed on the higher plane of international terrorism.

In *City of Masks* (London, 1982), Marshall Browne, former paratrooper and Hong Kong-based Australian banker, continued the tradition of well-designed credible thrillers on the murky fringes of Hong Kong business life, where threats to assassinate a self-made Chinese tycoon masked commercial crime.

William Leonard Marshall's 'Yellowthread' suspense novels, based on the adventures of Detective Chief Inspector Harry Feiffer, are in a class of their own, zany but not entirely incredible.[2] A former journalist and teacher, who spent a number of years in Hong Kong, Marshall depicted an imaginary Hong Bay district, 'where tourist brochures advise you not to go there after dark'. Sprightly, quickpaced, frenzied, the comic and brutal, mundane and bizarre go side by side. Feiffer's loving wife, cocooned cosily at home like the tourists in their hotels, watches American gangster movies on the television, while her husband wrestles with hair-raising, real-life crime.

In the novelist's Hong Kong, detectives, murderers, gangsters and drug-pushers rub shoulders with spies. Traditionally Hong Kong has been a watchtower, from which people have observed more troubled neighbouring regions in comparative safety and comfort. In post-war years professional China-watchers – intelligence officers, foreign correspondents and diplomats – congregated to exchange news and rumours.

The prototype of the secret agent reached Hong Kong in more relaxed pre-war days in *The Hong Kong Airbase Murders* (New York, 1937) by Francis Van Wyck Mason, then the leading American author of international espionage and intrigue. For Mason's hero, American military intelligence agent Captain Hugh North, globe-trotting in his country's defence, the Far East was a prime danger spot, which found him in Shanghai in 1933, the Philippines in 1936, Hong Kong in 1937 and Singapore in 1939. In Hong Kong, as everywhere, Westerners dominated the action, with the Chinese fulfilling simple stereotype roles as evil villains or clever detectives – though none so clever as North himself. The 'native city' provided a shadowy background, although modern readers can indulge a certain nostalgia for more spacious days when Aberdeen was a picturesque village, Repulse Bay an uncrowded beach, and shops only beginning to encroach on the plush Chinese residential district round Lascar Row.

After the war Hugh North, now a Colonel, pursued patriotism in different corners of Asia, leaving others to protect the Western world in Hong Kong. Two of Van Wyck Mason's contemporaries, prolific writers Ernest K. Gann and Simon Harvester (Henry Gibbs), turned their attention to the East, seeing the issue in black and white as a communist menace to Western democracy.

The American Gann, whose own pre-war escapades in China were more colourful than most fiction, told a straightforward tale in *A Soldier of Fortune* (New York, 1954) about an American wife coming to Hong Kong to organise her husband's rescue from a Chinese communist jail. Chinese villains and an American rogue with a heart of gold reinforced current American attitudes to Hong Kong as an arena in the Cold War, although the legendary Clark Gable failed to bring this anti-hero to life in one of Hollywood's and Gann's less memorable films.

Before the Second World War Englishman Simon Harvester, under his real name of Henry Gibbs, had already published *The Spectre of Communism* (London, 1936), a serious warning of the communist threat to China and the British Empire. It followed naturally that Harvester's fictional hero, battling communism in many parts of Asia, should later see service in Hong Kong in *The Bamboo Screen* (London, 1955), in Harvester's 'Asia in Turmoil' series.

Yet the bamboo curtain in the late 1950s and early 1960s was more transparent and less forbidding than Europe's iron curtain, as Eric Ambler told in his *Passage of Arms* (London, 1959). In this amusing and well-told tale about gun–running to Indonesia, Ambler's American businessman, doing the tourist run in Hong Kong, was surprised at the colony's defencelessness and the comparative freedom of contacts with China.

This situation changed dramatically during China's Cultural Revolution, which brought riots to Hong Kong in 1967 and a new violence into Western literature. As in Alexander Cordell's *The Bright Cantonese* (London, 1967),[3] told through a Eurasian Red China agent posing as a Hong Kong bargirl, which wove a web of rape, murder and intrigue, with the USA and China apparently set on a collision course.

Kenneth Royce's hero in *A Single to Hong Kong* (London, 1969) undertook a dangerous mission to the East and suffered torture in a communist Canton gaol in a fast-paced tale of violence, drugs and political treachery.

But pride of place in this category went to the two larger-than-life best-sellers by John Gordon Davis, who had worked for some years in Hong Kong and was well versed in its crime and the law: *The Years of the Hungry Tiger* (London, 1974), which views the spilling over of the Chinese Cultural Revolution into Hong Kong through the experiences of an English police officer; and *Typhoon* (London, 1978), with its triads, brothels, gang rape, corruption and spectacular typhoon. Vibrant, gripping, intensely exciting, this is rich fare.

Hong Kong often played a role – if sometimes a small one – in the thrillers of Soviet–China intrigue which became fashionable in the 1970s.[4] Outstanding among these was *The Honourable Schoolboy* (London, 1977) by John Le Carré (David John Moore Cornwell), in which Hong Kong was the launching pad for British intelligence forays into South-East Asia. This over-long convoluted novel contained some brilliant vignettes of the colony and the colourful band of journalists, intelligence agents and hangers-on who frequented its

Foreign Correspondents' Club. Life in Le Carré's Hong Kong was exhilarating and dangerous, but endowed with an air of unreality and glamour which came from viewing it from the former club's picture windows high above the city. Le Carré's interpretation of Hong Kong as as place of perpetual excitement, intrigue and sudden death was the authorised version for his faithful following in the Western world.

Other 'spy' novels were so lurid and violent that the background faded into insignificance. In *The Mandarin Cypher* (London, 1975), a Quiller action novel by Adam Hall (Elleston Trevor), the hero found that 'despite what the chamber of commerce says, the two chief industries of Hong Kong are narcotics and espionage', an experience already discovered in Franklin M.J. Davis Jr's *Secret Hong Kong: Spy-chase in a City of Sin and Death* (New York, 1962); in James Hadley Chase's *A Coffin from Hong Kong* (London and New York, 1962); and in Mignon C. Eberhart's *Message from Hong Kong* (London and New York,1969), her forty-fifth novel of mystery, murder and surprise. Terry Harknett's Australian detective in *Crown: Bamboo Shoot Out* (1975) penetrated the bamboo curtain in a welter of sex, violence, blood and gore. William Cord's *Death Run* (London, 1979) presented a 'new novel of intrigue and raw adventure sweeping from Hong Kong across the Orient'. By the time Nick Carter, No 1 AXE agent, reached Hong Kong in one of his Killmaster 'spy chillers', *Dragon Flame* (New York, 1968), the venue was of no relevance whatsoever.

Other writers turned to the historical novel. In *The Jade Alliance* (London, 1979) Elizabeth Darrell intelligently recreated the Hong Kong of the early twentieth century through the eyes of a Russian girl, who fled from the 1905 Revolution and fell in love with a British colonial official. 'The English did not adapt', she observed, 'they pre-ferred to take England with them wherever they went'.

Among the most popular scenarios for modern novelists were multi-generation family chronicles and the birth of Hong Kong during the first Opium War. Robert Elegant's *Dynasty* (New York, 1977), a mammoth Anglo-Chinese family saga, stretching from the beginning of the century to 1970, made absorbing reading. Played out against the background of the Chinese Revolution, of secret societies and the business world, its intricacies attracted a greater following than the more prosaic real-life view provided by two daughters of the most influential Eurasian family of this era: Jean Gittins's autobio-graphical *Eastern Windows, Western Skies* (Hong Kong, 1969); and Irene Cheng's biography of her mother, *Clara Ho Tung* (Hong Kong, 1976).

In an early attempt to bring Hong Kong's exciting and seamy origins to life, Mona Gardner's *Hong Kong* (New York, 1958) provided well researched historical background material about Canton, Macao, Hong Kong and the Opium war, but the characters and relationships were unreal.

Much more influential was James Clavell's *Taipan* (London, 1966), a vast panorama about the founding of Hong Kong and of a *taipan* with a vision of its future potential. Clavell claimed to be not a novelist but a story-teller, for whom escapism was a virtue. Never slackening pace, *Taipan* was a best-selling epic about cut-throat trading, ambition, lust, greed and the violence of man and nature, culminating in a devastating typhoon.

Fifteen years later Ernest V. Thompson used the same background for *The Dream Traders* (London, 1981), about honest clean-living Cornish hero, Luke Trewarne, his love for a Hoklo boat girl and his fight against opium smuggling. Told with sympathy by an author who served in Hong Kong waters in the navy and later as an officer in the anti-narcotics trade, *The Dream Traders* was a good story, but tended to superimpose values of the 1980s on the early nineteenth century.

Timothy Mo's *An Insular Possession* (London 1986 and New York 1987), which is also about the period of the First Opium War, set a new standard in Hong Kong literature. Being Anglo-Chinese, born in Hong Kong but brought up in England, Mo combined the traditions of English literature and the Chinese novel, which, as the author says 'moves in a path which is altogether *circular*', to weave a rich tapestry of language and character.

Whatever its literary merits and entertainment value, most modern Western fiction conveys a picture of Hong Kong as a den of iniquity and spectacular violence, a city living at fever pitch in an atmosphere of danger and excitement. Alongside this, the contemporary novel presents the worship of Mammon. Hong Kong is one of the world's most materialistic societies, in which men, both Oriental and Caucasian, are measured primarily by their financial standing. For Chinese, risking life and limb to escape in their thousands from the spartan virtues of the communist People's Republic, Hong Kong has long been 'The Golden Mountain where men eat fat pork' (Davis, *Years of the Hungry Tiger*). Greed and exploitation played a large part in Davis's *Typhoon*, but reached a crescendo in James Clavell's *Noble House* (New York, 1981), with the smell of money on all its more than twelve hundred pages. This mammoth novel, designed from conception to be a best-seller, brought the story of *Taipan* into modern times. In little more than one week's action in the early 1960s, Clavell crowded in twenty years of disaster: murder, kidnapping, mob terror, landslide, fire and flood, all dominated by obsession with the pursuit of wealth.

A third notable feature of modern Hong Kong fiction is the 'liberated woman'. A few women novelists still wrote romantic tales of lovely Eurasian heroines,[5] but for the most part the alluring, submissive Oriental charmer of Dawe and Halcombe, and the high-spirited but ultra-feminine Suzie Wong, lost ground to the new European woman, for whom all inhibitions disappeared in Hong Kong. Stunningly beautiful, she was independent, fearless, intelligent, giving full rein to her passions and appetites. The heroine of Davis's *Typhoon* was a terrifying challenge to any man's virility. And the 'modern' woman could be transposed to other times, as with Clavell's Mary in *Taipan*, an unlikely early Victorian damsel, who in the year 1841 found an antidote to incest in abandon with wealthy middle-aged Chinese lovers.

Often writing with an eye to the best-seller market and translation to the cinema or television screen, many modern writers have taken one aspect of life which is not necessarily false in itself but which is concentrated to the pitch of distortion. The effect is often gripping, vivid, sometimes masterly, but a meretricious parody of Hong Kong as a Sodom and Gomorrah of violence, sin, avarice and lust.

At the opposite extreme, a handful of writers revealed their sense of remoteness, particularly among the university faculty, insulated from the outside world in their ivory tower. Christopher New in *The Chinese Box* (London, 1975) wrote about a university couple in the 1967 political troubles; and Harry Rickett's *People Like Us: Sketches of Hong Kong* (Hong Kong, 1977) was a collection of glimpses into the detached isolated world of many Europeans.

In the 1960s a small body of fiction by local Chinese novelists began to emerge, not usually attracting a wide readership but written with feeling, integrity and understanding. Hse Yu's 'Strange Guest', in his *Woman in the Mist and Two Other Tales Set in Hong Kong and China* (Hong Kong, 1961) portrayed the alienation of formerly well-to-do Shanghai Chinese coming to Hong Kong after the communist takeover.

Lin Tai-yi, claiming at that time to be 'the only Chinese novelist writing in English about my people in my generation', portrayed in *Kampoon Street* (Cleveland and New York, 1964) the poverty of slums, the exploitation of women and the disillusionment of young people. C.Y. Lee (Li Chin-yang) in *The Virgin Market* (London, 1965) wrote realistically about the impact of modern life among the boat people in Aberdeen, where social practices and superstition died hard even in the face of rapid economic change. It gave a vivid portrayal of poverty, of the hard life of women, and of a well-meaning American doctor battling uncomprehendingly and ineffectively in a foreign world.

In his perceptive first novel, *The Monkey King* (London, 1978), Timothy Mo portrayed middle-class Chinese family life in the town and the rural New Territories against the colonial background, and he went on to produce a remarkable novel, *Sour Sweet* (London, 1982), about the alienation of a Chinese family who had migrated from the New Territories to London's Chinatown.

Lee Ding Fai's *Running Dog* (Hong Kong, 1980) described young people in colonial Hong Kong in the 1970s, including aspiring university students and enterprising refugees from mainland China who made good in Hong Kong's commercial world.

This literature was rich in its observation of character and the contemporary scene, and it revealed a dynamism and the opportunity to escape from poverty which characterised the Hong Kong emerging into the 1980s.

The increased international awareness of Hong Kong, coupled with uncertainties about the future, spawned a host of novels by journalists, civil servants and professional writers in the early 1980s. Some still used Hong Kong as a mere backdrop for scenes of mindless sex and violence, but generally the long-familiar themes of crime, corruption, drugs and Triad gangs were more accurately set in their local context.[6] *The Sanctuary* (Hong Kong, 1984), by civil servant and former police officer Anthony Cooper, dealt with the mounting problems which threatened to rip the colony apart: 'the centrifugal forces in this tiny Anglo-Asian crucible'. And in a lengthy novel, *Conspiracy of Amateurs* (Hong Kong, 1985), long-term resident Bill Lowe portrayed contemporary Hong Kong as a place where myths and illusions were soon shattered.

Strangely, the impending transformation of Hong Kong from British Crown Colony to a Special Administrative Region of the People's Republic of China has only captured the attention of a few novelists. *The Smile on the Face of the Tiger* (London, 1969 and New York, 1971), by Douglas Hurd and Andrew Osmond, was an exciting political thriller, which projected into the future (1976) a supposed Chinese ultimatum for the immediate return of Hong Kong. This novel attracted renewed interest when Douglas Hurd was Minister of State at the Foreign Office during the Sino–British negotiations about the future of Hong Kong. But by then the novel had been overtaken by events, and from the beginning Hong Kong was the occasion for the story rather than its subject. More recently, John Trenhaille's *The Mahjong Spies* (London, 1986) also treated Hong Kong as the background to an international game in which the USSR sought to undermine Hong Kong's prosperity in the countdown to 1997.

Meanwhile Macao, the older Portuguese colony lying some forty miles away across the estuary of the Pearl River, was being dragged belatedly from its picturesque backwater into modern life. Inevitably this quaint city began to provide the backdrop to modern thrillers: in Gavin Black's *The Golden Cockatrice* (New York, 1975) his regular businessman hero, Paul Harris, was caught there in a web of Russian-Chinese intrigue. And Nick Carter discovered Macao in 1981, *Macau: A Time for Death* (New York, 1981).

Nineteenth-century writers painted a picture of decline, Macao's past glories crumbled into decay, a sinister aura surrounding its gambling casinos, as in William Carlton Dawe's 'Fantan' story in *Yellow and White* (London and Boston, 1895). Nearly half a century later Maurice de Kobra wrote a sensational expose of the city's seamier side in *Macau, L'Enfer du Jeu (Macau, Gambling Hell)*, published in French in Paris in 1938, and in Portuguese translation as *Inferno do Jogo* (Rio de Janeiro, 1938).

But Kobra's novel roused considerable fury in Macao, where intermarriage between Portuguese and Chinese over the centuries had produced a distinctive Macanese way of life.

Unlike Hong Kong, in Macao China was not only felt but seen, for it enveloped the tiny peninsula in a tangible embrace. In the words of Stella Benson, Macao was 'old but it seems older than its years. Here you have China victorious. Portugal lies drugged and asleep in the arms of China.' (*The Little World*, London 1925 and New York, 1926).

The paradox of Macao was captured by W. H. Auden, who visited the colony in 1938,

> Churches beside brothels. . .
> This city of indulgence. . .
> And nothing serious can happen here.[7]

In contrast to Hong Kong, there was a long tradition of literature among the Macanese themselves, going back to the great sixteenth-century Portuguese poet, Luiz de Camões, who is reputed to have composed part of the *Lusiadas* in Macao.

Several prominent Portuguese writers spent part of their lives in Macao. The first book by Wenceslau de Morais, who lived there as a young man and later became an expert on Japan, was *Traços do Extreme Oriente (Traces of the Far East)*, published in Lisbon in the 1920s, short stories some of which described Macao in the late nineteenth century. The celebrated Joaquim Paco d'Arcos, son of a Macao

Governor, wrote about the city he knew in the 1920s in his *Amores e Viagems de Pedro Manuel (Loves and Voyages of Pedro Manuel)* (Lisbon, 1935), which went into several editions, and his *Navio dos Mortes (Ship of the Dead)* (Lisbon, 1952), a volume of short stories.

There were other writers of more local reputation.[8] But most of this fiction, though written with sympathy and affection and some-times rising to literary distinction, was available only in Portuguese, so that the readership was small, and Macao remained almost unknown outside of Portuguese territory.

Much of Macao's charm has come to Westerners through the paintings of George Chinnery, who spent most of his life in the East and died in Macao in 1852. Kathleen Odell's *Chinnery in China* (London, 1971), was an intelligent fictional reconstruction of Chin-nery's life in early nineteenth-century Macao as seen by the painter himself.

But old Macao is perhaps best known through *City of Broken Promises* (London, 1967) by the Englishman, Austin Coates. Described by the author as an 'authentic novel' of 'a city like no other in the world', *City of Broken Promises* told the unlikely but true story of Marta Meirop, a Chinese foundling who became the mistress of an English East India Company official and subsequently the wealthiest businesswoman and public benefactress on the China coast. The novel evoked the feeling of late eighteenth-century Macao at the zenith of its prosperity before Hong Kong was founded and inherited its trade.

Hong Kong itself figures hardly at all in the literature of the the-atre, although Noel Coward wrote most of the script for *Private Lives* in the confines of the colony's Peninsula Hotel during his brief visit in 1929.

Hong Kong's small inward-looking colonial society has a long tra-dition of doggerel and political satire in verse, written for a contem-porary local audience and largely unintelligible to the modern reader: from the anonymous, *Pill Poet's Street Ballads* (Hong Kong, 1857), a rather scurrilous collection of parodies, which originally appeared in the local press, through C. R. Thatcher's *The Hong Kong Distillery: A Rum Burlesque* (Hong Kong, 1871), to Robert K.M. Simpson's light-hearted *Diversions* (Hong Kong, 1933).

Probably for most Westerners the immediate image of Hong Kong in verse that springs to mind is Coward's lyric in 'Mad Dogs and Englishmen', in *Words and Music* (London, 1932):

In Hong Kong they strike a gong
And fire off a noonday gun
To reprimand each inmate – who's in late. . .
But mad dogs and Englishmen
Go out in the mid-day sun.

Yet one of England's most distinguished twentieth-century poets, Edmund Blunden, spent a number of years in the 1950s and early 1960s as Professor of English at the University of Hong Kong. Blunden remained *par excellence* a poet of the English countryside, seeking these same qualities in Hong Kong's remote islands and the peace of his own garden, so that the title poem of *A Hong Kong House: Poems, 1951–61* (London, 1962) reflected a sylvan calm of yesteryear, rare even in its day and since quite vanished.

Described by Stephen Spender as 'a god in Asia', Blunden put a generation of Hong Kong students under the spell of English literature, but failed to stimulate a strong indigenous tradition of poetry. In *Handful of Hong Kong: A Visitor's Verses* (Hong Kong, 1966), Joseph Jones, an American professor, offered witty, observant and affectionate little poems about familiar things in the lull before the Cultural Revolution. An anthology, *Hong Kong: Images on Shifting Waters* (Hong Kong, 1977) compiled by Joyce Hsia and T. C. Lai, comprised a small group of 'poems past', while the 'poems present' were largely by Western writers. The compilers referred to Hong Kong's beauty and indigenous culture, which Western visitors – and most Western residents – failed to see behind its more spectacular features. Yet the editors could find no 'definitive poem' and concluded that Hong Kong was 'perhaps an enigma that defies definition'.

So too with the novel: many authors have written about Hong Kong, some attempting to bridge the gap between the Chinese and Western communities, and more rarely between rich and poor. There have been intelligent novels, some exciting, skilfully constructed and gripping; some amusing; some true to life. Some have enjoyed contemporary acclaim; some were interesting from a historical perspective. Yet none survived its day to become an ageless classic nor achieved sufficient influence to change the course of events in Hong Kong or outside. None has captured the spirit and soul of this unique place.

Despite changing literary fashions, a number of themes recur: exotic escapism; safe, prim smugness; violence and danger; inscrutable Orientals and fantasy women; the Western world living in the shadow of an Eastern menace, whether it be Boxer rebels, Ch'ing mandarins, secret societies or communist spies. Much is stereotype, but a great deal of truth emerges: the gap between the races, between generations, between the affluent and poor; the exploitation of women; poverty and opportunity. This is not the grinding poverty of despair but a dynamic and energetic society in which wit, education and determination encourage upward mobility.

Hong Kong remains a paradox: a foremost international commercial centre in a colonial anachronism; nearly six million people crowded into one of the most heavily populated regions on earth, yet many living in pools of loneliness; 'Golden Mountain', capitalism in the raw; 'Fragrant Harbour', cesspool of the East. In the words of Han Suyin (*A Many Splendoured Thing*), 'Hong Kong where people come and go and know themselves more impermanent than anywhere else on earth. Beautiful island of many worlds in the arms of the sea. Hong Kong.'

Notes

1 First published in Chinese in Hong Kong in 1955.
2 William Leonard Marshall, *Yellowthread Street*, London, 1975, and New York, 1976; *The Hatchet Man*, London, 1976 and New York, 1977; *Gelignite*, London and New York, 1977; *Thin Air*, London, 1977 and New York, 1978; *Skulduggery*, London, 1979 and New York, 1980; *Roadshow*, London, 1985.
3 Published as *The Deadly Eurasian*, New York, 1968.
4 Such as Ian Stewart's political novel, *The Peking Payoff*, London, 1975; Christopher New's *Goodbye Mr Mao*, London, 1979; or Margaret Jones's *The Confucius Enigma*, New York, 1979.
5 For example, Carissa Ross in *Jade Princess*, New York, 1977, a story of life and mystery in Macao and Hong Kong; or Nita Rosemeyer, *The Bamboo and the Heather*, New York, 1980, about a Eurasian girl's romance with a German in Hong Kong at the time of the outbreak of the Second World War.
6 For example, in Sandy Gall, *Chasing the Dragon*, London, 1981; Keith Colquhoun, *Filthy Rich*, London, 1982; Peter Hill, *The Washermen*, London, 1982; Bernard Boucher, *Opalesque*, Melbourne, 1983; Geoffrey Thursby, *Miller*, Hong Kong, 1983; Robert Ludlum, *The Bourne Supremacy*, London 1986.
7 'Macau' in W. H. Auden and Christopher Isherwood, *Journey to a War*, London, 1939, p. 22.
8 Such as Emilio de San Bruno, whose *O Caso de Rua Volong: Scenas da Vida Colonial (The Case of Volong Street: Scenes of Colonial Life)*, Lisbon, 1928 was the autobiographical love story of a Portuguese naval officer in Macao. Francisco de Carvalho e Rego, a teacher and amateur actor, who came to live in Macao as a child,wrote *O Casa do Tesouro do Templo de A-Ma (The Case of the Treasure of A-Ma Temple)*, a story about a Chinese detective, first published in a Macao literary magazine, *Renascimento*, in 1943 and reissued six years later; and *Lendas Contos da Velhua China (Legends and Tales of Old China)* Macao, 1950. Luis Gonzaga Gomes also related Chinese stories about Macao in *Lendas Chinesos de Macau*, Macao, 1941, and *Chinesices*, Macao, 1952. Madam Castilho's A *Primeira Dama (The First Lady)* provoked consid-

F

erable local interest as a thinly disguised portrayal of a Governor's overbearing wife. Margarida Castel Branco, granddaughter of a Macao Governor, wrote *Aconteceu en Macau (It Happened in Macao)*, published in Lisbon in the early 1950s, one of a series of novels each set in a Portuguese colony and designed to give young people a picture of colonial life. Deolinda Conceição's *Cheong-sam* comprised rather sugar-sweet short stories largely about Macao's Chinese community. Henrique de Senna Fernandes, in *Nam Van: Contos de Macau*, Macao, 1979, told of Macao and Hong Kong in the 1940s and 1950s, with one story set in his grandfather's time, nostalgic for a fast vanishing gracious and unique way of life.

Reading list

Clavell, James, *Taipan*, London and New York, 1966.

Coates, Austin, *City of Broken Promises*, London, 1967.

——, *Myself a Mandarin*, London, 1967.

Davis, John Gordon *Years of the Hungry Tiger*, London, 1974.

——, *Typhoon*, London, 1978.

Elegant, Robert, *Dynasty*, New York, 1977.

Han Suyin, *A Many Splendoured Thing*, London and Boston, 1952.

Le Carré, John (David John Moore Cornwell), *The Honourable Schoolboy*, London, 1977.

Marshall, William Leonard, *Yellowthread Street*, London, 1975.

Mason, Richard, *The World of Suzie Wong*, London, 1957.

Maugham, W. Somerset, *The Painted Veil*, New York, 1924.

Mo, Timothy, *An Insular Possession*, London, 1986.

CHAPTER NINE

Journeys to Java

Western fiction about Indonesia
1600–1980

James R. Rush

As a political entity, the sprawling crescent of South-East Asian islands which forms modern Indonesia was realised only in the twentieth century. It had taken the Dutch more than 300 years of intermittent empire-building to bring the entire territory into its embrace as the Netherlands Indies. The world turmoil of the 1940s brought wartime occupation and a nationalist revolution to the Indies, and this made possible the transformation of Holland's huge tropical colony into an independent state. The Dutch departed for good in 1949. Within the framework they left behind, Indonesians have carried on ever since, very much in their own way.

The vast majority of Western writing about Indonesia occurred during the colonial period, most of it by Dutch men and women. More than anything else, therefore, novels and stories by Europeans about Indonesia reflect the imperial experience. In them we read of the involvement of Dutchmen and other Westerners with the place and its people. It is a limited involvement: confined to that small, dynamic intersection of Eastern and Western life in the colonial world occurring in towns, trading posts and plantations; dominated by the activities of administration and commerce; carried on by a disproportionate number of Europeans, Eurasians and other foreigners, and by Indonesians who are servants, coolies and functionaries. Characters of Western fiction seek adventure and fortune; they love and hate each other; they test their ideals and ponder the meaning of life within this limited realm. It is a small part of a large world, and in these stories we view it almost always through the special eyes of the coloniser.

Conquest, governance and Indies society

The first popular book in Europe about the Indonesian archipelago was not fiction, strictly speaking. Its publisher assured his readers on the title page that, 'Here you will find no trifling, nor dreams, nor fabulous imaginings.' Still, there are 'many wonderful and perilous happenings' in William Ysbrantsz Bontekoe's *Memorable Description of the East Indian Voyage*. It is a ship captain's tale of carrying gunpowder to Java in 1618 and his adventures thereafter: shipwreck in the Sunda Straits (the gunpowder blew up); a narrow escape from Sumatran 'savages'; and a timely arrival in the new Dutch haven of Batavia on Java. Later, Bontekoe relates several episodes of unabashed aggression by the Dutch East India Company (his employer) as it wrested a share for Holland of the lucrative spice trade. It is all in the book, and good reading it was for the stay-at-home Dutchman. In Holland, Bontekoe's fantastic account of his journey to Java was the most widely read popular book of the seventeenth and eighteenth centuries.[1]

Other works of purported fact offered readers of the time vicarious adventures in exploration and conquest. More deliberate works of fiction appeared only later. The earliest of these were verse dramas, like Onno Zwier van Haren's 1769 Enlightenment tragedy placed in Java called *Agon, the Sultan of Bantam*, and didactic novellas like those written by one Willem van Hogendorp around the turn of the nineteenth century on topics such as the importance of smallpox vaccination, and being kind to slaves.[2] Similar publications appeared sporadically in the first half of the nineteenth century, but it was not until 1860 that there emerged a serious novel. This was *Max Havelaar, or the Coffee Auctions of the Dutch Trading Company*, by Eduard Douwes Dekker. *Max Havelaar* established a tradition, and since then, the novel and the occasional short story have been popular forms of writing about Indonesia.[3]

Using the pseudonym 'Multatuli' – Latin for 'he who has suffered much' – Eduard Douwes Dekker wrote *Max Havelaar* following his stormy departure from the Dutch colonial service. The book tells of the frustrated career of a reform-minded colonial official in Java, someone much like its author. Depicting Java in the mid-nineteenth century, where Dutch rule had been mature and systematic for some time, Multatuli told his readers, as he put it, 'what is going on in the great Empire beyond the seas which belongs to the Realm of the Netherlands'. What was going on, he thought, was decidedly bad – the brazen exploitation of Javanese commonfolk by their own local chiefs in frank complicity with the ruling Dutch. *Max Havelaar* is a passionate book – 'I will be read', he insists – the first of many works of fiction about Indonesia whose purpose it was to arouse indignation among the Dutch public at home and to spur reform. Multatuli wrote it with such sharp wit and with such colourful language and imagery that it is today considered a classic of Dutch literature.[4]

In *Max Havelaar*, Javanese aristocrats who govern their districts under Dutch authority are despoiling the countryside by imposing vexatious taxes and illegal exactions. Havelaar is a flamboyant idealist: 'I'm very glad everything here is so backward and poverty stricken', he exclaims upon taking up his post, 'and . . . I hope to be here a long time'.[5] He soon falls foul of his superiors in the colonial bureaucracy, however, and ultimately it is he, not the larcenous chiefs, who is restrained and replaced. Multatuli is harsh when depicting the mentality of Dutch colonialism, and sentimental when depicting Indonesian villagers, especially a pair of star-crossed lovers named Saidjah and Adinda. Particularly good are his descriptions of the etiquette of race relations between the Dutch and their Javanese collaborators, and the humdrum, isolated, money-scarce domestic life of junior colonial officials. For Havelaar and his long-suffering wife, a can of cauliflower shipped from Holland is luxurious fare. Most importantly, Multatuli articulates what was for many Europeans the fundamental tension in the colonial relationship – that between honest and profitable stewardship on the one hand, and exploitation on the other.

Java of the later nineteenth century is depicted in M. T. H. Perelaer's *Baboe Dalima* or *Dalima the Nanny* (1888). Like Multatuli, Perelaer is concerned with the integrity of Holland's colonial purpose. His is a story of corruption in high places, wicked collaboration between Dutch officials and Java's Chinese opium merchants, and of the attempts by a few earnest reformers (Dutch, of course) to set things aright. Honest Dalima, a Javanese servant, is caught in the middle of all this.

Perelaer was a Dutch military man and popular writer who knew his subject. Lacking Multatuli's satirical gifts, however, his long-winded *roman-á-clef* is full of stereotypes. Having been once apprised of 'the faithful affection with which the Javanese do attach themselves to their master, if the latter will but treat them with anything like fairness and kindness', readers will not be surprised to learn on the last page that Dalima is, indeed, 'faithful to her trust until the end'.[6] Perelaer drove his point home. Published amid lively debate in the Netherlands about the Indies opium monopoly, *Baboe Dalima* helped to swing influential opinion in the direction of reform, just as *Max Havelaar* had done a generation earlier.

Not all literature of the period was so political. There emerged in the 1880s and 1890s in Java a new popular literature addressing the lives of the Indies colonial elite. This community had grown dramatically after 1870, the year Holland ended all restrictions on European immigration to the colony; and because European men most often came to the Indies alone and established families with local women, it included many Eurasians. Many of the new novels appeared first in serial form in the local Dutch-language newspapers, and they were meant to be entertainment. Where they addressed serious issues, they reflected the immediate social and economic concerns of their characters and their readers. Thus, we find stories of romance and marriage, of domestic intrigue, bureaucratic climbing, and of rising and falling fortunes, like P. A. Daum's *Ups and Downs of Life in the Indies* (1872).[7]

Questions of racial identity, legal status and social position play a prominent part in these stories. This reflects the emergence in Java and other Indies population centres of a social structure based fundamentally on race, in which one's all-important legal status as either 'European' or 'Native' often depended upon initiatives to be taken, or not taken, by white men – marrying their Indonesian concubines, for instance, or legitimising their Eurasian children. Of particular interest in this respect are several romances by women authors which take up the plight of women and children who were especially vulnerable to the caprices of the system. Some popular titles illustrate the contemporary concerns: *White and Brown* (1893), and *A Charming Little Blonde* (1886) by Marie Vanger-Frank; and Annie Foore's (F. J. J. A. Ijzerman-Junius') *Indies Marriages* (1887).[8]

The Hidden Force (1900), a fine end-of-the-century novel of Java by Louis Couperus, captures much of the spirit of the time and its literature. A prominent literary figure in Holland, Couperus had strong family affiliations in the East. 'The Indian tradition', he wrote, speaking of the Indies, 'had always ruled in my family'.[9] He had lived there as a child, and his wife was Indies-bred and born. During his long visit to Java in 1899, Couperus lodged with his sister and her husband, whose position as Resident of Pusuruan was the equivalent of governor of a province. Couperus was a knowledgeable and privileged observer.

The Hidden Force is a parable of East and West. Its hero is Otto van Oudijk, a hard-working and progressive Resident, proud and unstinting in his dedication to the welfare of Holland's native subjects. He lives for his work. But his work requires the collaboration of the princely Adiningrat family, two of whose members, as Regents, preside in feudal fashion over large territories within van Oudijk's Residency. It is van Oudijk's special pride that he has always maintained felicitous relations with the Adiningrats, having mastered the etiquette required to maintain a delicate balance between his authority and their prestige.

The crisis of *The Hidden Force* occurs when this balance is disturbed. Van Oudijk decides he must dismiss an Adiningrat Regent who has misused government funds and degraded his position by public drunkenness. Disgraced, the Adiningrats retaliate. Van Oudijk and his family are soon assaulted by a variety of 'hidden forces' – ghosts wail in the trees of their compound at night; glass shatters without reason; an invisible assailant spits betel juice upon van Oudijk's wife as she bathes alone in the wash house. His household servants flee terrified to their villages; and in the countryside the Adiningrats stir up rebellion.

Van Oudijk's crisis is not simply a crisis of authority. It is also personal. His first wife, from whom he is divorced, and all his children are Eurasian. Even in his domestic circle van Oudijk is partially isolated by race, and, following the conventional racial stereotypes of the Indies, by temperament. Doddie, his daughter, is dark, weepy and sentimental; his son Theo is an improvident, brooding layabout. His current wife, Leonie, though born to pure Dutch parents, was bred in the colony; like the others who surround him, she had absorbed its 'softness'. She is indifferent and faithless. All of them betray van Oudijk in one way or another. During the crisis, they too abandon him, leaving him to cope alone in the haunted Residency House.

In the end, van Oudijk and the state prevail: the voodoo ceases; the rebellion dies; the Residency returns to normal. But not without a cost, for a shaken van Oudijk pays the price of his confidence. 'But *that*, you see, the thing that happened . . . I never understood . . .'[10] He abandons his career. In Couperus's Java, the Dutch may exercise civil authority but the forces of Indonesian life, and not simply the 'hidden forces', possess a trancendent power all their own.

In the Indonesian islands outside Java, Dutch control was less uniform in the late nineteenth century. Many parts of the Indonesian archipelago remained independent or semi-independent. On Sumatra, Borneo and in the islands of Eastern Indonesia were hundreds of small states. Some of them were bound together in confederacies ruled by powerful chiefs or sultans; others had accepted the nominal suzerainty of the Dutch but were still beyond the reach of colonial adminstrators. Some, impinged upon, resisted. The times were turbulent and in disarray. This, not the mature colony of Java, was the Indonesia of Joseph Conrad's acquaintance.

Conrad first visited the archipelago in 1883 as second mate Josef Korzenioswki aboard the unlucky *Palestine* which burnt and sank near Bangka. Later, in 1887 and 1888, he sailed on the *Highland Forest* from Amsterdam to Semarang in Java, and made five trips from Singapore to East Borneo and the Celebes as first mate on the

S. S. Vidar.[11] These were brief encounters of stunning impact. In his career as a professional novelist, Conrad returned time and again to his Indonesian experiences. Here he came upon the tropical island world of his stories, with interminable shoal-guarded coastlines and dark rivers winding inland through the jungle; warriors' stockades and native villages, Arab bazaars and dusty towns with polyglot populations; here, too, he met traders, adventurers and dreamers from the four winds seeking their fortunes in this frontier 'country of land and water'.[12]

Indeed, Conrad wrote later that had he not met William Charles Olmeijer, a Dutch–Eurasian merchant who had established himself as confidant to the Sultans of Sambiliung and Gunung Tabur on the east coast of Borneo (and the model for Almayer, the hero of Conrad's first novel), ' . . . it is almost certain there would never have been a line of mine in print'. Olmeijer was legendary in the eastern seas: 'I heard of him in Singapore', wrote Conrad, 'I heard of him on board . . . I heard of him in a place called Pulo Laut from a half-caste gentleman there . . . I heard of him in a place called Dongala, in the island of Celebes . . .'[13] When he finally met him, Conrad was struck by the humble circumstances of his life and, as Conrad's biographer Jean-Aubry writes, by 'the pathetic contrast between his dilapidated condition and the enormous ambitions which he still cherishes'. Here, as Jean-Aubry observed, Conrad 'suddenly found himself confronted with an unusually elegant example of the discord between the power of the imagination and the weakness of human resources. This was to form the basis, the dominant theme . . . of the whole of his work.'[14]

Drawing upon his Indonesian experiences and a few books by others, notably the naturalist Alfred Russel Wallace and James Brooke of Sarawak, Conrad composed his trilogy of Borneo and Celebes, *Almayer's Folly* (1895), *Outcast of the Islands* (1896) and *The Rescue* (1919); also the novel *Lord Jim* (1900). Jim's Patusan is in Borneo and *Victory* (1915) is set in Java, Timor and the Flores Sea. Several of his short stories also depict Indonesia, including 'Karain: A Memory,' 'The Lagoon' and 'Youth'.

Conrad's European protagonists live on the fringes of authority, where the shifting sands of local politics and trade create opportunity for enterprising adventurers, and where exiles and outcasts can find sanctuary. His traders are busy exploiting the soft edges of the widening Dutch commercial monopoly in the islands, profiting from the 'quiet deal in opium; the illegal traffic in gunpowder; the great affair of smuggled fire arms'.[15] Jim, the disgraced seaman of *Lord Jim*, atones as a benevolent White Rajah in Borneo; and the wanderer,

Axel Heyst of *Victory*, lives in solitude on a remote island. In *Almayer's Folly*, Almayer dreams extravagantly of wealth and respectability in Sambir, a shabby little settlement in Borneo; and Laughing Anne, the ex-seaport prostitute of Conrad's 'Because of the Dollars', has settled down in obscurity along another river somewhere off the beaten track.

Indonesians in Conrad's stories – 'Malay adventurers, ambitious men of that place and time' – do what they can to manipulate local events to the advantage of one faction or another, sometimes acting to resist or escape the spreading net of the Dutch, but at other times conspiring to take advantage of it. The princely hero of 'Karain: A Memory', for example, had led his followers to Mindanao to escape the Dutch, whereas in *Outcast of the Islands*, the Malay chief Lakamba and his Chinese adviser Babalatchi scheme to 'apply to the Orang Blanda [the Dutch] for a flag, for that protection which would make them safe forever!'[16] By being shunted aside in the Dutch advance, or incorporated into it as subordinates and inferiors, Conrad's Indonesians become exiles of a kind, but exiles in their own lands.

Conrad's stories show us a vivid picture of regions of the Indonesian archipelago during the last moments of their autonomous existence. By the time *Victory* was published in 1915 virtually all the country of land and water had been incorporated firmly into the Netherlands Indies.

The romance and realism of high colonialism

Only a few episodes of this process of colonialism – strong-armed diplomacy and a string of small, brutal wars and pacifications – appear in works of fiction. The prolonged campaigns against Aceh, the tough Sumatran sultanate which held the Dutch at bay for thirty years, figure in some stories in so far as they caused hardships and uncertainty for Europeans. Later, in the 1930s, Madelon Szekely-Lulofs wrote a life of *Tjoet Nja Din*, a heroine of the Acehnese resistance.[17]

Perhaps the best-known novel depicting this period is *Tale of Bali*, a fictionalised account by the German novelist Vickie Baum of Balinese resistance to Dutch conquest during the years 1904–6, including the suicidal last stand of the nobles of Badung. This event marked the end of the old order in Bali, and it is symbolic of the many similar transitions occurring throughout the archipelago during these years. Baum wrote her book in 1937, only thirty years after the events she describes, but by this time colonial life under the

Dutch represented normalcy everywhere in the islands. Although she sympathised with the Balinese sentimentally, in writing of the subjugation of Bali, Baum reflected the views of her own day, which contrasted Holland's 'vigorous and sane colonial policy' with 'the heroic and medieval pride of arms of the Balinese noblemen'. Dutch Bali, she thought, was an admirable 'achievement in colonisation'.[18]

Much of the fiction written about Indonesia in the early twentieth century, until the Second World War, addresses aspects of this achievement and ponders the many qualities of colonial normalcy. These were years of enterprise and progress; of bringing modernity to the tropics in the form of new processing plants and machines, coaling stations, oil rigs, bridges, roads and cars, telephones, street lights, electric fans and massive new harbour works of the kind Louis Couperus observed at Belawan, Sumatra in 1922: 'a tremendous work – a work for Europeans'. This patina of modernity and the ever larger number of Europeans who came to the Indies to staff the growing bureaucracy and to seek their fortunes in the burgeoning colonial economy exaggerated further the perceptions of racial contrast between Indonesians and Europeans. As Couperus went on to observe, 'No oriental born out here, had ever undertaken or established a tobacco enterprise or a rubber plantation.'[19] It was a period, a brief period, of complete Western ascendancy.

This ascendancy is one of the major themes of the stories of Augusta de Wit. Born and raised in the Indies, de Wit saw in the dynamism of the West – its materialism, its lust for achievement, and its compulsion to *do* – the reason for its ascendancy over the static, spiritual and contemplative East. To de Wit, this was inevitable and good.

In de Wit's story 'The Vigil by the Bridge', (1923), Javanese villagers celebrate the building of a modern bridge across a turbulent river, remembering the difficult times before the bridge was built, how they all worked together to construct it and how the horrible flood threatened it when it was nearly finished. Most of all, they remember the Dutch engineer who designed and built the bridge and who alone was courageous enough to swim into the flooding river to divert a great tree trunk coursing towards its vulnerable foundation: 'Blessed be the Builder of the Bridge.' Late in the evening, Hadji Moosa recalls the history lesson he learnt from the Bridge Builder about the growth of cities, about empires bound together by straight roads and strong bridges, and how knowledge passed over these roads and bridges:

to people where as yet no knowledge was. When formerly the forest had been their Lord, and the strong beasts, the tiger, the wild buffalo, and the rhinoceros, the herds of wild swine, where the *alang-alang* had been their Lord and the impassable river, there came knowledge, by which man himself grows to be the Lord.[20]

But Augusta de Wit was also sensitive to the harmful side of this process. She joined many of her contemporaries in promoting an *ethical* colonial policy emphasising the welfare and education of Indonesians, and eventually she became a member of the Communist Party because it advocated independence for colonies. In her story 'A Native of Java', a prisoner being transported to an outer island to work on a labour gang broods over the beauty of his country: 'He loves the soil of Java . . . He loves the scent of Java . . . the sounds of Java . . . the colour . . . the daily labour of Java . . . All things of Java he loves.' On the morning before his arrival, the prisoner kills himself rather than accept a life of exile. In this story, with its suggestion of arbitrary justice, de Wit reflects the condition of 'those men of brown skin, the indelible mark of defeat and servitude'.[21] It is a strong anti-colonial parable.

Similar sentiments appear in the novels by Madelon Szekely-Lulofs which depict the city of Deli, Sumatra and its hinterland of plantations. This is a realm of private enterprise, where the prospect for gain has drawn together an unlikely collection of European and American planters (Lulofs herself was married to two of them, a Dutchman and then Szekely, a Hungarian *émigré*), together with contract coolies from Java, Japanese concubines, Dutch officials, Chinese shopkeepers, and traders and opportunists of all descriptions. Deli's is a rude frontier society, with none of the tradition and stability of Java. It had come alive overnight in response to world demand for tobacco and rubber, and Szekely-Lulofs describes it as desperate in its single-minded concentration on money-making, and foolish in its capacity for delusion. In *Coolie* (1936), for example, a Javanese villager is enticed to a contract coolie's life on a rubber plantation by a recruiter's promise of 'wealth, women, cheap gold and dice';[22] and in *White Money* (1933), a young Dutch couple seeks to recoup their fortunes after a family bankruptcy by putting in 'a few years – ten, fifteen at the most' with the Sumatran Hevea Company so that 'later', when we go back with a lot of money, how much more we'll enjoy Holland'.[23]

Unlike the romantic de Wit, Szekely-Lulofs is a realist. Her descriptions of Deli and of the routines of the rubber plantations are rich in quotidian detail. We learn in *White Money* that on American-managed plantations, khaki replaced white drill as the preferred working uniform among the Europeans, and that planters traded in their horse-drawn buggies for Fords – and later Overlands, Stude-bakers and, for the bosses, Pierce Arrows – as soon as prosperity made it possible. In Szekely-Lulofs colonial Indonesia, no one sees beyond the next payout. Planters and coolies alike are cells in a capricious and brutalising economic organism.

In *Malayan Tragedy* (1941), Johan Fabricius depicts Eurasian society in Batavia of the 1910s. Here, young urban half-castes compete with the envied pure-Dutch, called *totoks,* and with the Chinese and Indonesians for their own small share in the colonial economy. Getting on is difficult for Fabricius's Eurasian young men because they all suffer from the temperamental defects attributed by Europeans to mixed bloods. They are fun-loving, sensual, reckless and fickle. They feel sorry for themselves, brood over their failures and drink too much. Most of them cannot hold jobs; when employed, they are apt to dip into the till. Their sisters are lovely, flirtatious and easy. In *Malayan Tragedy*, Fabricius's hero, Boeng, unsuccessfully seeks work with the Opium Investigation Service, then involves himself with some nasty business spying on a brothel keeper, and finally beats to death a Chinese man whom he mistakenly believes has compromised his sister's virtue. It is a contrived tragedy which plays blatantly upon racial stereotypes, but it also provides a glimpse into Eurasian social and family life of the times – as perceived, that is, by *totoks* like Fabricius.

Amongst gentler depictions of the period are Beb Vuyk's story memoirs of life in the island world of the Moluccas. Here, she and her husband took up an abandoned tree plantation during the Great Depression. On the island of Buru they live a frontier life of simplicity, isolation and occasional danger in *The Last House in the World* (1941). Vuyk's corner of Indonesia has its turbulence, but it is the sort caused by storms, drought and the unpredictable market-place, not the political kind that Conrad knew. Dutch authority is firm and, although local chiefs still scheme and intrigue, nothing remains of the independent spirit observed by Conrad fifty years before. Vuyk's frontier is also unlike bustling Deli. It is a beautiful, severe place on the fringes of civilisation; the boat from Macassar, the nearest large outpost connecting Buru to Batavia and all the rest, stops only once a month. In this Vuyk found liberation from the intense colonial life of Java, 'so narrowly channelled between promotions, bonuses and raises'.[24]

W. Somerset Maugham's only Indonesian novel, *A Narrow Corner* (1932), also takes place in the eastern islands, but for no particular reason. An Englishman, Dr Saunders, has journeyed there from his medical practice in China to perform a cataract operation upon a rich

Chinese patient. Along the way he falls in with some engaging ruffians, and on the fictional island of Takana he encounters one of those quirky collections of expatriate Europeans which are the mainstay of Maugham's Eastern stories. The infrequency of inter-island transport makes Dr Saunders a temporary captive, and this gives him the opportunity to observe a modest romantic tragedy which ends in murder. Saunders ponders it all with detachment, and when he can next make connections to Singapore he takes leave from his brief Indonesian holiday considerably refreshed – as, no doubt, Maugham intended his readers to be.

Maria Dermout's *Ten Thousand Things* (1958) takes place on the spice-island Ambon. It relates the memories of Felicia, the last of five generations of an old Dutch line of spice-growers. Felicia lives in the Small Garden, a property which once produced nutmegs and cloves for the Dutch East India Company but now, in the 1930s, is no longer productive. Its once fine buildings are in disrepair and its population is reduced to Felicia and her servants. Some ghosts also visit the Small Garden, gathering at Felicia's invitation once a year – her son Himpies; a professor of botany; an Indonesian sailor; a police commissioner – all of whom were murdered. Through Felicia's memories we learn the history of her family and the stories of her spirit guests. *Ten Thousand Things* is a book rich in the physical beauty of Ambon: 'Now, as then, the gardens spread along both bays – outer bay and inner bay – the spice trees clustered together, kind with kind, clove with clove, nutmeg with nutmeg . . .'[25] Ambon, like Java, had been incorporated into the Dutch sphere in the early years of spice profiteering; in its colonial society Europeans, Ambonese and other Indonesians had accommodated to each other over centuries. In Dermout's Ambon dwell the remnants of a mature community of local people, some of whom, like Felicia, are by derivation European, but all of whom share the place and belong to it.

Yesterday (1959) is Maria Dermout's fictionalised recreation of her childhood in Java: of the big white house 'between the mountains Lawu and Wilis . . . deep in a walled garden under the dark green trees'; of her Javanese nurse, Urip, and the other servants who introduced her to the local spirits and magic places; of the sugar plantation where 'the air smelled prickly and sweet with dust'; and of the climate – 'Sunlight and dust and hot vibrating skies, hazy days, short twilights, and the long, clear tropical nights full of cool mountain wind and moon and stars'.[26] It is a lovely recollection, in which dark memories of tragedy and personal loss fuse with brighter ones of beauty and childhood delight, and in which an undercurrent of mystery pervades everything.

From 'the Indies' to 'Indonesia'

The sense of memory is strong in Maria Dermout's books in part because she did all of her public writing in the last ten years of her life, beginning when she was sixty-three years old with the publication of *Yesterday*. The year was 1951. By this time, the Netherlands Indies, where she was born and where she spent twenty-seven of her adult years, had in one swift decade ceased to exist. Japan's occupation of the colony and the Indonesian revolution which soon followed separated most Indies Dutchmen from their homes, positions and livelihoods, and abolished forever the context in which colonial life had existed. Gone was the luxury and the deference which had given to European life in Indonesia its special qualities of privilege. Gone, too, for many, were the places of their history. There is no overt sense of this loss in *Yesterday*, but because of it Maria Dermout's novel embodying the common images of an Indies childhood was especially poignant for the Indies Dutchmen.

Night Over Java (1946) is Johan Fabricius's tale of the early years of Japanese occupation in southern Java. The Dutch have fled or have been interned, and the houses in the European quarter are deserted. Standing watch over the district office, the bank, the school and the post office are Japanese sentries. In what had been the Dutch Club, Javanese 'sluts' entertain Japanese officers: Dasuki, a Javanese who has joined the resistance, 'stood and stared at them for a moment or two from a safe distance, astounded that the world could have changed so much in a few months'. Fabricius wrote this novel in London in 1942 and 1943, and it contains a good deal of wishful thinking. His Indonesian characters long for the return of the Dutch. Dasuki, speaking for them, resents the Japanese for making the 'white nyonyas' and their children sad, and concludes that 'this could only be a temporary phase . . . The things he saw with his own eyes made him feel quite certain that the white people would ultimately prove the stronger.'[27]

The years of occupation and revolution were uncertain for everyone. Would the Japanese prevail? Would the Dutch ever return? And then, after they had, could the Indonesian revolutionaries force them out again? Fiction about these years reflects the confusion, deprivations and violence of the times. Survival was a priority; but there were also new options which had been unthinkable in the stable 1930s. Stories of the time depict betrayal and loyalty, desperate experience – like Beb Vuyk's memory of Japanese torture in 'All Our Yesterdays'[28] – and the agonies of conflicting identity. Fabricius's anti-Japanese partisans in *Night Over Java* are led by a Captain

Mansveldt, a Eurasian army officer who has always suppressed the 'native' side of his temperament. In the throes of the occupation he recognises his deep affiliation with Indonesians, and in acts of revenge against the Japanese gives reign to his 'blood'.[29] Despite the racist caricature, Mansveldt's dilemma was that of many Eurasians, and it became more extremely acute during the years of revolution between 1945 and 1949.

The events of Dirk Bogarde's novel, *A Gentle Occupation* (1980), occur during a brief moment of transition. The Japanese have surrendered but the Dutch have not yet returned; in their place come the British to hold down the fort. As a young British officer, Bogarde went to the Indies as part of such a force, and Paradise Island in his novel is an abstraction of Java. The situation was, as he says, 'an appalling mess'. Outside a military perimeter, armed Indonesian nationalists operate at will – 'the natives are getting restless', comments a British major – and inside it the British attempt vainly to maintain order.[30] They restore essential services and distribute a few relief goods, and they also help to reunite Dutch families emerging from wartime internment camps. To staff their offices, however, the British must hire Chinese and Eurasians; the Dutch, angry with the British for not being more aggressive against the revolutionaries, refuse to help. Among Bogarde's characters there is little dignity and much opportunism. The British soldiers are reluctant occupiers facing unexpected hazards at the war's end; and for the people of the occupied city, it is time for yet another, if brief, accommodation.

For the next several years, life in Indonesia was one of occupied places, dangerous perimeters and revolutionary violence. In Dutch-occupied cities, the old pretence of civilised superiority could not be sustained. 'The Good Old Days', wrote Albert van der Hoogte in his novel of the period, *The Final Hour* (1953), 'are gone for good, and the Dutchman here is no more the lofty gentleman . . . These days he is a toiling proletarian, hatless and sweaty.'[31]

By 1949, those beyond the perimeters had won. The new state was truly Indonesian and, judging by the literature, it was dramatically less interesting to Western writers. With Indonesia's political disengagement from the West came a disengagement of the imagination as well. One is reminded of Harold Nicolson's exasperation during his 1957 *Journey to Java*, when a garrulous journalist presumes to tell him more information 'about the situation in the Federal Republic of Indonesia than I have hitherto ventured to acquire.'[32] Most recent Western fiction has been retrospective: historical fiction in the sense that it has sought to recapture moments of the past, like Dirk Bogarde's book; or qualities of the past, like those of Maria Dermout.

An exception should be made for a few works of adventure and spy fiction, such as those of Eric Ambler and Edward S. Aarons, and for a small crop of new Indonesia–based novels by Australian authors. Eric Ambler's *State of Siege* (1956) finds an English consulting engineer caught up in a rebellion in a corrupt and eccentric developing country with the giveaway name of 'Sunda' – Sunda being a major region of Java. Sunda offers an exotic setting for Ambler's adventure, warring generals provide the danger, and Rosalie, a beautiful prostitute (Eurasian, of course), the sex.

Edward S. Aarons's books chronicle the assignments of 'CIA superagent' Sam Durrell, one or two of which occur in Indonesia, sort of. Aarons invokes a hotchpotch of images: some plausible and others completely phony, all piled together willy-nilly in a fantasy of exotic escape. *Assignment Sulu Sea* (1946), for example, takes place on the east coast of Borneo not far from the Malaysian border. Here, Prince Chang, 'the richest and most loathsome man in the islands', runs a vice palace called the House of the Thousand Pleasures, controls the local gold miners and generally intimidates everyone, all the while doubling as a Red Chinese agent. He has, as our story begins, succeeded in stealing and hiding an American nuclear submarine: enter Durrell.[33] These adventure books recall Bontekoe's early travels, in which the Indonesian archipelago was an exotic place on the other side of the world where extraordinary things happened: good reading for today's stay-at-home Westerner.

Australia has only recently begun to yield a literature about Indonesia. This reflects a new awareness and curiosity about the country, and also a new immediacy. What used to be the safe Dutch territory to the north has become an independent Asian nation and a potential adversary with a population nearly ten times that of Australia. New Australian novels often depict Indonesia as a turbulent and hostile land on the fringes of home. In Jon Cleary's *The Long Pursuit* (1967) for example, a band of white men make their escape from Singapore to Australia through the inhospitalities of Japanese-occupied Sumatra; and in C. J. Koch's *The Year of Living Dangerously* (1978), another band of Westerners, newsmen this time, huddle together in a hotel bar amidst the virulent anti-Western climate of Sukarno's reign. Both books end with escapes, and curiously, a key Indonesian character in each is a Javanese interpreter who turns out, secretly, to be a high-ranking member of the Indonesian Communist Party. Indonesia is seen as a dangerous place where things are not as they appear. It is even a source of subversion of Australia's Aborigines; the solution to Arthur Upfield's mystery novel *The Will of the Tribe* (1962) turns upon just this suspicion.

But to Australians, Indonesia is also, unavoidably, a neighbour. *The Paper Castle* (1977), by Robert Macklin, tells of contemporary Australian politicians for whom Indonesia presents tricky questions of regional diplomacy and a profound social and political issue: 'Mr Speaker', says one protagonist as he addresses the legislature on the subject of immigration, 'The time has come for us to realise that we should not, we cannot, try to remain a European enclave on the tip of Southeast Asia. The time has come for us to turn our face to Asia, to our neighbours.'[34]

Common themes: race, power, wealth, alienation, home

Considered altogether, what are the common themes of these novels and stories about Indonesia? First of all, every one of them – from Multatuli's story of the righteous colonialist Max Havelaar to Eric Ambler's yarn about an innocent engineer in the wrong place at the wrong time – reflects some aspect of the forcible meeting of Western and non-Western cultures in modern times, a phenomenon once confidently referred to as 'advancing civilisation'. These stories present local variations on a universal theme, vignettes of the imperial experience as it occurred in the Indonesian archipelago. It is not in the least surprising that in these stories the images and activities of Europeans are in far better focus than those of Indonesians. One must remember that they were written by Europeans for European readers.

This accounts for the fact that we meet many vivid Western characters in these stories – like Couperus's Resident van Oudijk and Maria Dermout's Felicia – but seldom Indonesians of equal vividness. True, there are Malays and Javanese, Buginese and Ambonese, all differentiated, and they fill a variety of roles, but few come across as distinct personalities. What is more, having 'fallen prey to the Western race', Indonesians in these stories are on the losing side of life's critical encounters. We see them almost always in the positions of inferiority that colonialism reserved for them. They are poor peasants; they are cooks; they are bearers, sweepers, drivers, clerks, housekeepers and whores; they are rubber tappers, warehouse coolies and cane-cutters. Some are aristocrats in positions of subordinate administrative authority; others are rebels and thieves. Some, too, are heroes, defiant in the final moments of their independence. But they are tragically heroic, medieval men out of step with the times, like Vicki Baum's Balinese noblemen and Joseph Conrad's Buginese chieftains. More than any other writer, Conrad celebrated the exuberant independence of the Indonesian spirit, but he wrote fully conscious of the likely result of resistance. 'Advancing civilization', he wrote, would 'obliterate the marks of a long struggle in the accomplishment of its inevitable victory'.[35]

This inevitable victory encouraged the perception among Europeans that Indonesians – along with most other non-white peoples of the earth – were backward and inferior. It was most common to intepret this as a matter of race, and Western fiction about Indonesia abounds in racial stereotypes. Louis Couperus, for example, described the Malay as 'a born servant . . . It is in his blood and implanted in his soul.' Malays, and the Sundanese and Javanese, he thought, had no initiative and shunned responsibility 'on account of their contemplative, somewhat limited mentality'.[36] Couperus was expressing the conventional wisdom. Another part of it suggested that Indonesians were best understood as playful, pleasure-seeking, vulnerable children. But they could also be changeable – they could 'turn in a trice to cruelty', as one of Baum's Dutch officers says of the Balinese.[37] And Conrad, speaking of a Balinese prince, pointed to 'the sombre and desperate fury that is the peculiar inheritance of his race'.[38] It was a simple matter of instinct. As Szekely-Lulofs explains in *White Money* after a Javanese coolie murders a Dutch plantation manager, his 'instinct had had free run . . . It was a clash between primitive ages and the twentieth century.'[39]

The instincts of the primitive ages also bore other, finer traits. Some Western writers were eager to identify in Indonesians qualities of nobility which reflected what they believed to be an older, better stage in European society. Like others around the world, therefore, Indonesians sometimes became that other stereotype, the noble savage. These Indonesians were people of honour and strength, with aristocratic bearings of 'negligent elegance,' like Conrad's Rajah Hassim in *The Rescue*.[40] Reflecting the point of view of their creators, they were, as Jean Taylor has written, 'attracted instinctively by all that is finest in European civilization and repulsed by the coarseness, racism and arrogance of its bearers'.[41]

Although Indonesians ordinarily have only supporting roles in this fiction, they sometimes figure prominently in the plot; and Western writers have occasionally attempted to build an entire story around Indonesian characters. In the better of these books, such characters dress and behave outwardly in accordance with detailed observation, albeit not necessarily the author's. There is a good deal of verisimilitude in the activities of Conrad's Buginese warrior-traders like Karain and Rajah Hassim, derived in part from James Brooke's published Celebes journals. And in *Tale of Bali*, Baum succeeds in depicting many day-to-day aspects of Balinese life with an anthropologist's eye for detail, thanks to the tutelage of artist Walter Spies who was an expert. Yet, in both of these examples, when the characters are made to think – when they are given personalities – we soon recognise common stereotypes; and in Baum's case, we meet a familiar cast of personalities drawn from our own popular fiction.

But this literature is never really *about* Indonesians. It is about Europeans in Indonesia. Inevitably, *their* perception of things, and *their* preoccupations come to the fore in these stories. Prominent among these preoccupations is the use and abuse of power. Multatuli began the tradition of using fiction to address the problem of responsibility in the colonial relationship. In the nineteenth century, his novel *Max Havelaar*, and others, like Perelaer's *Baboe Dalima* and Annie Foore's *Indies Marriages*, dramatised examples of injustice and negligence in the colonial system, and pleaded the cause of Indonesia's common people and of women and children. In the twentieth century, colonial stewardship was a prominent theme in the works of Augusta de Wit, Madelon Szekely-Lulofs and others whose sensibilities rebelled at the harsh conditions of life for many Indonesians, and the arbitrary and capricious power Europeans so casually wielded because of their status. Some of these novels were overtly reformist, aimed at changing specific policies or practices like the Opium Laws, citizenship requirements or the coolie regulations; others sought only to give a 'true picture' of conditions in the Indies. None suggested anything so radical as an end to the colonial tie. European supremacy was a given; but the power which made it possible should be used, many argued, for the good of all.

Aside from reformist inclinations, power is central to these stories for a simpler reason. Organised force undergirded the whole colonial enterprise in Asia. It is this aspect of power which interests Louis Couperus. He is the best example of a writer who explored the subtleties of such power in a colonial setting, its complexities and its limits. As we see in *The Hidden Force*, in his battle of wits with his local Javanese subjects, Resident van Oudijk both wins and loses.

Closely related to the issue of power is the preoccupation among Europeans with race and status. These were inseparable in colonial Indonesia, in whose rigidly hierarchical caste system one was either 'European' or 'Native' by law. Since the privileges of the ruling class were reserved for Europeans, there was an acute awareness of status. This was heightened by the fact that European–Asian sexual liaisons and marriages in Indonesia had created a very large group of individuals who were of mixed ancestry. The existence of this Eurasian group, some of whom were legal Europeans but many of whom were not, made the question of race a very touchy matter. As we have observed, an elaborate conventional wisdom grew up which categorised people in terms of their racial purity, attributing to Eurasians qualities of weakness that were thought to result from their partial native ancestry. Eurasians, as Multatuli said, were 'not regarded as "one hundred per cent"'.[42] We have already observed Eurasian characters in Couperus's *The Hidden Force*, and in the novels of Johan Fabricius. Race thinking of this kind pervaded the literature from the beginning, just as it pervaded the society.

Even among that small group securely within the European niche there was keen awareness of one's place, of the inescapable pecking order. In official life, it ran from the novice Controller up to the Governor-General ('would not *her* Max be Governor-General of her beloved Indies some day', thought Havelaar's wife), and, in business, from a new assistant to the company head.[43] Social intrigue and status-seeking were popular elite activities, and these stories frequently contain depictions of the rituals of rank so common to colonial life – such as the rubber plantation tea party in *White Money* at which the colossal Mrs Stevenson, as wife of the Chief Manager, lords it over the wives of mere managers; and the officials in *The Hidden Force* who, always anxious for the possibility of promotion, 'sit studying the Colonial List and calculating on the illness of this man or the death of that . . .'.

Wealth, and hopes for it, also figure prominently in these stories. 'Almayer's thoughts were often busy with gold", Conrad tells us, and even Multatuli's selfless Havelaar 'could not shake off his dream of millions of money . . .'.[45] Among Indies Europeans, it was the common dream. After all, the prospect of prosperity and fortune had drawn many of them to the Indies in the first place. Some characters in these novels sought money to support a life of ease and luxury in the Indies. Others sought it as a reward for toil and deprivation – the heat, monotony, and sapped vigour of the tropics – which would secure a comfortable retirement in Europe. The thought, 'Later, when we go back', wrote Szekely-Lulofs, was for many 'the only foundation of the fleeting provisional existence of the tropics'.[46]

Thoughts of home, of Europe, of cool, wet Holland with its modern cities and its rich cultural life, and of one's distant relatives: such thoughts often nag the Indies Dutchmen of these stories. In Holland, one could feel fresh and alive. Life was vigorous there: one belonged; in the Indies, one didn't, not quite. True, one might have a mission or goal, responsibilities, and one might even commit one's whole life to these things, but one could never be fully at home. Even among those born and raised in the Indies there is often a longing for Europe. 'I have never been out of Java', bemoans Frans van Helderin in *The Hidden Force*. 'I feel there's something lacking in me because

I have never seen ice and snow . . .'[47]

The themes of power and status, and of wealth and home, which figure prominently in these stories are so fundamental that one might say they are simply universal. But there is more to it. It is clear in reading this literature that these preoccupations were exaggerated in colonial life. They were exaggerated because of the dramatic contrast Europeans observed between *their* achievements and behaviour and those of Indonesians – hence the race thinking – and also because of their vulnerability. The economy was capricious, and diseases like cholera could attack one's children, or oneself, in a swift, murdering epidemic. Europeans always counted for less than one per cent of the population of the Indies. They were a demographic veneer imposed artificially upon a vast Asian population. However secure they were by virtue of the state apparatus – its army and police, and all the other institutions of authority – personally they were at risk and often afraid. Discontented villagers might follow a local fanatic and kill off the whites in a small uprising; a coolie might run amok; one could fall sick without warning and die of an undiagnosed malady – a spell perhaps? If one were to believe these stories, being poisoned was one of the commonest ways to die in colonial Indonesia.

There were also things about life in the Indies which were, for the European, incomprehensible. Couperus wrote of Java's hidden force: 'deep in its soul, despite a cringing reverence, it lived in freedom its own mysterious life, hidden from western eyes . . .'[48] Novels of Indonesia are filled with talk of black magic, of omens, charms and ghosts. To a degree, this reflects acculturation to the spirit-filled Indonesian cosmos, but it also reflects an awareness, perhaps subconscious, of European vulnerability.

Vulnerability bred clannishness, the need to live in safe clusters, to keep up appearances, to be a good club member. This made expatriate social life cohesive, but negatively so. Conrad observed this in the real Almayer and his companion named Willems, who hated each other but dined together always on Almayer's veranda.[49]

The sense of deracination and tension does not occur everywhere. Through Ben Vuyk and Maria Dermout, for example, both of whom had deep roots in Indonesia as well as Indonesian ancestors, we are introduced to pre-war Indonesia as *home*. This friendlier accommodation reflects the experience of many members of what is called *Indisch* society, that group of Indies-born Dutchmen and Dutch–Eurasian families who recognised the Indies as home by heritage and by preference. They were, as the Dutch called them, the *blijvers* – the stayers. Their special European–Asian culture, nourished by the colonial system, was still in the forming in the 1940s when Indonesian independence abruptly aborted its development. Indisch writing is less concerned with power, status and money, and more attentive to family relations, cultural nuances and familiar details of living for those people, like writer Edgar Charles du Perron, for whom the Netherlands Indies was the *Country of Origin* (1935).[50]

This autobiographical quality in Indisch literature is characteristic of almost all Western writing about Indonesia, from Bontekoe's *Memorable Description* to the books of Maria Dermout and Dirk Bogarde. Our writers drew upon their own experience and feelings, and upon those of their acquaintances and relatives. Even in depicting Indonesians, as we have seen, it is essentially a Western understanding of things that comes through most clearly. How could it be otherwise? These stories represent a personal record of the Western experience in Indonesia when it was most intense, during the years of overt colonialism and its immediate aftermath. We can think of them as a collective memory, like a chest full of scrapbooks and letters home from all our relations who journeyed to Java.

Notes

1 W. Bontekoe, *Memorable Description of the East Indian Voyage, 1618–25*, translated by C. V. Bodde-Hodgkinson and P. Geyl, London, 1929. Quotations from Geyl's 'Introduction', and the frontispiece. See also R. Nieuwenhuys (E. Breton de Nijs), *Oost-Indische Spiegel*, Amsterdam, 1973, pp. 28–9.

2 In Dutch, *Agon, sultan van Bantam*, Nieuwenhuys, *Spiegel*, pp. 63, 67–8. See also A. Kumar, 'Literary approaches to slavery and the Indies Enlightenment: Van Hogendorp's *Kraspoekol*', *Indonesia* (Cornell South-East Asia Program), 43 (April), 1987, pp. 43–63.

3 For convenience, in this chapter the terms 'Indonesia' and 'Indonesians' will sometimes be used to apply to those places and people which *eventually* would be known as Indonesia and Indonesians.

4 E. D. Dekker (Multatuli), *Max Havelaar, or the Coffee Auctions of the Dutch Trading Company*, translated by R. Edwards, 1967, p. 318.

5 Dekker, *Max Havelaar*, p. 97.

6 M. T. H. Perelaer, *Baboe Dalima*, translated by E. J. Venning, London, 1888, p. 556.

7 P. A. Daum (Maurits), *Ups and Downs of Life in the Indies*, translated by E. Q. Sturtevant and D. E. Sturtevant, Amherst, Mass., 1987.

8 See J. S. Taylor, 'The world of women in the colonial novel', *Kabar Sabrang*, 2, 1977, 26–41.

9 L. Couperus, *Eastward*, translated by J. Menzies-Wilson and C. C. Crispen, London, 1924, p. 15.

10 L. Couperus, *The Hidden Force*, translated by A. T. de Mattos, London, 1922, p. 311.

11 G. Jean-Aubry, *The Sea Dreamer: A Definitive Biography of Joseph Conrad*, translated by H. Sebba, New York, 1970, p. 97; G. S. Resink, *Indonesia's History Between the Myths: Essays in Legal History and Historical Theory*, The Hague, 1968, pp. 307–8.

12 J. Conrad, *The Rescue*, New York, 1926, p. 3.

13 G. J. Resink, 'Joseph Korzeniowski's voornaamste lectuur betreffende Indonesie', *Bijdragen tot de taal-, land- en volkenkunde*, CXVII, 1961, 218–19; quotations from J. Conrad, 'A Personal Record' (1912), in *A Conrad Argosy*, Garden City, NY, 1942, pp. 703, 708.

14 Jean-Aubry, *Sea Dreamer*, p. 123.

15 J. Conrad, *Outcast of the Islands*, London, 1949, p. 8.

16 Conrad, *Outcast*, pp. 50, 57.

17 Taylor, 'The world of women', p. 26.

18 V. Baum, *Tale of Bali*, translated by B. Creighton, Garden City, NY, 1937, p. xi.

19 Couperus, *Eastward*, p. 67.

20 A. de Wit, 'The Vigil by the Bridge', in *Island India*, New Haven, 1923; see also, Nieuwenhuys, p. 324.

21 de Wit, *Island India*, pp. 32–4.

22 M. Szekely-Lulofs, *Coolie*, translated by G. J. Renier and I. Clephane, New York, 1936, p. 24; Nieuwenhuys, pp. 349–56.

23 M. Szekely-Lulofs, *White Money*, translated by G. J. Renier and I. Clephane, New York, 1933, p. 33.

24 B. Vuyk, *Het laatste huis van de Wereld*, (*The Last House in the World*), Utrecht, 1941, p. 11.

25 M. Dermout, *Ten Thousand Things*, translated by H. Konigsberger, New York, 1958, p. 3.

26 M. Dermout, *Yesterday*, translated by H. Konigsberger, New York, 1959, pp. 1, 24–5.

27 J. Fabricius, *Night Over Java*, New York, 1946, p. 40.

28 B. Vuyk, 'All our yesterdays', translated by E. Debrot, in C. N. Moore (ed.), *Insulinde*, Honolulu, 1978, pp. 138–44.

29 Fabricius, *Night*, p. 157.

30 D. Bogarde, *A Gentle Occupation*, New York, 1980, Author's Note and p. 199.

31 A. van der Hoogte, *Het Laatste uur*, (*The Final Hour*), Amsterdam, 1953, p. 8.

32 H. Nicolson, *Journey to Java*, Garden City, NY, 1958, p. 176.

33 E. S. Aarons, *Assignment Sulu Sea*, Greenwich, Conn., 1964, p. 31.

34 R. Macklin, *The Paper Castle*, Sydney, 1977, p. 20. Another Australian novel depicting Indonesia is B. D'Alpuget's, *Monkeys in the Dark*, Sydney, 1980.

35 From Conrad, *The Rescue*, p. 3.

36 Couperus, *Eastward*, pp. 151, 267.

37 Baum, *Tale of Bali*, pp. 257–8.

38 J. Conrad, *Almayer's Folly*, Garden City, NY, 1933, p. 167.

39 Szekely-Lulofs, *White Money*, p. 207.

40 Conrad, *The Rescue*, p. 65.

41 Taylor, 'The world of women', p. 5.

42 Dekker, *Max Havelaar*, p. 41.

43 Dekker, *Max Havelaar*, p. 110.

44 Couperus, *The Hidden Force*, p. 98.

45 Conrad, *Almayer's Folly*, p. 3; Dekker, *Max Havelaar*, p. 112.

46 Szekely-Lulofs, *White Money*, p. 43.

47 Couperus, *The Hidden Force*, pp. 97–8.

48 Couperus, *The Hidden Force*, p. 150.

49 J. Conrad, *Outcast of the Islands*, London, 1949, Author's Introduction to the 1919 edition, p. x.

50 E. C. du Perron, *Country of Origin*, translated by F. Bulhof and E. Daverman, Amherst, Mass., 1984; Rob Nieuwenhuys (E. Breton de Nijs) *Faded Portraits*, (1955), Amherst, Mass., 1982, is the best example of nostalgic Indisch writing available in English.

Reading list

Aarons, Edward S., *Assignment Sulu Sea*, Greenwich, Conn., 1964.

Ambler, Eric, *State of Siege*, New York, 1956.

Baum, Vicki, *Tale of Bali*, translated by Basil Creighton, Garden City, NY, 1937.

Bogarde, Dirk, *A Gentle Occupation*, New York, 1980.

Bontekoe, William, *Memorable Description of the East Indian Voyage, 1618–25*, translated by C. V. Bodde-Hodgkinson and Pieter Geyl, London, 1929.

Cleary, Jon, *The Long Pursuit*, London, 1967.

Conrad, Joseph, *Almayer's Folly* (1895), Garden City, NY, 1933.

——, *Complete Short Stories*, London, 1933 ('Lagoon', 'Youth', 'Karain, a Memory', and 'Because of the Dollars').

——, *Lord Jim*, London, 1900.

——, *An Outcast of the Islands* (1896), London, 1949.

——, *The Rescue* (1919), New York, 1926.

——, *Victory*, Garden City, NY, 1915.

Couperus, Louis, *The Hidden Force* (1900), translated by Alexander Teixeira de Mattos, Amherst, Mass., 1985.

Daum, P. A. (Maurits), *Ups and Downs of Life in the Indies* (1892) translated by Elsje Qualm Sturtevant and Donald W. Sturtevant, Amherst, Mass., 1987.

Dekker, Eduard Douwes (Multatuli), *Max Havelaar, or the Coffee Auctions of the Dutch Trading Company* (1860), translated by Roy Edwards, Leiden, 1967.

Dermout, Maria, *Ten Thousand Things*, translated by Hans Konigsberger, New York, 1958.

——, *Yesterday*, translated by Hans Konigsberger, New York, 1959.

Fabricius, Johan, *Night Over Java*, New York, 1946.

IJzerman-Junius, F. J. J. A. (Annie Foore), *Indische huwelijken (Indies Marriages)*, Amsterdam, 1887.

Koch, Christopher J., *The Year of Living Dangerously*, Melbourne, 1978.

Macklin, Robert, *The Paper Castle*, Sydney, 1977.

Maugham, W. Somerset, *A Narrow Corner*, Garden City, NY, 1932.

Nieuwenhuys, Rob (E. Breton de Nijs), *Faded Portraits* (1955), translated by Elsje Qualm Sturtevant and Donald W. Sturtevant, Amherst, Mass., 1982.

Perelaer, M. T. H., *Baboe Dalima*, translated by E. J. Venning, London, 1888.

Perron, E. C. du, *Country of Origin* (1935), translated by Francis Bulhof and Elizabeth Daverman, Amherst, Mass., 1984.

Szekely-Lulofs, Madelon, *White Money*, translated by G. J. Renier and Irene —, Clephane, New York, 1933.

——, *Coolie*, translated by G. J. Renier and Irene Clephane, Amsterdam, 1936.

Upfield, Arthur, *The Will of the Tribe* (1962), New York, 1984..

Vanger-Frank, Marie (Katja-Mata), *Een Lief blondinetje*, Dordrecht, 1886.

——, *Blank en bruin*, Amsterdam, 1893

Vuyk, Beb, *The Last House in the World* (1941) in E. M. Beekman (ed.), *Two Tales of the East Indies*, Amherst, Mass., 1983.

Wit, Augusta de, *Island India*, New Haven, 1923.

CHAPTER TEN

Fear and fascination in the tropics

A reader's guide to French fiction on Indo-China

Milton Osborne[1]

It is an ironic fact that among South-East Asian societies, those of Indo-China are among the least accessible through the medium of English-language fiction. For almost a decade before it ended in 1975, the Second Indo-China War was a dominant feature of American life, causing controversy which spread throughout the Western world. Yet, in the West today, the region where the war was fought remains little known or understood. Disappointment awaits readers of English who would augment through fiction their knowledge of the histories, cultures and peoples of Indo-China.

The number of French-language novels and short stories dealing with Indo-China is large, but most of these works are obscure and, outside of France, to be found only in specialised or research libraries. Towards the end of the 1920s, Albert de Pouvourville, a French writer long associated with the Indo-Chinese region, estimated that, over the years, his compatriots had published some three thousand books on 'Far Eastern' subjects, of which approximately one-third were novels. No complete bibliography is yet available, but many more novels set in East or South-East Asia, including Indo-China, were written in the years up to the end of the French colonial presence in Cambodia, Laos and Vietnam in 1954.

Despite their number, these books had only a limited impact outside colonial circles, or even within them. In his 1934 survey of the history and character of French writing on Indo-China – *L'Exotisme indochinois dans la littérature française depuis 1860 (Indo-Chinese exoticism in French literature since 1860)* – Louis Malleret noted that these works were virtually unknown in France, and their existence barely guessed at in some parts of colonial society.

Background

French fiction on Indo-China is mainly about the European experience of Asia. Deep insights into the indigenous society are rare. Intentionally or not, the typical author portrays the position of the alien Western intruder within an 'exotic' society.

By far the most important locale for French books and stories about Indo-China is Vietnam, rather than Cambodia or Laos – a circumstance reflecting the much greater economic and political importance to France of Vietnam compared with the other two segments of colonial Indo-China.

Finally, one gains much more from French writing about Indo-China when the fiction is read in conjunction with non-fiction produced at the same time. By comparing the fiction with non-fictional accounts, one can appreciate better the overall character of the French experience in Indo-China. Contemporaneous works of fiction and journalism or biography often mirror the same concerns. Novels and stories offer more freely subjective perspectives on vital issues raised in non-fictional commentaries on colonial affairs.

This complementarity is most evident for the period from the mid-nineteenth century, when the French began their colonial adventure in South-East Asia, to the early twentieth century, when they finally overcame Vietnamese resistance and established themselves throughout Indo-China. With some exceptions – notably, novelisations of the Franco–Vietminh war – fiction written later in the colonial era focused more on private matters that were less subject to public discussion.

Flowing from this historical background, certain key themes permeate French fiction on Indo-China. Above all, there is a sense of inaccessibility, of the remote and incomprehensible nature (to a Westerner) of Vietnamese society, and to a lesser degree of Cambodia and Laos as well. The French coloniser observes, but cannot enter into or even understand, what is being seen. Along with this central theme is a preoccupation with the perceived inherent cruelty of the peoples of Indo-China, particularly the Vietnamese. Taken together, these two interacting images, of the unfathomability and inhumanity of Indo-China, form a foundation for other perceptions: a sense of expatriation, of being outside one's 'normal' existence as a Frenchman in France; an obsession with opium and a nearly equal fascination with the Vietnamese concubine, or *con gai*; and a persistent anxiety, turning sometimes to fear, of attack and death at the hands of the Vietnamese. With the passage of time, this last preoccupation grows.

French colonial writing on Indo-China must be set in the context of the assumptions which inspired the colonial advance. Beyond the supposedly practical considerations which brought the French to Indo-China, including such visionary but unworkable ideas as trade with China up the Mekong River, less purely material motivations were at work. The most significant of these was the French concept of their civilising mission *(mission civilisatrice)*, the belief that France possessed a superior culture which could transform an alien society into something similar to France itself. As hindsight has shown, this project was impossible. But the French believed in it strongly, and this helps to explain why they became so intensely disappointed with the results of their efforts in Indo-China. Faith in the desirability and universality of French culture led to an expectation that colonised peoples would hasten to embrace the French language and accept French political control.

Frenchmen living in Indo-China were deeply disturbed to find that, for the most part, the local population did not see matters this way. The peoples of Indo-China treasured their own cultures and values. The Vietnamese, in particular, showed a persistent readiness to fight against foreign rule. Dissappointment that this should be so is a subtle but striking feature of much of the work of French authors on Indo-China.

Each of the four main historical phases of colonial administration gave rise to a distinct set of themes in French fiction written at that time. The Literature of the first period, the so-called 'heroic age', is focused on discovery and struggle. Many of these writings were inspired by the autobiographical accounts of pioneers – explorers and early administrators – and by the authors' own personal experiences on the Indo-Chinese frontier.

By the early twentieth century, a more reflective element becomes apparent. The broad themes are much the same, but the treatment is new. While the picture given of the *con gai*, for instance, is still almost always critical, she becomes somewhat less of an anonymous stereotype, acquires a more defined individual personality and is described in greater detail. The locales change also. In keeping with the consolidation of colonial exploitation and administration, more and more novels have urban or partially urban settings. Finally, the authors of this second phase begin, with varying success, to tell stories set in Vietnamese society as such, without a European element.

The end of the 1920s brings intimations of a third period, one marked most strongly by disillusion. Whatever the hardships and difficulties portrayed in the earlier literature, there is no sense that France was wrong to have undertaken its colonial enterprise. Nor, indeed, is there any dramatic swing towards such ideas in the novels published after the mid-1920s. Rather, there is a growing reflection of tiredness and uncertainty, of the sterility of life in the colonies, and of an ill-defined but persistent concern that the 'natives' might rebel, as individuals or collectively, against their colonial overlords.

The fourth and final phase of French fiction on Indo-China, from the end of the Second World war, yielded little of literary value. For this period, journalism provides the best insights. Among possible exceptions are novels by Jean Lartéguy and Marguerite Duras. As might be expected, Lartéguy confronted issues of life and death during a protracted colonial war. Duras is best left for discussion later in the context of the acclaim she has recently received in France and abroad. Suffice it to say here that her work both before the French retreat in 1954 and afterwards, while set in Indo-China, concentrates on the thoughts and feelings of individuals to the virtual exclusion of a sense of place.

For the most part, with the end of the First Indo-China War – the Franco–Vietminh War – the torch passes from French hands and a new phase of writing in the English language begins.

Review

From the time of their first arrival in Indo-China, French colonisers recorded their attempts and failures to penetrate and understand local societies and cultures. Some of the most telling fictional evocations of this travail can be found in the writings of Jules Boissière. Boissière went to Indo-China in 1886 as a member of the staff of Paulin Vial, one of the leading colonial officials in the first three decades of the French presence, and later edited a colonial magazine. He died in 1897. While in Vietnam, Boissière became addicted to opium. The importance of opium in the lives of his fictional characters runs parallel to his own feelings about the colonial world in which he lived: its depressing drabness and monotony from which opium was an escape. An example is 'Une Ame' ('A Soul'), one of a collection of Boissière's short stories entitled Fumeurs d'opium: Comédiens ambulants (Opium Smokers: Strolling Players).

'Une Ame' is in the form of a diary written by a young French soldier who is about to executed by a firing squad. His crime is desertion, made more heinous by the fact that, to save his own life, he went over to the rebel side and fought alongside the Vietnamese against his own countrymen. He also became addicted to opium. The story seems to suggest that the young man's death resulted as much from his drug habit as from the brutalities of colonial war on hostile terrain – as if smoking opium were for Boissière a doomed gesture of affiliation with indigenous society. Warranted or not, this interpretation underscores Boissière's fascination with what he saw as a virtually unbridgeable gulf between the world of the French and that of the hostile Vietnamese.

From the late nineteenth to the early twentieth century, the French were engaged in a protracted military pacification of northern Vietnam. Reinforcing and symbolising the actual danger, and the associated perception of Vietnamese as enemy aliens, was the alienation of the French from a strange tropical environment. Illustrating this double preoccupation is 'Dans la forêt' ('In the Forest'), another story from *Fumeurs d'opium*. Here Boissière evokes the despair of an opium-smoking French officer whose unit is carrying out operations in an apparently endless forest in northern Vietnam. The forest in its immensity, darkness and lack of definable form holds for Boissière's character a promise of death, and seems to incarnate the ultimate futility of France's mission in Vietnam: 'We will not leave the forest – the dark, formless forest that stretches from the Tonkin delta to the measureless and shifting frontier of Kwangsi; we will never leave the forest; we are meant to die here' (p. 9).

In the work of writers such as Boissière, the menace of unchartered nature frames the cruelty of the unknowable Vietnamese, and the resulting tableau seems at once to attract and repel the author. Taking the work out of its historical context, it is easy to see and deride the double standard whereby the French colonial observer dwells on Vietnamese cruelty while ignoring the French violence and brutality. Many colonial writers, however, sincerely believed that Vietnamese and French values differed completely, and that while Europeans held life sacred, the Vietnamese were ready to kill and injure without compunction. A sense from another of Boissière's stories, '*Comédiens ambulants*' ('Strolling Players'), in which a Vietnamese mandarin orders and enjoys the execution of the actors who have just performed before him, may be simply the product of the author's imagination. But the horror Boissière seeks to conjure up in this scene was historically grounded in actual instances of cruelty, which the French believed the Vietnamese enjoyed, or were at least morally indifferent towards. In Boissière's story, the mandarin Liet, having indulged his wish to kill what is beautiful, takes pleasure in the sight of dead flesh and the colour of blood spilling over the props which have just been used by the performers. To a modern reader, Liet's pleasure seems bizarre and macabre, but that may not have been the reaction of a Frenchman in colonial Indo-China. The earlier reader would have been aware of the atrocities committed by

Vietnamese and Chinese against French military forces in the savage, if limited, campaigns which continued through the 1890s: for example, the execution of French soldiers by Chinese 'Black Flag' bandits, who impaled their victims on iron hooks set into fortress walls.

The non-fiction of Albert de Pouvourville would also have been available to colonial readers. Writing under the pseudonym Mat Gio, Pouvourville recounted the deaths meted out by the Vietnamese resisting French control. An example is his description – in *Deux années de lutte, 1890–1891 (Two Years of Struggle, 1890–1891)* – of one Lieutenant Ehrer as having been 'cut into pieces and atrociously hacked about'. French readers in Indo-China may also have witnessed, as had Boissière, executions in which neither the Vietnamese victim nor the Vietnamese onlookers displayed emotion.

Unyielding foreignness, dead-pan cruelty and inhospitable landscapes were historically associated with the experiences of pioneer soldiers and explorers in the early phase of French colonialism. But these themes did not disappear in later years. Well into the twentieth century there were authors who preferred to recreate in their work the atmosphere of the earlier period. A case in point is Charles Valat's (writing under the pseudonym of Henry Daguerches) novel *Le Kilomètre 83 (The 83rd Kilometre)*, published in 1913 – a tale of death, jealousy and murder amongst Europeans building a railroad north through Cambodia to Battambang in a remote and isolated part of Indo-China. (To a colonial reader, the number of coolies and Europeans who die in the novel would have recalled the human cost of building an actual rail link between Hanoi and K'unming in southwestern China just a decade before.) As the novel's chief protagonist, the engineer Tourange, prepares to leave Indo-China, he feels the accumulated effects of living under a torpid atmosphere in repellant surroundings, in which he has seen 'too many deaths', and where a piece of himself seems almost to have died as well.

More 'Kiplingesque' are the echoes of early French colonialism to be heard in the work of Jacques Deprat, a writer who deserves comparison with some of the more accomplished writers of English fiction in Asia. In *Dans les replis du dragon (In the Dragon's Coils)*, published in 1926 under the pseudonym Herbert Wild, the dangers and ironies of being French in Indo-China are summed up in a dedication which remembers the pioneers: 'To those who, disregarding indifference and ingratitude, have suffered or are dead in the wilderness of the Far East to add to the grandeur of France.'

In the 1920s, while literary interest in the founders of a French presence faded, French writers remained preoccupied with the sinister opacity of indigenous Indo-China. Jean Marquet's two novels of northern Vietnamese life, *De la rizière à la montagne (From the Ricefield to the Mountain)* and *Du village à la cité (From the Village to the City)*, return again and again to the supposedly negative features of Vietnamese life. Marquet's concern in these works is to contrast French and Vietnamese values to the detriment of the latter. Again, the purported cruelty of the Vietnamese is reiterated. Marquet appears to have written some of these scenes from a near pathological obsession with violence. A few of his Vietnamese characters are sympathetically portrayed, but they are exceptions, and their appeal is neutralised with evidence of their foolishness or improvidence.

When Marquet concentrates on the clash of the French and Vietnamese cultures, as he does in another novel, *La Jaune et le blanc (Yellow Woman and White Man)*, he emphasises the disdain of the French for people and things Vietnamese, and the incompatibility between colonialist and colonised. At the same time, in this work, the European is attracted by what disgusts him. Rivolet, the French protagonist of *La Jaune et le blanc*, is filled with 'hatred for all that is' Vietnam (p. 79); yet, like so many male European characters in French colonial fiction, he keeps a Vietnamese mistress.

French fiction on Indo-China, written early or late in the colonial era, shows European men obsessed by native women, and suffering difficulties and disasters in consequence. Sexual relations between colonial males and local women are examined with frequency and pessimism. Only rarely is it suggested that combined barriers of race and gender could be overcome through genuine love in a lasting accommodation. It might be argued that in stressing the obstacles and misfortunes associated with relationships involving men and women from different cultures, French writers were merely illustrating yet again the unapproachability and danger of Indo-China. But ill-fated inter-racial sex is more than a subtheme – in many novels and short stories it overshadows all other issues of France's colonial imbroglio. Here too, contemporaneous non-fiction can be used to underpin novelistic impressions. From the earliest years of France's endeavours in Indo-China, cross-cultural sexual liaisons are treated explicitly and negatively by French observers. With few exceptions, the early commentaries criticise Vietnamese women – in contrast to Cambodian and Laotian women, about whom the authors show more ambivalence.

In fiction this pattern is extended: the alien quality ascribed to female Vietnamese characters makes them distinctive even in the context of an already alien society, and they appeared strikingly malicious and dirty even against the background of an Indo-China already seen to be unfriendly and unclean. In these impressions, differences of gender apparently intensified those of culture. Nevertheless, these were women, in a setting which for the most part offered no other female companionship, and so they were used for physical relief, as French writers frankly acknowledged. As early as 1896, in an autobiography published that year, *Tonkinoiseries: Souvenirs d'un officier (Things Tonkinese: An Officer's Memories)*, Jean Léra established the conflict of emotions which were to be repeated so often in later fictional works: simultaneous lust for, and repulsion from, the dehumanised image of a Vietnamese woman. Léra recalls how he purchased a *con gai*: how he found himself drawn to her body but revolted by her red betel-stained teeth; and how, finally, he 'succumbed to the brutish feeling of violent desire' (p., 46).

In *La Jaune et le blanc*, published more than thirty-six years later, Marquet recreates this attitude by having Rivolet ask only 'one thing from his *con gai*: animal passion that one indulges day or night, at will; an animal passion that clears the brain and reposes the body' (p.25). Even as sexual conveniences, Frenchmen appear to have preferred other women to the Vietnamese. According to one of Rivolet's acquaintances, a sexually deprived European male is better off with a Japanese prostitute than with a *con gai*, because 'with a Japanese woman you at least have cleanliness and calm' (p. 51) Not every fictional presentation of the *con gai* is so harsh, but even when a Vietnamese mistress is more sympathetically portrayed, she tends to be unapproachable in European terms, or to prove ultimately untrustworthy. Such is the case with the principal female character in Henry Casseville's novel, *Sao, l'amoureuse tranquille (Sao, the Peaceful Lover)*. Sao is the local mistress of a French army sergeant. When he is posted up country, she readily becomes another man's *con gai*; is saddened, briefly, when the sergeant dies of fever and almost immediately becomes the mistress of yet a third Frenchman. Like Sao, Thi Hai, the principal figure in Jean Cotard's *Thi Hai*, is loved by a French sergeant, Benezech. She prefers a simple Vietnamese soldier. When Benezech dies, the tragedy is presented as a direct consequence of Thi Hai's refusal to love the Frenchman as he had hoped she would.

As has been noted, the French took a more charitable view of Cambodian and Laotian women. As early as the 1860s, the explorer Francis Garnier recorded with embarrassment his favourable impression of Laotian women, wondering if there might be some touch of the European in their appearance. In novels from the first three decades of the twentieth century, such as Roland Meyer's *Saramani, danseuse khmèr (Saramani, the Khmer Dancer)* and George Groslier's *Le Retour à l'argile (The Return to the Clay)*, Cambodian

women are portrayed with a sympathy seldom accorded their counterparts in Vietnam.

The fictional picture of French women in Indo-China is only
somewhat less critical than that of the *con gai*, even when the author
is herself female; but the criticism is different. There is a consensus
in French fiction that when significant numbers of European women
arrived in Indo-China intending to stay, the basis was laid for a new
class of dissatisfied foreigners, whose ennui and peccadilloes would
further corrupt colonial society. French women in novels on Indo-
China written in and about the 1920s and 1930s are almost universally bored – offended and enervated by their tropical surroundings.
Life for these fictional women is a succession of sterile gatherings at
which they find fault with servants and husbands, bicker over imagined slights and deplore their absence from France. Joyless infidelities
help to pass the time. Typical of the novels evincing these themes are
George André-Cuel's *La Jonque immobile (The Stationary Junk)* and
Christiane Fournier's *Hanoi, escale du coeur (Hanoi, Stopping Place
for the Heart)*. The first book depicts the emotional pressures on
European women in an isolated mining settlement, while the second
chronicles the discontents of a bored *femme* in Hanoi, who has a
lover to take her mind off the daily monotonies of life in the tropics.

The need to situate French fiction on Indo-China in historical context, and to avoid unfair judgements, cannot alter the fact that rarely
in this literature does an author attempt anything beyond a superficial rendering of colonial existence. Concern with the surfaces of
things reflects the artificial nature of colonial life itself, and carries
with it an avoidance of deeper and more sensitive subjects.

One such subject is the role of the Eurasian, the *métis* of colonial
society – almost always the product of a union between a Frenchman
and a Vietnamese woman. To the extent that Eurasians are dis-
cernible at all in French colonial fiction, their characters are not central to it but on its margins – as they were indeed marginal in the
society itself. Up to the Second World War, the pseudoscientific view
of the inferiority of Asians to Europeans then prevailing among the
French in Indo-China sustained the idea that Eurasian 'half-castes'
were necessarily – that is, biologically – less capable than those
whose European blood had not been degraded by mixture with a local
source. The debasement, shame, tragedy and prejudice associated
with this under presented topic do appear in full view in one novel,
by Jehan Cendrieux, *François Phuoc, métis (François Phuoc, Eurasian)*.
Although Cendrieux originally dedicated the work to those who
sought to improve the lot of Eurasians in Indo-China, the novel has
more recently been condemned for adopting the very biases that

[167]

G

besieged people of mixed blood in the colonies. At the centre of Cendrieux's convoluted plot is François, born to a Vietnamese mother and a French father. Abandoned by his father, François experiences discrimination first in Vietnam and later in France, where he goes to study. In Europe he makes friends with a boy who, unbeknown to François, is actually his half-brother – his father's pureblooded son by legal marriage to a French woman. Also unknowingly, François meets and falls in love with a pure-bred European girl who is, in fact, his half-sister. François's discovery of the origin he shares with his friend and loved one leads to the final tragedy: he is knocked down on a Paris street and dies in the arms of his father. While the book and its contrived plot have little literary merit, the story of François does illustrate an aspect of colonial life in Indo-China about which most writers, of fiction and non-fiction alike, were silent.

One theme which surfaces more frequently in non-fiction than in fiction is the anxiety bordering on fear felt by many French colonials. It would be wrong to claim that such emotions governed, or even constantly accompanied, the lives of the French in so large an area over so many years. French apprehensions in Vietnam, for example, were typically more intense than in Cambodia or Laos. French writing suggests, however, that by the third and fourth decades of the twentieth century a kind of background anxiety, or latent fear, had become a standard feature of colonial existence. To an extent, these were realistic trepidations. The French were unsure of the loyalty of those whom they had colonised. The subservience of the indigenous peoples could conceal hostility, and that could flare suddenly into violence. When 'native treachery' was confirmed, the fears of the French bred brutal and public retribution. When a Vietnamese convinced of killing anyone French was executed, the colonial press covered his punishment in detail in order to discourage rebellion, perhaps even to execute the fear of rebellion itself. The scale and intensity of colonial revenge against the insurgent peasantry of Nghe An and Ha Tinh provinces in the early 1930s also illustrate this point.

Where does realistic fear stop and paranoia begin? Certainly, the latter mentality helped to undermine the colonial project. As more and more Vietnamese became 'potential enemies', the number of 'reliable natives' shrank. Christiane Fournier's previously noted *Hanoi, escale du coeur* captures this tendency for mistrust to expand. The novel's female protagonist is involved in a car crash while travelling in the countryside with her lover. As she reacts to the event, the possibility occurs to her that the crash was not an accident, that it could have been a deliberate attempt by her Vietnamese driver to kill her. From this thought it is not far to wonder whether any Vietnamese could ever be trusted – an anxious, nagging uncertainty which suffuses Fournier's novel.

Useful as a summary in retrospect of this and other themes in French colonial fiction is *L'Appel du dragon (The Call of the Dragon)*, by Jean Bach-Sisley and Claude Gimbert. Like so many of its neighbours on the colonial shelf, the novel is little known. Unlike most of them, it appeared in 1947, at the beginning of the decline of the genre after the Second World War.

Against an accurately drawn historical backdrop, *L'Appel du dragon* illuminates the nature of bourgeois colonial society in Vietnam. Issues neglected in other works are addressed, including the role of Eurasians. More successfully than many colonial novels, the book conveys the mood of isolation felt by the French in Indo-China: the feeling of being inescapably an alien, unable fully and self-consciously to relax; of being subtly menaced by strange people unreconciled to their subjugation. In a passage which captures all the forced artificiality of the French experience in South-East Asia, Bach-Sisley and Gimbert describe the effects of an outbreak of native violence in northern Vietnam on a small community of Frenchmen and women in a provincial capital:

> So their minds were always brought back to the contemplation of this weighty danger that was floating about them like spirits, like the evil genii that the natives fear so much and see everywhere. The Annamites [Vietnamese] chase them away by making a noise. . .
>
> One could say that the [French] colony of Do Son did the same. What fine croquet and tennis parties took place in the Hugues' grounds! [p. 33]

The bulk of French colonial fiction has not been translated. But the language barrier does not wholly block literary access in English to the French experience in South-East Asia. Though extremely small, the openings are of two kinds: translations into English; and works written originally in English. Two examples (one of each type) deserve review: *La Voie royale*, by André Malraux, published in French in 1930 and reissued in translation as *The Royal Way*; and *The Quiet American*, by Graham Greene, which appeared in 1955, just after the end of French rule. These two are not the only novels to deal in English with French Indo-China. But their literary merit greatly exceeds that of, say, the thrillers of Jean Hougron or Jean Lartéguy, which have been translated at various times; or of Clotilde Chivas-Baron's *Three Women of Annam*, if the latter book can be found. *The Royal Way* and *The Quiet American* are, in contrast, minor classics.

The Royal Way is a dense novel, appreciable on six different levels. Especially rewarded is the reader who brings to the book some knowledge of the French part of South-East Asia and Malraux's experiences there. As previously argued, fiction and non-fiction on Indo-China are complements, not alternatives.

At a first level of appreciation, Malraux has written an adventure story, an account of an expedition to Cambodia mounted by a young Frenchman determined to combine research on aesthetic exotica with some profitable trading in antiquities. As the quest proceeds, the protagonist, Claude, and his older companion, Perken, move steadily deeper into unknown territory in a fictionalised area somewhere north of the real ruins of Angkor. In this distant region, where aspects of Thailand, Laos and Cambodia combine, the adventurers become entangled in a revolt of hill people against lowlanders. The book closes with Perken dying and Claude's fate unclear.

At another level, *The Royal Way* is a well-embellished account of Malraux's own experiences in Vietnam and Cambodia in the 1920s, when, despite warnings not to do so, he involved himself in the unauthorised removal of stone carvings from the Angkorian temple of Banteay Srei. Few would now argue that Malraux manages in the novel to justify his actions, any more than he did in the legal defence which he presented at the time. But, while his apologia fails, the novel succeeds in its vivid rendition of the repressive worlds of colonial officialdom in Saigon and Phnom Penh against which Malraux was reacting.

Apart from this third level at which *The Royal Way* can be appreciated, as a politico–literary critique, the novel richly evokes what then remained of the Indo-Chinese frontier: those unexplored or partly explored regions which still existed beyond the pale of colonial society in the 1920s, as if to remind the French just how narrow, even at that late stage, was their colonial footing. Order might have been imposed on most of Indo-China. Urban settlements might have been constructed, comforting architectural remembrances of southern France. But beyond the perimeter, the bush remained, emanating danger.

Malraux himself, in a later explanation of his reasons for writing the book, introduced a fifth level of interpretation. One of his motives, he said, was to retrace in literature the remarkable life of a French adventurer, Charles David – 'King' Mayrena – who set out, like James Brooke in northern Borneo, to carve for himself a kingdom out of the mountains of central Vietnam, where he planned to rule the apparently primitive hill peoples who lived there. Malraux's discussions of his intentions as an author (*Antimémoires*, pp. 185-267) is absorbing, even if much of what he wrote must be discounted as *ex post facto* rationalisation. However, the question of veracity is best left to students of Malraux's literary methods and reputation, and need not diminish the value of *The Royal Way* as an entry into colonial Indo-China.

Malraux's book can be read, finally, on a sixth or philosophical level. His principal characters are, or seem to be, obsessed with death. How should men behave in the face of what is both a threatening unknown and a necessary, even familiar part of human condition? That Malraux chose to ask it in a Franco–South-East Asian context does not reduce the unversality of the question: the Cambodian jungle itself promises the death that everyone must face.

Graham Greene's novel, *The Quiet American*, is no less a classic but its origins are altogether different. As a young unknown in his twenties, Malraux travelled to Indo-China at a time when colonialism dominated the region and much of the rest of the world. Greene went as a famous author in his late forties, when the colonial era was closing all over the globe. Greene's disclaimers to the contrary notwithstanding, it is hard to believe that the novel's narrator, the English journalist Fowler, does not voice many of Greene's own feelings about the First Indo-China War – *la sale guerre* ('the dirty war'), as the French called it.

The Quiet American is a remarkable novel in its spare but effective characterisation and its presentiment of American naivete and failure. The story takes place in Vietnam around 1952, at the time of the departure of Marshall de Lattre de Tassigny. Pyle, a Harvard-trained CIA man, the quiet American of the title, has been seduced by the myth that somewhere between aggressive communism and colonial anti-communism there is a 'third force' among Vietnamese which can be cultivated and made viable. The costs of Pyle's ingenuousness are brilliantly drawn by Greene, as is Pyle's personality, for which the experienced, world-weary Fowler is an almost perfect foil.

Only one of the principal characters is less than fully credible. This is Phuong, the narrator's Vietnamese mistress, for whom Pyle develops an unrealistic and rather unconvincing passion. What is striking about Phuong in the context of this review is the extent to which she mirrors earlier French characterisations of the *con gai*. She, too, is a woman lacking real principles, ready to switch men without hesitation for what seem to be essentially venal reasons. In this regard, for all its merits, *The Quiet American* reflects a traditional debility of the genre: the difficulty of creating persuasive characters on the other side of fictional Indo-China's double – that is, racial *and* sexual – divide.

Within its short span, Greene's novel contains some marvellous set-piece descriptions of Vietnam during the First Indo-China War: the Roman Catholic bishopric of Phat Diem under siege; life in the bars and cafes of Saigon, where drinkers and diners are always aware of the ever-present threat of a grenade attack, and, perhaps most memorable of all, the visit to the Cao Dai temple at Tay Ninh, followed by Fowler's and Pyle's brush with death in the paddyfields after their car has broken down on the way back to Saigon. These and other scenes in *The Quiet American* combine to provide an unusually effective fictional introduction not only to the First Indo-China War but, because of the parallels and the prophetic treatment of Pyle, to the Second (the American one) as well.

A few more English-language entries into French Indo-China warrant brief consideration. The first is the writing in translation by Marguerite Duras, which has recently become well known outside France, mainly because of the success of her Goncourt Prize-winning short novel *L'Amant*. *L'Amant* appeared in French in 1984 and in English, as *The Lover*, the following year. Previously, to the extent that Duras was familiar at all to English speakers, she was known as the author of the Franco–Japanese love story, *Hiroshima mon amour (Hiroshima, My Love)* which was written as a screenplay for the movie of the same name. The critics have generally favoured Duras, though more for her novels than her screenplays. Yet the qualities for which she has been praised – a pessimistic preoccupation with the interplay of relationships of love, passion and destruction – seem to divorce her stories from their background. This judgement may seem curious, since it is in Indo-China that crabs and the sea sabotage the mother's efforts to tame the land in *Le Barrage contre le Pacifique* (published in translation as *The Sea Wall*); while in *The Lover* it is Saigon that locates the affair between her protagonist, a French girl of fifteen, and a much older Chinese. But the novels lack a sense of place despite the exotic settings, or perhaps because of them, remembering the tendency of most French novelists on Indo-China to play down the indigenous. In any case, a sense of place is not Duras's intention. In her 'Indo-Chinese' novels she is concerned with the internal, the psychology of individuals, almost regardless of historical time or physical place.

The documentaries, *The Quicksand War: Prelude to Vietnam* by Lucien Bodard and *The Battle of Dienbienphu* by Jules Roy, are the last two English-language works worth citing here. What makes them valuable as an entry to Indo-China and suitable for inclusion is their achievement in reporting the Franco–Vietminh war accurately but with a sense of drama found more often in works of the imagination.

Colonial Indo-China is at least as inaccessible to fiction buffs who do not read French, and to those who know the language but lack the time to search for out-of-print titles, as the indigenous societies of Indo-China were for the Europeans who actually lived there. For other parts of colonial South-East Asia, fiction in English is much less scarce, and some of it has acquired lasting stature; one need think only of Joseph Conrad's *Lord Jim* or of the short stories of Somerset Maugham. In some of this material, indigenous societies are in the foreground: *She Was a Queen* by Maurice Collis comes to mind. But for Indo-China, there is nothing to equal Kipling's *Plain Tales from the Hills* to shed light on ways of life that were, and remain, as interesting as any others. The French fictional literature which does exist forms a large, but extremely uneven, body of work, much of it hard to find and most of it preoccupied with the tight little worlds of the overseas French to the neglect of indigenous life. Under these conditions, the non-specialist reader is obliged to encounter colonial Indo-China equipped with little of the stimulation or insight that fiction might have provided.

Note

1 The views expressed by the author of this chapter do not reflect, nor should be regarded as representing those of the organisation for which he works.

Reading list

André-Cuel, George, *La Jonque immobile*, Paris, 1926.

Bach-Sisley, Jean and Gimbert, Claude, *L'Appel du dragon*, Lyon, 1947.

Bodard, Lucien, *La Guerre d'Indochine*, Paris, 1963 (in English, *The Quicksand War: Prelude to Vietnam*, Boston, 1967).

Boissière, Jules, *Fumeurs d'opium: Comédiens ambulants*, Paris, 1925.

Casseville, Henry, *Sao, l'amoureuse tranquille*, Paris, 1928.

Cendrieux, Jehan, *François Phuoc, métis*, Paris, 1929.

Chivas-Baron, Clotilde, *Trois femmes annamites*, Paris, 1922 (in English, *Three Women of Vietnam*, New York, 1925).

Cotard, Jean, *Thi Hai*, Paris, 1946.

Deprat, Jacques (Herbert Wild), *Dans les replis du dragon*, Paris, 1926.

Duras, Marguerite, *La Barrage contre le Pacifique*, Paris, 1950 (in English, *The Sea Wall*, New York, 1967).

——, *Hiroshima, mon amour (scénario et dialogues)*, Paris, 1960 (in English, *Hiroshima, mon amour [screenplay]*, New York, 1961).

——, *L'Amant*, Paris, 1984 (in English, *The Lover*, New York, 1985).

Fournier, Christiane, *Hanoi, escale du coeur*, Hanoi, 1937.

Greene, Graham, *The Quiet American*, London, 1955.

Groslier, George, *Le Retour à l'argile*, Paris, 1929.

Hougron, Jean, *Tu récolteras la tempête*, Paris, 1950 (in English, *Reap the Whirlwind*, New York, 1953).

——, *Mort en fraude*, Paris, 1953 (in English, *The Fugitive*, London, 1955).

——, *Rage blanche*, Paris, 1951 (in English, *Ambush*, London, 1956).

——, *Soleil au ventre*, Paris, 1952 (in English, *Blaze of the Sun*, London, 1954).

——, *La Terre du barbare*, Paris, 1958 (in English, *Barbarian's Country*, London, 1960).

Lartéguy, Jean, *Les Centurions*, Paris, 1960 (in English, *The Centurions*, New York, 1961).

——, *Le Mal jaune*, Paris, 1962 (in English, *Yellow Fever*, New York, 1965).

——, *Les Tambours de bronze*, Paris, 1965 (in English, *The Bronze Drums*, London, 1967).

——, *Enquette Sur un crucifié*, Paris, 1973 (in English, *Presumed Dead*, London, 1974).

Léra, Jean, *Tonkinoiseries: Souvenirs d un officier*, Paris, 1896.

Malleret, Louis, *L'Exotisme indochinois dans la littérature française depuis 1860*, Paris, 1934.

——, *Antimémoires*, Paris, 1967 (in English, *Antimemoirs*, London, 1968).

Malraux, André, *La Voie royale*, Paris, 1930 (in English, *The Royal Way*, New York, 1935).

Marquet, Jean, *De la Rizière à la montagne*, Paris, 1920.

——, *Du Village à la cité*, Paris, 1922 (?).

——, *La Jaune et le blanc*, Paris, 1926.

Meyer, Roland, *Saramani, danseuse khmèr*, Saigon, 1919.

Pouvourville, Albert de (Mat Gio), *Deux années de lutte, 1890 – 1891*, Paris, 1892.

Roy, Jules, *La Bataille de Dien Bien Phu*, Paris, 1963 (in English, *The Battle of Dienbienphu*, New York, 1965).

Valat, Charles (Henry Daguerches), *Le Kilomètre 83*, Paris, 1913.

CHAPTER ELEVEN

The Philippines in
mass-market novels

Morton J. Netzorg

The Philippines is a country about which much is stated in an authoritative tone. Much of what is stated is either wholly untrue or is made up of guesses that have been repeated so often that they have come to be accepted as wholly factual. The subject I shall dwell on here has no such drawbacks, however, simply because it has had practically no attention.

That subject is novels, with a Philippine locale, that have had some chance of shaping American public ideas or impressions about the Philippines. This means almost exclusive attention here to books that have appealed to a mass audience. Until now such books have rarely earned even a passing reviewer's nod because they were not aimed at a supposedly elite public of discriminating readers. Most of them have been either pulp fiction or related to it; they were published as paperbacks or in hard covers for a paperback readership.

Almost all of these books are by Americans. This is because few books by Filipinos have been published outside the Philippines, and most of those have not had a mass audience as the target. Among these few, however, have been works by Filipino authors of exceptional skill in Western languages and their literary forms. Although only briefly, these writers did enjoy a flicker of American vogue, and I shall discuss them first. They are José Rizal, Carlos Bulosan, Stevan Javellana and Edilberto K. Tiempo. Two of them are notable for having left a body of work not only in fiction but in the form of poetry and autobiographical writing.

José Rizal, 'The Pride of the Malay Race' (1861–96), is the Philippine national hero and man of all knowledge. He died before a firing squad as his penalty for being too bright, too logical, too outspoken, and for outdoing Spaniards whenever he came into competition with them. He was a man of rich intellect and broad interests, and became a political man only because the times forced it upon him as spokesman for a set of ideas whose time had come and which he personally embodied. He spent much of his short life in Europe as a student, a scholar and a publicist. One form his publicising took was the writing of message-laden fiction, including two novels, *Noli Me Tangere* (Berlin, 1887) and *El Filibusterismo* (Ghent, 1891). These were written in Spanish, a language today closed off from nearly all Filipino readers; they simply will not learn a language for the sake of reading two books that embody allegorically Filipino nationalist hopes of a century ago and that satirise the Catholic clergy and Spanish governmental bureaucracy in the Philippines of that day. Within a dozen years of Rizal's death there were in Spain several Spanish editions of these two novels, as well as (in 1907) a scholarly biography by W. E. Retana, once his detractor. Even earlier than this, William Dean Howells had written an essaylet on Rizal's greatness and there had been two translations into English of abridgements of his fiction. In 1912 there appeared the unabridged Derbyshire translation of the two novels. These are, to this day, still in print – despite competition from numberless other translations into English aimed at the Philippine textbook market. Different in character and in quality from all others in style is the translating done by Leon Ma. Guerrero. (He makes it a point to reflect in his English the type of language that appears in the Spanish – the formal is formal, the slangy is slangy, the idiomatic is idiomatic.) For him the *Noli* is *The Lost Eden* (1961); *El Filibusterismo* is *The Subversive* (1962). Ironically, there is no particularly well-thought-of translation into any Filipino language, in spite of numerous attempts.

Carlos Bulosan was quite another type of man. He was the son of peasant parents, and in his late teens he went to America and made of himself a man of letters in English, against all odds and barriers of language, poverty, racial discrimination and ill health. His book best-known to Filipinists is *America Is in the Heart* (1946), an autobiography about his early years in America that is factual but with great poetic licence.[1] It is a fine book, though it is short on dates and a good many names are disguised and some of the events, though factual in someone's life, may not be facts of Bulosan's own experience. For his later life there is the splendid autobiographical narrative published in the Philippines as *The Sound of Falling Light* (1961).[2] In addition to these two books of autobiographical bent, Bulosan wrote several volumes of innocuous verse, about which there is little to say but that it is innocuous.

Bulosan was an immense reader with an immensely retentive memory but, like so many others, he was not particular about remembering what came from where. Accordingly, the book that brought him a big readership also brought charges of plagiarism. I doubt very strongly that there was any conscious plagiarism, but instead believe that what he had read somewhere at some time floated into memory and got woven in with his stories that purport to be tall tales about his wacky father, and wacky neighbours and wacky relatives in rural Luzon. These stories are probably the only ones by an ex-field hand ever to appear in *The New Yorker*. Later they came out in book form as *The Laughter of My Father* (1944). They make no strong claim to be other than the author's imaginative fiction. (There are parallels here and there in it to Paul Bunyan or Febold Feboldson or Br'er Rabbit, in a mingling of the indigenous with booming Bulosanic creations and half-remembered reading.) As Kipling put it, 'When 'Omer smote 'is bloomin' lyre, 'e 'eard men sing by land and sea, and what 'e thought 'e might require, 'e went and took.' The tales have the virtues of good anecdotal stories told with zest; the only Filipino follow-up in their genre is Alejandro Roces's *Of Cocks and Kites* (1959), whose small readership has been in the Phlippines. Neither Roces's little book nor Bulosan's has the form of a novel, but in each the short stories weave together to have much of a novel's effect.

A third writer is Stevan Javellana, whose only published book was *Without Seeing the Dawn* (1947). This novel of the Second World War in the provincial Philippines won critical acclaim and sold well in the United States. It has had much attention from Filipinos, both qualified critics and unqualified rave writers. The book is that rarest of rare things among Filipino books, a book that was reprinted (in 1976) a generation after its first appearance. I find *Without Seeing the Dawn* to have discrepancies in characterisation but not so great as to make one dump it unceremoniously into the class of melodrama for melodrama's sake. It is a flawed but substantive work. It was written after its author was rejected for military service because he was asthmatic. His comment was that if he couldn't fight he could at least observe. And he did. At this distance in time it seems to me that the book was overpraised because here at last (and after quite a few false starts) was a novel in English by a self-coached Filipino – indubitably, unquestionably and by any standard a novel.

Be that as it may, I find the war novels of Edilberto K. Tiempo better written and better thought out than Javellana's book. There are three of them that are wholly or partly about the Second World War in the Philippines and the guerrilla years. One of them (*Cry Slaughter*, 1957) was mass-marketed in the USA as a paperback. It is one of the few books that mingles melodrama and style and that can be taken as a fairly reliable indicator of real attitudes in a real place at a real time.

Once we leave these few Filipino writers, each in a class of his own and apart from one another, we find ourselves in a domain of American writing that spans about a century and that contains an unknown number of works, most of which nobody alive has ever seen or read.

Much of what I shall describe is really the most formal part of a special kind of pulp fiction. This is the fiction for men that appeared in short stories or novelettes in such magazines as *Adventure*. What appeared in these magazines had a tendency to focus on the adventures of straw men among Moros (Muslim Filipinos), and to be accurate in its version of the people of Mindanao as felt rather than seen by enlisted men of the US army, navy or merchant marine. The stories tend to be pure hokum though written with a precision and skill and an accuracy of grammatical nicety that is out of keeping with the content.

Overlapping this type of fiction is the type I hereby dub the thud-and-blunder type (no spoonerism). In it a hero goes after an objective to which heavy-handed opponents interpose violence of various kinds, and the thuds are the sounds of night sticks or their equivalents against the hero's body. He blunders through to a happy ending.

Such stories in a Philippine setting go back to the turn of the century and continued into the 1960s. The earliest and in some ways the most engaging is Archibald Clavering Gunter's *Jack Curzon* (1898). In its wonder world a lot of fantasy weaves in with a very little fact to present an adventure story with great amounts of plot and sub-plot. It can be read for intrinsic interest as a period piece and with broad grins over such little things as taking a raft journey across an area that is guarded by one mountain range after another and where the rivers actually flow in a direction opposite to where the raft drifts gently down the stream in the story.

Perhaps as good an example as any of this type of fiction is Lee Gifford's *Pieces of the Game* (1960). This is tough guy fiction with much of the action on, in, or under Manila Bay at the time of the Second World War. This part of the yarn is followed up an indefinite number of years later by battles of wits, knives, bullets, and a crucial spear gun when the diabolical but intellectual and exquisite Colonel Yamata makes his illegal and surreptitious play to grab a buried hoard of silver. (There really was such a hoard; near the start of the Second World War the beleaguered Americans dumped several million dollars in Filipino coins into the bay to prevent the Japanese from getting the money.) In the battle of wits and violence, Colonel Yamata abducts the hero, who is supposedly the sole remaining diver who knows just where the silver is. The author creates many characters with considerable skill only to have his Japanese kill them off so that as dead men they can tell no tales. The writing is unusual, there is ingenuity that makes the highly improbable temporarily acceptable for the sake of getting on with the story. The time scale of the war period is anachronistic and the Manila scenes are pure fakery, while off in the distance lies the sugar plantation in Bontoc (which is just a handy name; no vast acreage of sugar cane actually grows there). The bits on Corregidor and Manila Bay indicate either ownership of a map or contact with someone who had actually been there. The language of all Filipinos in the story is Spanish. The hero's Spanish is called 'perfect,' but it errs in gender, number, tenses and idioms.

Other 'thud-and-blunder' books that depend upon pace to cover inadequacies of background are two by Alan Caillou (pseudonym of Alan Lyte-Smyth). Both are laid in what purports to be the Muslim Philippines. They are *The Mindanao Pearl* (1959) and *The Walls of Jolo* (1960). In books such as these one must not be surprised to find Muslims as swiggers of beer in public saloons. Earlier, and run serially in *Blue Book* magazine, was Charles Clifford's short novel, *Typhoon Dawn* (1942), sited in just-before-World-War II Mindanao. I know only the first and last of its three instalments, in which a much-stirred pot finally comes down to a happy simmer in spite of untrustworthy everybody but Americans; at the end, one hero ends the stereotypes by taking the heroine in his arms. In fact, I quote the final words, which are these: 'I took her in my arms.'

A recent 'thud-and-blunder' book that has had surprisingly many readers is George Fox's *Amok* (1978). This somewhat dizzying tale seems aimed straight at a celluloid bull's eye. Its action is placed in 1975, but it is filled full with castings back to the Cagayan Valley of Luzon during the days of Japanese occupation. The characters are many and they are well individuated. In particular, some lesser figures (for instance, the conscience-torn Japanese ex-officer, the Filipino doctor, the Filipino constabulary officer) have more that is human about them than the two not very convincing or consequential American protagonists, the usual he and she twosome headed towards bedding. Indeed, these two seem to have strayed out of *Gone with the Wind* for a confrontation with Stonewall ('King') Kong masquerading as a seven-foot-tall Japanese straggler still unsurrendered, still on the rampage, and still wielding his four-foot-long samurai sword. In this book the wild and tightly jammed cogon grass grows taller than the tallest corn, but the huge Japanese wends through it with his sword on his shoulder without getting snarled and without leaving the trace of a trail for enemies to follow. The American planters who live in the Cagayan Valley have the amenities of Waikiki condominiums when that suits the story, the rest of the time they live a harsh, rugged backwoodsy life. The author seems unaware that a lot of amnesty has been in effect for a long time, and that the present generation of Filipinos looks on Japanese more as potential trade partners than as enemies who made grandpa's and grandma's lives nightmarish.

Some books give evidence of once-upon-a-time popularity by the fact that they went through more than one edition. Such a book is William H. Thomes's long adventure yarn, *Life in the East Indies,* called *A Manila Romance* in some editions. Across a span of many years the author tinkered (or some might say tampered) with this story, so that in one format it appears to be a book for teenage boys, in another it edges more toward a love story for misses who like their romance spiced with danger. Despite its original title, the scene is laid wholly in the vicinity of Manila. It is (subject to correction) the earliest book-length fiction in English that is wholly devoted to doings in the Philippines; its first appearance was in 1872. Other editions or versions appeared in 1875, 1892, and 1898 – and perhaps at other times between; for instance, there is record of an 1890 edition in the Detective and Adventure series. In Thomes's book the heroine has an athletic life, escaping from abductors and climbing up and down ladders in and out of convents and the Asylum of San Sebastian ('a private prison'), and otherwise showing courage, spirit, and a neat ankle. She is a paragon of modesty too. She refuses to climb down the rope-ladder in the dark until the men at its foot move far enough away so that no possibility remains of their seeing any display of uncovered flesh.

A much later book, a whodunit, has one of the characteristics of Thomes's novel, which is that in the course of time the author rewrote the story but this time without changing the title. The book is Van Wyck Mason's *The Sulu Sea Murders* (1933). The book first appeared with this on its title page: 'A Case for Captain North, D.C.I. What had a dying pearl diver in Zamboanga to do with the terror at Fort Winfield, where the stormy Sulu Sea washed the walls of grim Killers' Castle? Little enough, thought Captain North . . . until the first man died with a knife in his back, and red gates of murder opened wide.' (The three dots do not indicate an elision, they are a peculiarity of the writing style of the day.) The book appeared in the Crime Club series in the United States, and three years later achieved the distinction of a British first edition. ('An Eldon Book . . . entirely new, 3/6 net.') The story is a variation, in part, on the locked room type of mystery: 'How could a man be murdered on an empty tower top, with guards all around him and only the sea and the jungle outside?' The answer is telegraphed to anyone who is acquainted with lesser detective fiction of the 1890s, for the trick of the man trap set off by sunlight focused by a lens had been used in a short story in *Harper's Magazine* of that vintage.

In 1958 an abridged edition appeared of *The Sulu Sea Murders*, as a pocket book, 'completely rewritten by the author'. The rewriting is drastic as far as trappings are concerned. Hugh North has been promoted from Captain to Colonel, and the story is now (says the front cover) 'about a top-secret microfilm, a fortune in pearls and a killer who would do anything to get both!' However, the creaky old device for no-hands murder is retained, though now Fort Winfield has been converted to a base for guided missiles.

Most of the authors I have brought to your attention so far wrote one or two or at most three books set in the Philippines. Even Thomes and Mason, who each wrote much fiction, wrote only one novel apiece about the Philippines. As a contrast I turn to discussion of a man whose fiction ran to more than fifty volumes across the time span between 1883 and 1909, with several of them set in the Philippines.

Charles King came from a distinguished New York family, with, on his family tree, a US senator, a president of Columbia University, a signer of the US Constitution, and John Eliot, the early apostle to New England Indians. He himself began a military career when he was sixteen years old and the Civil War was on. By the time the war ended he was an officer; he detoured through West Point, then continued in the military service across many years of Indian warfare that later provided the background to his 'romances of frontier chivalry.' He served in the Spanish-American War and was a general of volunteer troops in the Philippines. Remarkable as it may seem, General King's last military command was in France in 1918, during World War I, after nearly 60 years of a soldier's life.

King wrote several books about the bravery of American soldiers in the Philippines, and their inability to stand up to the charms and wiles of American women – who were miraculously there in considerable numbers as officers' wives or offspring even while the fighting was going on. In his Philippine tales King pays no heed to lowly American civilians, while his Filipinos are a rabble. To today's taste King's fiction is overly sweet and overly tied to conventions whose juices have been squeezed out and evaporated by changes in customs and beliefs, but at the century's turn he was the one writer who had a regular following for his fiction about the Philippines. This comprised at least four novels – *Found in the Philippines* (1899), featuring love, loyalty, bravery and blackmail, printed, reprinted, and pirated a number of times; *Ray's Daughter: A Story of Manila* (1901); *Comrades in Arms: A Tale of Two Hemispheres* (1904); *Captured: The Story of (Lieutenant) Sandy Ray* (at least two editions in 1906). In addition, he published another book that seems to me several cuts above the others in distinction but that bears no signs of ever having had the popularity the others achieved. This is *A Conquering Corps Badge and Other Stories of the Philippines* (1902). In all there are nine of these stories, of which the first and longest is as long as a short book – sixty pages. This is the book's title story, 'A Conquering Corps Badge.' There is also one beautifully evocative piece of non-fiction that I herewith commend to the attention of historians. This piece, 'The Fate of Guadalupe', tells of what befell the church at Guadalupe ('the richest and finest on the river') and how it became 'one of the sorrows of the campaign'. Through the misfortunes of war 'that grand old church was a white elephant on our hands', and was destroyed by American nitroglycerine, leaving 'only a . . . blistered ruin . . . and only the massive wall . . . standing'.

King's books are a gentleman's books written with gentility for others presumed to be gentlefolk. They contain more illustrations than is customary for their period. These are more or less in the Gibson Girl tradition, with more emphasis on the women than on men. There is in the writing little of the poorly disguised contempt for the Filipino leadership and the Filipino masses that seeps through typical military accounts of the day.

Little of the American fiction I have so far discussed strove for authenticity of background or of character depiction. There were exceptions and a few books did achieve a sort of popularity with special readerships. Perhaps the most important period piece of fiction about Americans and Filipinos in a recognisable Philippines has never had an American edition and indeed was not aimed at Americans in America. It was written by an American for Americans *in the Philippines* at a time when there was still a large enough American population there to make publishing such a novel more than an appeal to a tiny in-group, though by then American tinkers and tailors and teamsters and ostlers and bricklayers were rapidly being squeezed out by their more diligent and less rowdy Filipino counterparts. The book was by Chauncey M'Govern, its title was *When the Krag is Laid Away* and it bears the imprint of the Escolta Press, Manila, 1910. By the time this book reached the public,

M'Govern had written three other books, one of which, *By Bolo and Krag* (1907), begins with seven pages of soldier slang – for instance:

Beno:	a vile-smelling, stomach-rotting liquid, distilled by Filipinos from grass, etc., and ruinous to an American soldier who gets a craze for it.
Dog-Robber:	A soldier who does chores for an officer.
Gold-Fish:	Canned salmon.
Mystery:	Corned beef hash.
San Miguel:	Beer; so named after the only brewery in the Philippines.
Squawman:	An American married to a native of the lower class – or living with her without marriage.

When the Krag is Laid Away has a title page somewhat in the eighteenth-century manner, with this to say: 'The story of lively adventures of a young man from a small town who went to New York City to set the place on fire; romantically thrown into the American army; lands in the Philippines in the midst of the scrapping; where he finally becomes an uncrowned king.' It's that last phrase that raised eyebrows and a ruckus, because M'Govern made it pretty clear that he thought well of marriage to a Filipina and hoped for the foundation of a squirearchy of hacenderos living patriarchally with local mates, in opposition to the 'high society' hen house that was in process of being built among Americans resident in the Philippines, on the British colonial model; in it men were condoned in any kind of relation at all with local women – as long as it was quiet and didn't involve marriage. In the meantime, by some occult means, some coteries of women (e.g., Eastern Star) voted themselves into little elite groups. They made it stick among the others, and went from there to considerable bluenosery and laying down the rules of decorum in a country where a nubile American girl was a social high trump card because there were perhaps ten American men ready for mating for every conventionally eligible woman. (In passing, we may note that quite many of these invading male heroes wore their first long pants at about the time they enlisted for service abroad.)

M'Govern's little section titled 'After-thoughts' comes appropriately at the start of the book, and begins with 'Days of Empire.' At that time 'Adventurers from America flocked to the Philippines . . . Females were almost as numerous as the males.' But, says he, things have changed: 'An American civilian could be ignorant and remain in the Archipelago. He or she could hold any views . . . however contrary to the ideas of the Government. But any man or woman with a white skin who behaved, morally or socially, in a manner not approved by the all seeing Police was summarily handed passage on the next Army Transport to San Francisco.' (I may add that in later pre-war days the ticket-handing was reputedly a part of the affairs of the American Chamber of Commerce.)

One of the odd things about eternal fame and eternal love is how evanescent they are. Maxima Ferrer's so careful *Union Catalog of Philippine Materials* (1970) deals with today's holdings of about 200 Philippine libraries – public institutional, private. For M'Govern it lists two copies of the seventh printing of *Sergeant Larry*, another of his novels, and zero copies of any of the others in the entire Philippines. To the best of my knowledge, what I write here is the first published attention to any of M'Govern's books in perhaps half a century. I commend them to historians who have taken documents and public statements too seriously and have had no corrective from the sociology floating in suspension in the fiction of the American period.

The sort of things M'Govern wrote about were stirring to Americans in the Philippines. In contrast, books that depicted more usual contemporary American lives in the colony appear to have made no impression on the home folks. Americans tend to be adventuresome under pressure, but by and large their interests in any year are like those expressed in a letter I have before me as I write this. It is from Nell, in Ionia, Michigan, to her sister Cora V. Bartlett of Dansville, Livingstone County, New York. Nell's letter has the date of January 10, 1871: 'Have you got your green dress made and how is it made, do the girls wear cloaks like yours down there and how do they wear their hair also do the ladies wear such large waterfalls as they did here. Has Aunt May got a melodean so you can exercise your musical talents and has she got a sewing machine.' (Punctuation is Nell's. So is the spelling.)

The novels I speak of were published by reputable houses, but a scanning of the bookish journals of their day shows them as seldom given a review and even seldomer given an advertising budget. Between about 1904 and 1942 it was an act of unrequited faith to publish a novel about the Philippines. The writers were people who had lived in the Philippines, the writing was usually sober and not sensational, and the authenticity was high in such works as Rowland Thomas's *The Little Gods* (Little, Brown, 1909), once considered the high point of fictional representation of Americans in the Phlippines. Other books were C. L. Carlson's *The Taming of Calinga* (Dutton, 1916) and Mary Fee's *The Locusts' Years* (McClurg, 1912). Some excellent writing and a considerable feeling for the provincial Philippines is in the short stories in James Hopper's *Caybigan* (McClure, Phillips, 1906). Apparently more popular than any of these was Walter Elwood's *Guimo* (Reilley & Britton, 1915). This book had at least two printings within a year after publication. It is a lush novel, written with considerable flair, but it holds more interest as evidence of what an American didn't know about Filipinos than for what it shows he did know. This novel is probably unique in one sense, which is that though it is by an American it centres on the life story of a Filipino *mestizo*, the illegitimate son of a Spanish friar. The action spans the last years of the Spanish period and the earlier years of the American period.

Perhaps the most-owned book with a Philippine setting, as evidenced by its continued presence in today's antiquarian bookstores in no small numbers (with the majority of copies autographed), is a novel-in-spite-of-itself. It is about a man who contracted a then incurable but long-protracted disease. The book is *Who Walk Alone*, by Perry Burgess; the disease is leprosy. The book is mainly careful historical fact interspersed with some fictional characters and more than enough amateurish dialogue. Burgess at the time he wrote the book was president of the Leonard Wood Memorial, whose mission was to work toward the eradication of leprosy. In the year of his book's publication (1940) it was one of only three to receive the National Book Award. By April 1947 it was in its twenty-seventh American printing, and in 1942 it was widespread in Great Britain through the Readers Union, a book club. The book, mostly centred on Culion Leper Colony, is not particularly well written, but it has real Filipinos in it and real Americans. They are cast in roles other than pullers of triggers in a 'bang-bang shoot 'em up.' One curious thing about this supposed biography is that you can turn hundreds of pages without finding a single date and mighty few outside events to orient you to the outside world's history. The book begins at the time of the Rough Riders, while a word near the end (about the fall in the death rate among lepers) reveals that the events have spanned about thirty years. Though Burgess's book was in its day considered a biography, it was, as I have intimated, actually a historical novel. No other historical novel with a Philippine setting challenged it in popularity.

Totally different in type are the books in which Isa Glenn seems to have specialised. Her fiction (*Heat*, 1926: *Transport*, 1929) depicts the life of the American army officer and his lady in, or en route to, the Philippines. It turns out to be Main Street life magic-carpeted to the tropics; life there is shown as made alternately piquant by small-town rivalries, and sullen by *ennui* and the toll on vitality of a pre-air-conditioned era. At the turn of the century American military regulations classified service in the Philippines as a hardship, with time spent there counting $1^1/2$ usual service time in totting up both seniority and eligibility toward retirement. This was fully justified at the start; then in all the Philippines there was, for instance, not a single ice plant and a taste for warm beer and flaccid canned butter had to be cultivated by the sociable. I suspect the lady's novels were a rearguard action to keep perks operative quite long after the conditions that had justified them were almost wholly gone. By the late 1930s American army officers in the Philippines led a life where they shut up shop an hour or two after noon, and they were then thrown on their caste-conscious own. There was much golf and some gambling at cards and dice and quite a lot of social drinking, and not very much making of small scandals. It took little rubbing to bring out self-pity in people sitting on top of the world in semi-idleness. (I suspect that this has been so back into B.C. whenever military forces have gone into cantonments.)

I do not know what prevented the writing of cloak and dagger novels about the Spanish period; for nearly 250 years Philippine Spaniards wore cloaks, while daggers and swords were much in evidence and sometimes in use. The only person to write much fiction (short stories) about this period was Percy A. Hill, who flourished as a writer in the 1920s. It is curious that the cloak and dagger story about the Philippines was also a scarce product in Spain. I know of only one historical novel in English about the Spanish period. This is Linda Ty Casper's *The Peninsulars* (1964), a well written and well researched novel, which has made no mark in the United States in spite of its goodness.

A few novels produced in America have been historical either as social documents or as military history shoehorned into American minds as background to a yarn. A quite competent example is Elinor Chamberlain's *The Far Command* (1953), which deals with bloody Samar in 1902. It appeared simultaneously in hardback and paperback. Here are words from the back cover of the paperback: 'Tells the story of that band of Americans . . . whose task was to win the friendship of the people and put down the marauding guerrilla bands. It is the story of Captain Morrow and Lucy Leslie, the school teacher; of Ramos, the shrewd sergeant and of the mysterious rebel chief, Faustino.'

Quite different in intent is Richard O'Connor's *Officers and Ladies* (1958), where the treatment is less serious and restrained than in *The Far Command*. (When the O'Connor novel was republished as a paperback it bore a new name: *The Sulu Sword*.) The *Wilmington News* said of O'Connor's book, 'This novel of . . . the Philippines . . . of 1898 is exciting and gory . . . coupled with plenty of romance. It is the tale of the wild Moros . . .' and we have come almost full circle to what I said near the start of this essay: Moros captured and retained the American imagination, but once the Christian Filipinos ceased their resistance they passed almost wholly from the consciousness and attention of stateside Americans.

One striking exception, however, is Benjamin Appel's *Fortress in the Rice* (1951). This is fiction at length, in depth, and with several missions. These are to show the rawness of guerrilla war in Central Luzon during the Japanese occupation, the nobility and selflessness of the peasants who formed an anti-Japanese resistance movement and exercised self-government, and to depict the crass betrayal of these people by the American military and the Filipino landowners and their controlled politicians and uncontrolled Filipino soldiery. At least that's what the main emphases were in the big, thick, but non-rambling original edition. When, in 1960, it was 'edited and revised by the author' (i.e., greatly abridged) for appearance as a paperback, it continued to be 'dedicated to the nameless humble peasants . . ., the taos' – but more emphasis in what remained was now on the number-one American and his romance with the 'honey-skinned exotic'. In either form, the example is of an author who writes with passion that sometimes gets a little out of control because his characters and their emotions manipulate him. There were quite many other novels by Americans about the Second World War in the Philippines; I know of no other that seeks to make Filipino peasants and their motives and actions understandable to people who have never had to live in terror or in near starvation.

A novel about terror and degradation in the Philippines that rises to the level of literature with a capital L is written neither by a Filipino nor an American but by a Japanese, Shohei Ooka. Its Japanese title was *Nobi* (1952). A superb translation by Ivan Morris appeared in 1957 titled *Fires on the Plain*. The story is set in Leyte during the American re-invasion and has no plot at all. It needs none, for it compassionately but unswervingly tells of descent into Avernus, the degradation and moral death of a Japanese foot soldier who experiences fear, hunger, hallucinations and eventual madness – an imaginative treatment of the author's own experiences.

A new subject for a novel with a Philippine setting based on an author's personal experience is *Ants Have No Taste* (1980) by Juliet S. Blanchard. Blanchard's lively, readable story centres on her life in the Philippines as a Peace Corps Volunteer in the 1960s.

There is yet another genre of novels that, because I dislike it, I will mention only very briefly. This is the cheap novel shoddily written and shoddily produced as a companion piece for a grade-D movie. Its reason for existence was to be sold in movie theatre lobbies. A good example is Randall White's *Salute to the Marines* (1943), a mixture of bits of corn sloppily ground up with bits of ham.

Most of the books I have paraded before you, though not great, are
quite good as story-telling; they are interesting not only as stories but
as evidence of what publishers thought Americans would deign to
read. They are interesting too for their revelations both of knowledge
and, more notably, of ignorance; much of this fiction is false and
bloated and full of misconceptions. But that's the way conceptions
about Philippine things were in the United States from the beginning.

The crassness and the extent of American ignorance of the
Philippines is hard to bring out in a few words, but it was, to a
degree, of the sort that appears in this semi-litany that local
Americans could and did recite to one another:

A: I hear you're going back to the Philippines.
B: Yes.
A: I have a second cousin in Melbourne.
B: So?
A: So when you bump into him give him my regards.

Aside from the presence of misinformation in novels about the
Philippines, what was absent also bred misconceptions. Not in the
literature, for example, is the quite impudent and barefaced cheerful-
ness in discriminatory wage scales that prevailed for so very long and
that had nothing to do with merit but everything to do with promotion in business houses whose home base was in 'the States.' There
was a wage scale for Filipinos, and a remarkable Filipino could rise,
by diligence, to the eminence of a chief clerk. There was a wage scale
for locally hired whites, at three to five times the pay of Filipinos,
with opportunity to do actual brain work and make the main deci-
sions. There was yet another wage scale for certified grade-A pure
Americans hired in the United States and sent out with no knowledge of the country or its customs. These tended to be decorative
people (who at heart never left home); they were paid three to five
times the wages of locally hired Americans. Some of them grew to
eventual leadership, but the duds were plentiful.

During the American period there was a great deal of Filipino
whooping and hollering about racial discrimination but really there
was no great desire among normal Filipinos to fraternise with
Americans. What they resented was being made painfully aware that
the American (girls') rules said 'no fraternisation,' i.e., that they
couldn't have what they didn't want. Of course, there were rebels,
and of course some of the rebels were among the Best People; it was a

privilege and a pleasure, for instance, to be asked to one of Janet Walker's multinational tea-salons. The multi-nationality was in the participants, not in the economics; American, Filipino, Chinese, German, Italian, East Indian, and other visiting and resident firemen were there. Janet and her sister were usually the only American women present, though quite many elite Filipinos were there – usually the elite of brains rather than of money.[4]

Discrimination in the 20s and 30s was peculiar and had its own special bounds. For instance, there was little discrimination in athletics (except in polo) and none in stamp clubs, coin clubs, chess clubs, or public bowling alleys. There were also some saloons that played the role of pubs in the British sense, with no racial discrimination but with the ordinary Filipino priced out of the running and the rumming.

None of this shows up except between the lines in the fiction of the time or since, and none of it has been recorded by sociologists or anthropologists or social historians. Another fact that none of the fiction revealed was the enormous complexity of social relationships and the tendency of people towards cleavage into minorities along social fracture lines, with or without real issues. There was not only, for instance, a British community in the Philippines, there was a Scotch community and two Irish communities within the British community. There was cleavage between married and single Britons, and further cleavage partly governed by mates of different nationalities and backgrounds.

There was also cleavage within the Chinese community, by reason of place of origin, political beliefs, business interests and the degree of Philippineness in blood lines. The Spanish community had not only its main Spanish components but also its Basques and Catalans and its Balearic Islanders; they all tended to be cliques apart. There was a subtle gradation of blood lines from lily-white Castilian to not quite purely Filipino.

In addition to cleavages by nationality and racial mixture there was stratification by sex and religion and social grace and hobby and age and wealth and intelligence and number of kinds of languages spoken. No man was an island but every man was an expert hopper from one atoll to another with comfort and accuracy.

To a large degree, of course, similar conditions have prevailed in the United States and in spite of Fourth of July oratory there have been numberless and persistent sub-cultures within 'one nation indivisible'. In fact, the concept of a main stream is largely a statistical convenience for the use of people who tire when they cope with much diversity.

Let me speak to a nice, round phrase that has had currency but no precise meaning over nearly three-quarters of a century. This is 'special relationship' to describe what supposedly existed between Filipinos and Americans. There was indeed a special, ever-changing relationship, but it was political and economic, not cultural. It existed as a fragile creation always in process of mutation. Its features resulted from the pull and haul between a very limited number of influential Americans and an even smaller number of influential Filipinos. Between them they constituted a not quite open conspiracy of the two elites.

The Americans manipulated the Filipino leaders and the Filipino leaders manipulated the American leaders. It all started as a stately masked contra-dance but, as the years went by, the tempo changed to that of a polka and it kept getting harder and harder to keep the masks in place or to keep a straight face when a mask slipped.

As continues to this day, the biggest and boldest semi-fiction was what was in the newspapers and news magazines, and truth was distorted by aversion of the attention from many subjects. For instance, nobody seems to have written a novel about even one of the thousands of 'little ladies more than dead' who have lived for at least three generations on the fringes of Philippine–American society, and there is only one novel, Robert O. Bowen's *Bamboo* (1953) that deals honestly with American gobs (seamen of the US navy) shacked up in Manila. Of the enlisted man's life in Corregidor or Cavite or Olongapo, there is only one fictional depiction (in Marcus Goodrich's *Delilah*). I know of no novel about the peacetime US Marines who sang their taunting song – 'Ten thousand gobs laid down their swabs to lick one sick marine.' There was only a handful of Marines, but their strut put all the world in its place.

On the whole there is a sort of truth in books by American authors that has not been much noted. This is that in them are few recognisable individuated Filipinos, while on the whole Americans are notably absent in the novels Filipinos have written for the microscopic Philippine market. This reflects the fact that in our century it has been quite possible for a provincial Filipino to live for many years between the time when he lays eyes on one American and when he sees the next. After the Days of Empire the number of Americans in the country was only a few thousand among the Filipino millions, and most of them clustered in a few places – such as Manila, Iloilo, Cebu, Baguio, Davao, Zamboanga. Filipinos who made it to high school or college came in contact with a few American teachers. There was a sprinkling of zealous American missionaries all over the country, and there were plantation owners or managers in many parts of the country. The Americans were influential in running the transportation network, especially the bus lines. In the main cities, there were American doctors and American lawyers who had Filipino clients, just as there were some Filipino doctors and lawyers who had Americans among their clients. However, on the whole there was minimal intercourse on a formal social level between Americans and Filipinos.

The Americans as a whole had no social contact with adult Filipino peasants, while there was practically no Filipino middle class and there were no Americans as small town shop keepers. Before the Americans came, the Filipino elite had had its ties to Spanish culture and this group and its descendants did not hanker after anything from America except luxuries of one kind or another; by and large the American businessman's company was sought only by other American businessmen. Perhaps the least stand-offishness between races and cultures existed in retired enlisted men and in the men and women of the print media – the better magazines and the English-language newspapers. There existed genuine friendliness and real rivalry among these latter people.

Just as there was no first-rate portraiture of Filipinos by Americans, there has continued to be a great dearth of good portraiture of Americans in the novels Filipinos write. In fact, perhaps the most successful portraiture of Americans is in the work of a man who even a few years ago would not have been eligible for coverage in this chapter.

Bienvenido N. Santos has spent a lifetime as a man of letters. He has won recognition as a writer of great capability and his many books of short stories and his highly literate novels have won repute in the Philippines and have had bestowed upon them prizes and laudatory reviews. But across decades they did not sell in any mass way, even though a story here and there has been included in one or another mass market anthology. More recently, Santos, who is an expatriate from the Philippines, had a collection of his stories published as a University of Washington Press paperback, *The Scent of Apples and Other Stories* (1980). This now stands in a class of writing that may yet have a mass sale – though the odds are still against it. If you are interested in the starkness of life of Filipinos in America in the period of the 40s, before the influx of Filipino doctors and nurses, there are but a few books to bother to read. I have already mentioned two by Bulosan. Their only peer is Santos's *You Lovely People* (1953). These three books tell more and tell it more powerfully than all the tracts, dissertations, government documents and sob-stories combined. Further, in Santos's novel, *The Volcano* (1965), there is portraiture of an American family that is caught in the Bicol provinces during the years of the Second World War. The family is recognisably American, its worries and biases and interests and attitudes and responses are acceptable to an American reader without a great deal of strain and with no smirks over gross errors of delineation or understanding. Critics have not been particularly friendly towards Santos's depiction of an American missionary, but the critics err: they are intellectuals who never personally rubbed against the mixture of unsullied idealism, practicality, brotherly love and childish priggishnes that made nearly all pre-war American missionaries so hard to understand and deal with, and that put so many of their children into revolt against their upbringing and upbringers.

The fiction I have discussed in this paper was almost wholly of a kind aimed at a genuine mass market that wasn't really there. You must bear in mind that though nearly all these books were the least unsuccessful ones in a commercial way, all but a few of them are now in limbo: I stir their dust. Their impact on current popular perceptions of the Philippines is probably minimal. If a writer's intent is that his words shall bring later generations to see as he sees, there has been practically no success at all. The limited success has been of the Filipinos I have named, not of Americans.

As for the future, I expect that most Americans and most Filipinos will continue to ignore one another or to talk past one another. I expect that (as ever) books of American fiction will continue to have less cultural influence in the Philippines than American movies and TV programmes and much less than American dances and pop songs.

All these are subjects for other writers, on some other day; all are poorly documented and remote from today's conventional scholarship. Perhaps tomorrow will be different? As someone didn't quite say, it is a consummation devoutly to be inched forward to.

Notes

1 Republished as a University of Washington paperback in 1973.
2 Edited brilliantly by Dolores Feria.
3 See Morton J. Netzorg, 'Little Jack Horner in the Philippines: The Philippines in American literature for children at the turn of the century,' *Kinaadman* (Philippines), 1979, pp. 84–6, partially quoted here.
4 Janet Walker shows up in Gregorio Brillantes's 'Excerpts from the autobiography of a middle aged Ghost Writer with Insomnia', in *The Apollo Centennial* (1980). She's there under the transparent disguise of Janice Wacker, as the hostess to the writers who goggled at Ernest Hemingway and Martha Gellhorn during their 1941 visit to Manila. See pp. 172 ff.

Reading list

Appel, Bejamin, *Fortress in the Rice*, Indianapolis, 1951.

Blanchard, Juliet S., *Ants Have No Taste*, New York, 1980.

Bowen, Robert O., *Bamboo*, New York, 1953.

Bulosan, Carlos, *The Laughter of My Father*, New York, 1944.

Bulosan, Carlos, *America is in the Heart*, New York, 1946.

Bulosan, Carlos, *The Sound of Falling Light* (ed. Dolores Feria), Quezon City, 1961.

Burgess, Perry, *Who Walk Alone*, New York, 1940.

Caillou, Alan (Alan Lyle-Smith), *The Mindanao Pearl*, London, 1959.

Caillou, Alan, *The Walls of Jolo*, New York, 1960.

Carlson, C. L., *The Taming of Calinga*, New York, 1916.

Casper, Linda Ty, *The Peninsulars*, Manila, 1964.

Chamberlain, Elinor, *The Far Command*, New York, 1953.

Clifford, Charles, *Too Many Boats*, Boston, 1934.

Clifford, Charles, *Typhoon Dawn*, 1942.

Elwood, Walter, *Guimo*, Chicago, 1915.

Fee, Mary, *The Locusts' Years*, Chicago, 1912.

Fox, George, *Amok*, New York, 1978.

Gifford, Lee, *Pieces of the Game*, Greenwich, Connecticut, 1960.

Glenn, Isa, *Heat*, New York, 1926.

Glenn, Isa, *Transport*, New York, 1929.

Gunter, Archibald Clavering, *Jack Curson; or, Mysterious Manila*, New York, 1898.

Hill, Percy A., *Romance and Adventure in Old Manila*, Manila, 1928.

Hill, Percy A., *Philippine Short Stories*, Manila, 1934.

Hopper, James, *Caybigan*, New York, 1906.

Javellana, Stevan, *Without Seeing the Dawn*, Boston, 1947.

King, Charles, *Found in the Philippines*, New York, 1899.

King, Charles, *Ray's Daughter*, New York, 1901.

King, Charles, *A Conquering Corps Badge and Other Stories of the Philippines*, Milwaukee, 1902.

King, Charles, *Comrades in Arms*, New York, 1904.

King, Charles, *Captured*, New York, 1906.

Mason, Van Wyck, *The Sulu Sea Murders*, New York, 1933.

M'Govern, Chauncey, *By Bolo and Krag*, Manila, 1907.

M'Govern, Chauncey, *When the Krag is Laid Away*, Manila, 1910; 1936.

O'Connor, Richard, *Officers and Ladies*, Garden City, NY, 1958.

Ooka, Shohei, *Fires on the Plain*, (trans. Ivan Morris), New York, 1957.

Rizal, Jose, *The Subversive* (trans. Leon M. Guerrero), Bloomington, Indiana, 1962. Original: *El Filibusterismo*, 1891.

Rizal, Jose, *The Lost Eden*, (trans. Leon M. Guerroro), Bloomington, Indiana, 1961. (Original: *Noli Me Tangere*, 1887).

Roces, Alejandro, *Of Cocks and Kites*, Manila, 1959.

Santos, Bienvenido N., *You Lovely People*, Manila, 1953.

Santos, Bienvenido N., *The Volcano*, Quezon City, 1965.

Santos, Bienvenido N., *The Scent of Apples and Other Stories*, Seattle, 1980.

Thomas, Rowland, *The Little Gods*, Boston, 1909.

Thomes, William H., *Life in the East Indies*, Boston, 1872.
Thomes, William H., *A Manila Romance*, Chicago, 1898.
Tiempo, Edilberto K., *Cry Slaughter*, New York, 1957.
Tiempo, Edilberto K., *More Than Conquerors*, Manila, 1964.
Tiempo, Edilberto K., *To Be Free*, Quezon City, 1972.
White, Randall M., *Salute to the Marines*, New York, 1943.

CHAPTER TWELVE

Taking Japan seriously

Some Western literary portrayals of the Japanese during the climax of their national self-assertion c. 1905–c. 1945

D. N. Lammers

We have it on good authority that, at least up to 1900, the images of, and attitudes to, Japan commonly held in the Western world did not amount to 'taking Japan seriously'. Whether Japan's astonishing successes in arms and industry thereafter dispelled the 'cherry-petal exoticism' which characterised Victorian perspectives on the Island Empire is less certain. Some scholars believe that the earlier attitudes changed 'fairly dramatically' after about 1900, while others share the view of Edwin O. Reischauer, who wrote: 'The Japanese were maddened before the war [of 1941–45] by our refusal to take them very seriously, because our obliviousness to the Japanese threat implied a certain degree of contempt.'[1] Proceeding from a consideration of what 'seriousness' may mean in this context, this chapter reviews some Western novels and shorter fictions about Japan to see whether these literary portrayals of things Japanese do, in fact, amount to taking the country seriously.[2]

To achieve seriousness in the realm of imaginative writing, one may argue, is to produce work which eschews stereotypes and condescension, which prefers characterisation to plot development, and which aspires to pass beyond descriptive accuracy (hardly unimportant in itself) in pursuit of what might be called 'moral accuracy' – a sensitive and careful portrayal of the strivings of complex individual natures in a context created by social forces having both historical and psychological verisimilitude. To be called a 'serious' writer in this sense is to be highly praised. It is not something that would readily be said, for instance, of the authors of such popular works as *Stopover Tokyo*, *The Bridge Over the River Kwai*, *Sayonara*, *The Teahouse of the August Moon*, *You Only Live Twice*, *Shōgun* and *Shibumi*.[3] Whether it deserves to be said of the books and authors about to be discussed remains to be decided.

Like most novelists in most times and places, the half-dozen writers being considered here – 'John Paris' (Frank T.A. Ashton-Gwatkin), William Plomer, Pearl Buck, 'Robert Standish' (Digby Gerahty), Oswald Wynd ('Gavin Black') and Laurens Jan van der Post wrote out of their own experience, bending it to their individual purposes, which were various, and augmenting it in at least two cases with wide or selective reading.[4] All of them spent an appreciable amount of time among the Japanese, mostly on a voluntary basis, though two of them (Wynd and van der Post) were prisoners for much of the Second World War. With the exception of Ashton-Gwatkin, every one of whose published novels dealt with Japan-inspired subjects, all of them wrote other books in which the Japanese figured marginally or not at all. Chronologically arranged, their experience of Japan ran from Ashton-Gwatkin's arrival in 1913 as a junior consular official to Pearl Buck's visits as an acclaimed writer and humanitarian after the Second World War. None of these observers, therefore, needed to invent impressions in order to achieve plausibility, though all of them, by virtue of their foreignness, inevitably made the acquaintance of mainly those features of Japanese public and private life which were readily accessible to visitors, in general, and to specialists in diplomacy or the literary arts, in particular.

The foremost consequence of this is that whatever preoccupations they brought with them, these writers acquired very little direct experience of certain aspects of contemporary Japanese life which, on a long view, turned out to be extremely important and which might, perhaps, have been better appreciated outside Japan if these novelists themselves had been better placed to gauge their significance and implications. The reference here is to the military, industrial and political strands of the Japanese social fabric, particularly in their higher reaches – a tightly interwoven region into which Western writers had virtually no entrée.[5] The absence of intellectually and psychologically compelling literary portrayals of intention and capacity in these dynamic and ambitious socio-economic sectors, while easily explicable in terms of the novelists' limited exposure to them, may well have handicapped Western leaders in general in formulating their responses to Japanese policy in the run-up to Pearl Harbor – the negatively charged equivalent to the kind of superficial rendering of the Japanese by 'Pierre Loti' which is alleged to have built Russian over-confidence before Port Arthur.[6] However that may be, it is hardly a proof of 'unseriousness' on the part of these novelists that, by remaining largely faithful to their own experience, they did not, in the main, give desirable dramatic and moral weight to those forces in Japan which were dedicated to changing the main contours of Asian politics, if necessary by resort to war.

The dozen or so 'Japanese' novels produced by these writers displayed several widely shared characteristics and preoccupations which might well be summarised before turning to individual works. It is, first of all, worth noting that none of these writers ever tried to describe an exclusively Japanese experience altogether from the 'inside' – a telling reflection of their acceptance of the ultimate limitations of their angle of vision. Without exception they approached the 'Japaneseness' of things by counterposing Japanese characters to non-Japanese ones – usually Westerners, but also Chinese in the case of Pearl Buck's *The Patriot*. Thus, they created situations in which unfamiliar (to Western readers) social institutions and behaviours required explanation, which came either in the form of authorial asides (as happened regularly in Ashton-Gwatkin's books) or of exchanges between the characters themselves. However it was managed internally, all of these novels contained varying amounts of descriptive prose, the principal focuses of which were religious beliefs and practices, family structures and authority, sexual customs, marriage and prostitution, educational values and practices, and, invariably, suicide. Much of this material, so far as one may judge, meets very high standards of accuracy (including value neutrality) as those might be applied by a cultural anthropologist or ethnographer. Whether this same level of accuracy was reached when it came to fathoming and describing Japanese feelings and motives, not to speak of characterising the society as a whole, is a more complicated and important question. At this point it is sufficient to say that any lingering traces of 'cherry-petal exoticism' present in Ashton-Gwatkin and Plomer evaporated in the heat of the Far Eastern crisis, so that the novels of Buck, 'Standish', Wynd and van der Post delivered undeniably stern judgements on the Japanese people and the deliberate, perverse choices of their national policy; judgements that will raise yet again the question of the West's capacity to interpret the East in other than racial and stereotypical terms.

As Frank Ashton-Gwatkin, the Balliol-educated son of an Anglican cleric, 'John Paris' enjoyed a successful career in diplomacy, beginning in 1913 with a six-year posting to Japan. From this experience he drew material for five works of light fiction, the last of which was published in the early 1930s. By his own admission, 'John Paris' should be remembered as 'an impermanent member of the exotic school of novelists', a writer whose early work was 'rather too Lafcadio Hearn, perhaps', in its affinities for the 'succulent school of description' deriving originally from *Madame Chrysanthème*. Again, by his own admission, the passage of time dimmed his memories, so the books that most exactly captured his perspective on Japan were those published in the early 1920s – *Kimono* (1921), *Sayonara* (1924) and *Banzai!* (1925), all collected for reissue in 1927 under the title *Japan Revealed*.[7] By the time *Matsu* appeared in 1932, Ashton-Gwatkin had long since left the Far Eastern section of the Foreign Office and was deeply immersed in the economic and political fall-out from the Great Depression. Also by then the struggle within Japan, which pitted the liberal, democratic forces embodied in the trade unions, the intellectuals and the commercial classes against the nationalistic, authoritarian forces embodied in the *zaibatsu*, the army and the bureaucracy, had been decided in the latter's favour, with all the consequences that victory implied for the future of the West in Asia. As a former supporter of the Anglo–Japanese Alliance on the optimistic calculation that the liberalising forces would prevail, Ashton-Gwatkin was predictably disappointed by this ominous turn of events.

Whatever else may be said about Ashton-Gwatkin's novels, they abound with accurately realised descriptions of Japanese cultural traditions and social behaviour – indeed, they deserve to be read on this count alone. Yet, while the tone is invariably genial and 'enlightened' by contemporaneous Western standards, the governing perspective itself could hardly be called uncritical. On the eternally fascinating subject of the treatment of women, for example, Ashton-Gwatkin wrote at length in both *Kimono* and *Sayonara*, and in ways which aroused official Japanese ire. Protesting that the accounts of regulated prostitution in *Kimono* were 'anti-Japanese' because they portrayed this long-standing social practice ' in an unfavourable light', the government tried to ban the book – with a predictably stimulating effect on sales. It then pursued the matter to the point of persuading the author to promise not to sell the movie rights, and it subsequently spoilt his chances of appointment to the legation at Peking on the grounds that his novels 'had given much offence to the Japanese'.[8] On the face of it, at least, one may conclude that 'John Paris' did, indeed, take the Japanese seriously, though not always in ways that flattered their rather brittle self-esteem at the time.

While the eye of 'John Paris' ranged widely over the Japanese cultural landscape, it would be fair to say that the subject which most consistently caught his attention was sexual relationships, especially cross-cultural (or racial) ones. All of his storylines twine around miscegenation and its implications. It would not be too great a simplification to say that, for this novelist, inter-racial marriage figured as a microcosmic, fictional representation of the possibility of an authentic partnership, a genuine merging of values and affections, between two great island peoples. In each of the novels such a union occurred, but only in the first did it survive, barely, the great shocks of cultural discovery that regularly caught their victims unprepared. In every case, moreover, the intending couple moved through a cloud of conventional wisdom on the subject of mixed marriages, almost all of it pejorative. In *Kimono*, for instance, a British diplomat put the point this way: 'Keep the breed pure, be it white, black or yellow. Bastard races cannot flourish. They are waste of Nature'. To judge from the survival of just such a marriage in this story, 'John Paris' was not personally averse to them, but any optimism he may have felt about them quickly died away, perhaps partly in response to the rising strain in Anglo–Japanese relations following the non-renewal of the Alliance in 1922. In *Sayonara*, when the earnest young English missionary proposed to marry a *joro*-girl in order to save her from the brothel, his sister expostulated, 'I don't think you've any right to make such drastic experiments with the breed'; and his bishop, quoting Kipling at him, warned against half-castes, who are invariably 'feckless, futile and pathetic'. By this time the writer knew how to show that many Japanese also opposed such matrimonial experiments, and he contrived to have this one end in a ritual double-suicide (involving not the English husband, but the wife and her Japanese lover). In the last of his novels, *Matsu*, the match was between a glittering young English debutante and an Oxford-educated Japanese religious leader, who was also a 'living Buddha'. After only a short stay in her new husband's country the disenchanted bride abandoned the marriage, concluding that although the Japanese people 'aren't very different from us, *the life* is'. If by 'the life' was meant the whole cultural matrix that gives shape and direction to human activity, then the narrative outcome may be read as a pessimistic judgement of the possibility that East and West would soon find a way to get onto the destiny-merging terms symbolised by a successful marriage.

Sized up in the most general terms, Ashton-Gwatkin's fiction exuded something of the sophisticated, ironically flavoured and heavily romanticised ennui that characterised an important current of British imaginative literature in the 1920s. The modern, secular insistence on the relativism of ethical systems and social conventions had an essentially approving presentation in his novels, where the point was repeatedly, and often cleverly, made that Western religious beliefs and practices frequently, and quite understandably, looked unintelligible or hypocritical to Japanese eyes. And yet, for all his apparent commitment to a position of tolerant detachment on

[199]

H

such cultural issues, even to the point of preferring Japanese ways to Western ones in some cases, it has to be acknowledged that Ashton-Gwatkin's relativism with respect to values was incomplete. Beneath his playful chivvying of the British for their own foibles and short-comings, the position remained that the Western perspective on the real world of cause and effect, with its logical and experimental ways of reasoning, amounted to something different in kind from other, non-Western ways of comprehending and dealing with the realms of nature and culture. Organically conjoined here to certain political-*cum*-spiritual values, of which individual freedom protected by law was the foremost, this Western cast of mind constituted a kind of 'absolute'. Some portions of it might be appropriated by others, most conspicuously the Japanese. But the master question was whether any non-Western people could internalise the whole system of ideation, value and practice, and then naturalise it, so to speak, in a cultural milieu which continued to be fundamentally unlike its origins.

In short, Ashton-Gwatkin's answer was 'not really'. Although he freely credited the Japanese with very great proficiencies and awesome powers of adaptation (theirs was 'the least Oriental of Asiatic lands'), he never really abandoned the notion that the Japanese, in general, were rent by a racially specific tension between their intellects and their souls. Of the young heroine in *Kimono*, for example, he wrote that her eyes were those of an Oriental girl, 'a creature closer to the animals than we are, lit by instinct more often than by reason, and hiding a soul in its infancy, a repressed, timorous uncertain thing, spasmodically violent and habitually secretive and aloof'. And of the Japanese people more generally (speaking here through the persona of a British diplomat), that they were 'extraordinarily quick . . . the most adaptable people since the ancient Greeks, whom they resemble in some ways. But they are more superficial. The intellect races on ahead, but the heart lingers in the Dark Ages.' As a result, Japan remained for him 'the Land of Inverted Thought'.

But unlike so many of the putatively passive societies of Hither Asia, whose golden age of achievement lay buried in the past, Japan was unmistakably growing in power; it was already 'the Britain (or 'the Prussia') of the Pacific'; even, in some formulations, 'the nation of the future'. Given Ashton-Gwatkin's academic background and professional training, therefore, it is particularly unfortunate that he focused his literary effort on aspects of Japanese national life which, while undeniably fascinating, afforded very little insight into the modernising forces which were transforming the country's political agenda. Despite obvious efforts to realise individual characters in fiction, he never really got much beyond giving the reader a gallery of types – the Westernising student, the *joro*-girl, (prostitute) the religious leader, the *ronin* (masterless man). Instead, in his final novel, 'John Paris' expressed a kind of defeated puzzlement: the Japanese were 'correct, orderly, efficient, but somehow ambiguous. These people, who were like us and yet not like us, one did not know how to take them.'[9]

The only other British writer to give anything like so much attention to Japan between the world wars was William Plomer. Born in the Transvaal of English parents, Plomer made an early start on a literary career which ultimately brought him critical acclaim and a permanent home in the UK. For most of his adult life he enjoyed the friendship of another migratory native of the Transvaal, Laurens Jan van der Post, of whom something will be said later. If Earl Miner is correct in saying that 'no great novel has been written on Japan', nothing certainly of the stature of *A Passage to India*, he is also correct when he adds that 'the example of Plomer proves that it is now possible to treat Japan as a fictional subject apart from the intolerable exoticism or condescension which for so many decades has prevented any mature treatment of Japan in our literature'.[10]

Plomer's Japanese *oeuvre* consists of two books, a collection of stories published in 1929 – *Paper Houses* – and the novel *Sado*, published two years later at the Hogarth Press. Both works drew heavily on his personal experience among the Japanese, acquired during a protracted visit in the late 1920s, when he supported himself by teaching English and literature. Although he shared this occupational history with Lafcadio Hearn, in every other respect Plomer wanted to dissociate himself from his famous American precursor, whose 'indiscriminate japanegyrics' did little justice to their proper subject and much injustice to the race he did not leave behind when he donned the kimono. Of his own work Plomer said that it aimed to avoid being either 'romantic' or 'realistic', or, for that matter, offering a 'complete' or a 'bird's-eye' view:

> it is no more than a search for an honest approach to a very few aspects of the Japanese character, in which are involved so many complications and contradictions; an extraordinary cerebral agility mingles with a fatal apathy of spirit, a puritanic strain with a dionysiac; human faults abound; but honesty, gentleness, truth, culture and style, courage, loyalty, ambition and even – I dare hope – originality survive and reappear, everywhere and always, through all the unallayable turmoil, until achievement flowers from setbacks.

How did he do with this 'modest' assignment?

The timing of Plomer's visit to Japan enabled him to observe the final stages of the ongoing struggle of the liberal, democratic forces to avoid repression by the nationalistic, authoritarian forces then obviously on the rise. Affirming his capacity to respect and love Japanese as individuals, he went on to say:

> But I disbelieve in their enslavement of women, and I detest their tendency to nationalistic paranoia and their particular politico-religious superstitions, which I believe to be more insidious and locally almighty than those of nearly all countries, Russia and Italy included, and which, if persisted in, will have terrible results; some predict a revolution; some hope for one.

In the stories 'A Brutal Sentimentalist' and 'Mother Kamchatka' he redeemed the implied promise of these passages by providing a remarkably acute rendering of a mature Japanese personality from within; and by subjecting many features of Japanese public life, including Emperor-worship, *bushido*, resolute self-deception and the ruthless suppression of 'dangerous thoughts' to a satirical scorching of Swiftian quality.[11] In this admixture of respectful sensitivity and discriminating criticism at least the shadow of seriousness may be found.

The novel *Sado* and the story 'A Brutal Sentimentalist' resemble E. M. Forster's masterpiece, *A Passage to India*, in having as their focal point the question of whether the East and the West can ever achieve the friendship of equals. Assuming that an approximate parity of self-esteem was the indispensable foundation of true friendship, Plomer first addressed the feelings of inferiority then often ascribed to the Japanese. In his view a sense of inferiority was not necessarily a source of self-defeating behaviour, for the conviction that things could be improved might in fact spur 'the whole vast effort of human betterment'. In other words, he would not hold against the Japanese their earnest strivings to catch up. Instead, taking a spacious, philosophical view of things, he believed that 'there is a kind of natural balance between East and West', a complementarity of skill and temperament which, in the Japanese people themselves, engaged a second, corresponding dualism that often took the form of personalities divided asymmetrically between 'activist' and 'quietist' traits. Whether these are circumstances out of which fully self-respecting friendships could be made across cultural and racial lines – whether a relationship between 'unlikes' could become one of true equality – was the preoccupying psychological and moral issue in the texts.

Plomer never provided an unambiguous answer to his master question, but it is a mark of his honesty and his artistry that he left the matter unforgettably posed and searchingly examined. In 'A Brutal Sentimentalist' the Japanese protagonist (Tonoki) came to trust and respect his English friend (Wilmington) because of the latter's indomitable intellectual honesty: 'he had definite opinions, was without fear, could speak his mind straightly, was singularly free from prejudice, seldom frivolous, and never, even when silent, never dull'. While Tonoki liked to believe that '[i]t is a great gift of the Japanese people that they can assimilate foreign civilisations without their real character changing', his greatest satisfaction came when he candidly acknowledged the sentimental and brutal strains in his character and was told by Wilmington:

> My true thoughts are that you're quite all right. You've always done your duty, and you'll keep on doing it. . . . You've been able to hesitate, to doubt, to question yourself. I have always felt that you were not introspective enough, but now I see that we may make a good European of you yet. I tell you, for the fact that you don't take everything for granted, I really admire you.

Through the cloud of condescension it is easy to see that, in Plomer's view, if there was to be a genuine meeting of East and West it must occur on ground prepared by the self-critical, astringent scepticism of the modern European intellectual tradition.

The same motif, extended and embroidered, reappears in *Sado*, a luminous portrayal of a relationship, gently undercast by the theme of homosexuality, between a young English artist (Lucas) and a Japanese student (Sado). With a deftness of touch that led one critic to write of 'Bloomsbury in Japan', Plomer described the ripening of this acquaintanceship to the point of intimacy, all the while making it clear that Sado, precariously poised 'between the lotus and the dynamo', had more at stake than Lucas in terms of self-esteem – that he lacked the kind of authority over himself which the Englishman, however beset by the social and intellectual rip-tides of the age, still knew how to assert. Indeed, Lucas's aim was to bring Sado 'to stand squarely on his own feet', an especially daunting task because Sado believed himself to be 'too different' ever to get equal treatment from Lucas, and that Lucas, 'while fond of him, *in his inmost heart despised him*'. Although Lucas failed in his larger purpose, and greatly offended Sado by carelessly omitting to honour a social commitment, the two re-founded their friendship on the understanding 'that one was too confident and the other too little confident in himself', and Lucas sailed for home respecting that 'certain calmness of spirit' which Sado had latterly found at the centre of his own being.

The dextrous treatment of the subject of self-esteem distinguishes

Plomer's work but does not exhaust its interest. For he also knew how to express trenchant and provocative general views on the subject of East and West, encompassing formal religion, artistic taste and sexuality. While no paraphrase can do them justice, it may be said that these views developed very powerfully the ideas of inextinguishable difference as between Lucas and Sado ('each bore the incubus of a hemisphere, a saddle not to be bucked off by the wiriest soul'), and natural complementarity as between Europe and Asia. Approaching the latter point through art:

> [Lucas] saw Western painting, then, mainly as power and freedom continually tempered and controlled by feminine influences, Mariolatry, domesticity, love; and Eastern painting as an expression of feminine conventionality and good taste. But now that the East had begun to imitate the West it had lost its elegance and tried to acquire power instead, just as some women today, becoming masculine, have lost grace; while the virtues of contemporary Western culture are largely feminine. Was it, he wondered, solely due to his imagination that in this age not only the sexes, but West and East, sometimes appeared to be gradually changing places?

Although 'the present chaos of transition in East and West' left thoughtful people in both hemispheres adrift, in Plomer's view the only course for Lucas and Sado alike was one of 'trying to base every thought and action on a sound understanding of what is constant and necessary to human nature – a proper balance between heart and head, the need for religion and idleness [the East?] as well as for work and science [the West?], and the recognition that it must always take all sorts to make a world'. No one who reads these books would have an easy excuse for stereotypical thinking about the people of Japan or their relations with other countries.

While both 'John Paris' and William Plomer drew attention to the highly unstable combination of repression and ambition which characterised Japanese public and private life, it took the violent application of Japanese power, first in Manchuria, then in North China itself, to induce Western novelists to 'take Japan seriously' in the sense of attempting imaginative explorations of the roots and implications of Japanese aggression. The results, judged as literature, were neither especially happy nor memorable in the main, but they deserve some consideration here because of the obvious relation they bear to the general theme of the chapter.

When she published *The Patriot* in 1939, Pearl Buck was perhaps at the summit of her popularity, having won the Nobel Prize for Literature the previous year on the strength of her fictional portrayals of Chinese society caught up in the winds of revolutionary change.

While her deeply humanitarian interests were broad enough to take in all of Asia (at least), the prime focus of her literary effort was the Chinese people, with whose sufferings and aspirations she identified herself very closely indeed. Of Japan she knew, and wrote, comparatively much less, but on two occasions she did attempt fairly extensive treatments of Japanese subject matter, once before the attack on Pearl Harbor in *The Patriot*; the other in the early 1950s, in *The Hidden Flower*.[12]

Nothing, one may suppose, would have come more naturally to a writer already committed to the cause of Chinese nationalism than a keen interest in the 'China Incident' and the unfolding of Japan's role on the Asian mainland. In *The Patriot*, written not long after the 'Rape of Nanking', Pearl Buck gave an account of the psychological background to both Japanese aggression and Chinese resistance. The story, which followed a well-born Chinese student revolutionary (I-wan) for more than a decade (from 1926 to 1938), included a lengthy exploration of the customs and mentalities of the Japanese middle-class family (the Murakis) with whom I-wan lived during his years of exile – the result of his association with Chinese communists at the time of Chiang Kai-shek's coup. On balance, the depiction of Japanese family relations – the disciplined affection, the love of order, the unfailing courtesy, the zest for work, the particularly intense struggle between the 'traditionalists' and the 'moderns', over marriage policy, for example – showed sensitivity, and the fact that I-wan willingly married Tama, the daughter of his host, supports the view that Buck had no objections on principle to such unions even across what she called 'the infinite difference of race[!]'. What is more, she acknowledged the authentic variety of Japanese personality structures when she explained how one son of the household (Akio) could choose suicide rather than re-enter the army to fight an unethical war in China. A few jarring words about the 'simian physiognomy' of the Japanese apart, the book also gave respectful treatment to the capacity of ordinary people to take disaster (whether in the form of earthquake damage or the return of the ashes of the war dead) with silent dignity, and their continued personal friendliness to I-wan even after China became 'the national enemy'.

In her portrait of the younger son (Bunji) of the Muraki family, Buck made her most deliberate effort to show what was wrong with Japan. An amiable, hard-working and not especially imaginative young man, Bunji had internalised the insistently presented official teachings about duty to the state and emperor, along with the geo-political perspective that featured Japan as an embattled, have-not nation which must contemplate war against one or more of the larger nations if it were to survive. Sent off to China after the shooting began, Bunji returned much coarsened by his experience there, which included murder and rape, induced when his commanding officer, whose conduct he strictly emulated in the hierarchical fashion of the Japanese, had himself begun to brutalise Chinese women. Though the episode caused Bunji much mental anguish and led him to heavy drinking, his deeply imprinted sense of duty and attachment to the national mission were proving stronger than any promptings of conscience or recognition of the higher claims of common humanity. As with Bunji individually, then, so with Japan as a nation – a conclusion neither original nor profound, perhaps, but one which did, at least,identify and indict some of the cultural preconditions,some deliberately fostered emphases of national life, which distorted reality in ways that made an expanding war a strong possibility, never mind the odds.

No novel about a 'national enemy' written in the midst of a twentieth-century war is likely to take broad, balanced views of its subject – a point amply confirmed by *The Three Bamboos*, published in July 1942 by 'Robert Standish'. Dedicating his book to the women of Japan, 'to the gentle, self-effacing and long-suffering mothers of the cruellest, most arrogant and treacherous sons who walk this earth', the author avowed in the preface that he did not really understand the Japanese, even though he had lived amongst them on three occasions between 1920 and 1930. Intending none-the-less to portray them accurately, he warned against assuming

> that the Japanese are entirely vile, for nothing entirely vile could have survived, untouched by other influences for several thousand years [sic]. No creature that is brave is wholly bad! Common fairness, furthermore, demands that one admits that much of the vileness of modern Japan is of western origin. That the Japanese seized it avidly is also beyond dispute.

Having thus established his perspective, 'Standish' proceeded to tell the Buddenbrooks-like story of a samurai family (the Furenos) which emerged from obscurity in the later nineteenth century and helped to direct Japan's drive for hegemony in east Asia, – a gamble, perhaps the greatest in history, 'planned with the utmost deliberation over fifty years ago'.

Here, at last, was a book which purported to examine the inner workings of the economic-*cum*-military power structure which controlled the shaping of Japanese policy in the expansionist era. The greater the misfortune, therefore, that it should have borne all the marks of moralising didacticism which, while permitting the transmission of much accurate information, fatally corrupted the springs of imagination. As a result 'Standish' produced a story which illuminated the history of the sub-class, the lesser samurai, that did most to modernise the country after 1857, but he did not achieve any portraiture having weight, depth or refinement, nor did he disclose any human dilemma having much grip or edge. The reader comes away, therefore, with a sense of having perused an outline history of the modernisation of Japan as recapitulated in the experiences of a roughly typical entrepreneurial family whose matrimonial adventures gave the author a welcome occasion to write approvingly about the women involved, the men belonging mostly to the category singled out for scornful comment in his preface. While he had the creditable aim of making Japanese dynamism intelligible, 'Standish' pursued it by manipulating obvious character types, and thus created a work which succeeded neither as history nor as art.

Although this novel underscores the point that novelists who stray from their personal experience are likely to produce bad books, *Three Bamboos* did give a circumstantial account of some of the anger and resentment that fueled the Japanese drive for domination, even as it was holding up to ridicule the Japanese pretension to be the 'People of the Gods'. Simply stated, the argument of the narrative was that the Western nations, the English foremost among them, had inconsiderately and greedily wounded the pride of the Japanese while simultaneously acquainting them with the techniques of self-strengthening. In the event, the leaders of the modernisation movement (like the Furenos) chose to make wealth and power their lodestar, thus betraying their more restrained and estimable samurai tradition and setting their feet on the fateful path of conquest. Although some members of each generation clung to the honourable ways of their ancestors, the unscrupulous power generated by the new wealth moved inexorably towards expansion, adroitly managing the symbols of national unity and greatness in the process. Along with intensified emperor worship came the worked-up code of *bushido* ('a fantastic travesty of samurai ethics') and the control of national politics through assassination societies and a venal press. 'Standish' brought his tale to an improbable end by having the youngest of the male Furenos rediscover samurai virtues and follow them to a watery death in the attack on Pearl Harbor. The net effect is morally confusing, for the author appears to conclude that the Japanese erred by not cleaving to their ancient and honourable traditions, when that is precisely what the instrusive, insolent West would not allow them to do. He was on solider ground, perhaps, when he suggested that the Japanese (like most of the rest of us) have rarely known how, culturally or politically, to keep acquisitive instincts under control. However inept he was at individuating Japanese in his novel, he most assuredly understood that Japan was a paramount force in East Asian politics, one whose psychology and history suggested that it would not steer a middle course between mastery and ruin. In the short run he was right, and the Japanese experienced both.

Of the novels about Japan published after 1945, two may serve to frame a discussion of Japanese behaviour as it could be observed (or imagined) by prisoners of war during the great final climacteric of Japan's bid for regional domination. The first of them, *Black Fountains*, won a literary prize for Oswald Wynd when it was published (1947) and launched him on a career divided between serious fiction and the production, under the name 'Gavin Black', of mystery/adventure stories often set in exotic places. The son of Scottish missionaries to Japan, Wynd made of *Black Fountains* a kind of *roman à thèse* no less acerbic and rancorous than *Three Bamboos*. Although willing to acknowledge the existence in Japan of 'a small nucleus of people who were capable of maintaining their concepts of human dignity and justice and who bore these convictions openly to the very threshold of death', he took a generally pessimistic view of the prospects of democracy in Japan and wanted the victorious Allies to be especially alert to politico-cultural movements that might, under such rubrics as 'Resistance in Peace', aim at refashioning Japanese hegemony in East Asia by (unspecified) non-military means.

To flesh out this perspective Wynd constructed the story of a Japanese-born, American-educated young woman (Omi Tetsukoshi) who returned home in 1938 to find her country in the midst of a radical renunciation of Western ways and values. Over the next seven years she struggled to align her hybridised cultural background to the increasingly disagreeable facts of national life in wartime. Beginning as a spirited defender of things Japanese, on the grounds that history had proved that her people must be either 'warriors or slaves', she finally reached the painful realisation that her country's policy was really founded on irrational fear, a desperate craving to avoid self-scrutiny and the need for change:

> 'Dangerous thoughts!' That phrase sums up a national philosophy. There has never before been such a race of men who loved tradition so much because they are so afraid. For a thousand years our houses have remained the same, our clothes, our manners. Everything. The modern buildings and tramcars are only a surface movement.They're a necessary evil. We acquiesce to Western developments to this extent only because we must do so to preserve the stability which is our real belief. Even our religion is a worship

of form. It has no imperative of morality, only the morality necessary to retain the terrible stability.

Choosing to give her support to the liberal Countess Kamaibashi, whose 'dangerous thought' was birth control, Omi found herself stigmatised as a 'political unreliable' and rusticated to a mountainside retreat near Kobe. There, protected by the wealthy, doting father with whom she had already had many a contretemps over an arranged marriage, Omi wrote an outline history of her country as part of a deliberate search for self-understanding.

Like Plomer's Japanese protagonists, Omi established a kind of peace with herself only after reaching a level of self-critical awareness that enabled her to see the record she had been creating for what it actually was. Out of the spectacular, improbable victory over Russia had come 'a feeling of confidence in arms which has been maintained to the present day . . .a philosophy of invincibility. . . the superman myth in Oriental form'. 'Only a Japanese [she continued] can ever really understand how we combined the most effective and quite ruthless cynicism with this new mysticism [*bushido*].' Adding that the Japanese 'will never change with victory', she declared herself

> oppressed by the meaning of what she admitted to herself. It meant for one thing that war as a form of national expression was an essential to the Japan that had come into being and not merely the kind of war that was going on in China but the acceptance of greater challenges to the code, to the national faith. It meant that war would be sought to prove the supernatural power of the soldier creed.

Then came the epiphany:

> She smiled to herself.
> It also means that most of what I have been writing has been sheer nonsense! I started out to show how my country had been forced to resist the pressure of the white man in order to survive. That's part true. But unfortunately a lot more is true. In addition to having made ourselves a first-rate military power we've come to worship ourselves, or the projection of ourselves in this myth of national destiny. And I've been writing often as a Japanese when I wasn't even aware of it.

Finally disenthralled, Omi committed a self-redeeming act of rational courage by betraying the 'Resistance in Peace' movement to the American occupation forces.

Captured by the Japanese while leading a guerrilla movement against them in Java, Lieutenant-Colonel Laurens Jan van der Post spent the final two-and-a-half years of the Pacific War as prisoner in harrowing

[209]

circumstances. As a younger man he had visited Japan with his countryman, William Plomer, and, like Plomer, he had subsequently combined a literary career with a settled life in England. Now he was to
experience firsthand some of the brutality which, while present in
his friend's books, had until then been kept in check by other elements in the Japanese cultural make-up. In particular, he was tried,
tortured, sentenced to death and forced to witness the execution of
many of his subordinates. A decade later he gave a portrayal of a
Japanese military mentality in a novella whose penetrating power
and stylistic elegance were inversely proportional to its short length.

A Bar of Shadow recounted an odyssey of understanding which
began in the Japanese prison camp where the protagonist's life hung
on Serjeant 'Rottang' Hara's whim and ended several years later in
the executioner's cell where Hara awaited the hanging to which he
had been sentenced by the War Crimes Tribunal.[13] The amazing
vivacity of the observation both of people and settings argues strongly for the presentation here of virtually unretouched personal experience. In the hardest way imaginable – in a relationship which
exposed him to casual beatings, torture, death-threats and countless
lesser manifestations of cultural contempt – the narrator, John
Lawrence (Laurens Jan), had fathomed the racial and psychological
springs of Hara's behaviour. Their roles reversed in 1945 by the
Allied victory, Lawrence sought a way to help Hara accept the tribunal's verdict, which struck the Japanese as being unjust in view of
the nature of the war and the actual unpunished misdeeds of others.
In Hara's last hours Lawrence told him:

> 'You can try to think only with all your heart, Hara-san, that unfair and
> unjust as this thing which my people are doing seems to you, that it is done
> only to try and stop the kind of things that happened to us in the war from
> ever happening again. You can say to yourself as I used to say to my
> despairing men in prison under you, "There is a way of winning by losing,
> a way of victory in defeat which we are going to discover." Perhaps that too
> must be your way to understanding and victory now.'

Hara's reply closed the link of comprehension: 'That, Rórensu-san',
he said, with the quick intake of breath of a Japanese when truly
moved, 'is a very Japanese thought'.

The passages in the wartime and post-war novels which explored the
psycho-cultural pathology of Japanese aggression read somewhat
strangely now,. 'Standish' wrote in terms of the fateful corruption of
some estimable Japanese 'original' by a combination of malign
Western influence and Japanese moral failure. Buck and Wynd, the
latter very forcefully, took the position that the core cultural values

in Japan were themselves fatally flawed, and that Western intervention only exacerbated an already unhealthy condition by setting up new and terrible tensions between the attractions of continuity and the imperatives of modernisation. With a greater taste than the others for metaphor, van der Post delivered some stunning comments on what was a central concern for all these writers, the relentlessly 'dis-individuating' power of Japanese cultural tradition. Thus, a man like Serjeant Hara 'was an embodiment of myth more than a conscious human being', and his countrymen 'were all still deeply submerged like animals, insects and plants . . . subject to cosmic forces beyond their control to an extent undreamed of in the European mind and philosophy'. John Lawrence

> had always felt even when he was in Japan that the Japanese were a people in a profound, inverse, reverse, or if I preferred it, even perverse sense, more in love with death than living. As a nation they romanticised death and self-destruction as no other people. The romantic fulfilment of the national ideal, of the heroic thug of tradition, was often a noble and stylised self-destruction in a selfless cause.

Entrapped in this mythology, the Japanese forsook their claims to individuality at birth. Instead 'they were socially not unlike a more complex extension of the great insect societies in life . . . a sort of super-society of bees with the Emperor as a male queen-bee at the centre'. Warming to his theme, Lawrence next spoke of:

> how strangely, almost cosmically, propelled, like an eccentric and dying comet on an archaic, anti-clockwise and foredoomed course, Hara's people had been. They were so committed, blindly and mindlessly entangled in their real and imaginary past that their view of life was not synchronized to our urgent time. Above all they could not respond to the desperate twentieth-century call for more precise individual differentiation. Their view of life refused to be individual and to rise above their own quaking and volcanic earth, as if there was always a dark glass or the shadow of the great dragon's wings of their own submerged selves between them and the light of the individual mind, a long blackness of their own spinning globe between them and the sun, darkening the moon for which they yearned so eagerly, and some of the finest stars. He was sorry if it sounded fantastic but he could put it no other way.

It is not the least of the ironies present in this literature that van der Post's comprehensive collective indictment of the Japanese, while working to excuse Serjeant Hara for any Western-style personal responsibility for his deeds, should appear in a work that succeeds remarkably in delineating an individual Japanese character, thus satisfying one major criterion for 'taking Japan seriously'.

[211]

While it would be foolish to deny the presence of much bias, arrogance and condescension in this English-language fiction about the Japanese during the first half of the twentieth century, it would be almost equally foolish to dismiss these works too summarily on the grounds that their provenance disqualifies them from making truthful and relevant observations about Japanese society, sometimes in a spirit of disinterested, even affectionate, tolerance. The fact that the most thoughtful of these writers saw fit to stress the great desirability of inter-cultural friendship, on the basis of something like parity of self-esteem, does credit to their understanding of the real seriousness of the underlying issues, even though they often wrote as though the only obstacles to this outcome were problems endemic to Japanese culture. Whether the reshaping of Japanese national life after 1945, the attainment by Japan of at least parity with the leading Western industrial powers, and the virtually complete disappearance of the old imperia in Asia have made it possible to 'take Japan seriously' in new and more satisfying ways, in literature as well as in politics and economics, must become the subject of another occasion.

Notes

1 E. O. Reischauer, *The United States and Japan*, Cambridge, Mass., 1950, p. 17. For the contrary view, see J. P. Lehmann, *The Image of Japan: From Feudal Isolation to World Power, 1850 – 1905*, London, 1978, p. 49; and E. Miner, *The Japanese Tradition in British and American Literature*, Princeton, 1958.

2 The approach taken here is to treat the question as one which is answerable in principle by appeals to evidence. Thus, I make no attempt to grapple with the large theoretical issues raised by E. W. Said in *Orientalism*, New York, 1978, where it is strongly argued that the hegemonic power exercised by Western societies over non-Western societies, by its very existence, has foreclosed the possibility of treating the latter as authentic, discrete elements of a common humanity.

3 J. P. Marquand, *Stopover Tokyo*, Boston, 1957; P.Boulle, *The Bridge Over the River Kwai*, translated by X.Fielding, New York, 1954; J. Michener, *Sayonara*, London, 1954; V. J. Sneider, *The Teahouse of the August Moon*, New York, 1954; I. Fleming, *You Only Live Twice*, London, 1964; J. Clavell, *Shōgun: A Novel of Japan*, New York, 1977; and Trevanian, *Shibumi*, New York, 1979. Without intending to be lightly dismissive of these fictions, which are sometimes written with skill and verve, the position taken here is that these plot-centred entertainments often show, at best, a secondary interest in Japanese motivations and values. That they have done much to create and/or reinforce the images (often stereotypical or downright fantastic) of Japan and the Japanese held by their readers is no doubt true and constitutes a suitable subject for another essay.

4 'John Paris' wrote *Kimono*, London, 1921; *Sayonara*, London, 1924; *Banzai!*, London, 1925; *The Island Beyond Japan*, London, 1929; and *Matsu*, London,

1932. For his reaction on learning of the publication of James Michener's novel called *Sayonara*, see F. T. A. Ashton-Gwatkin, 'The life and times of John Paris', *Bulletin of the Japan Society of London*, 51, 1967., 11–16, where much may also be learned abut the novelist's intellectual background. William Plomer wrote *Paper Houses*, New York, 1929, and *Sado*, London, 1931. Pearl Buck wrote *The Patriot*, New York, 1939, and *The Hidden Flower*, New York, 1952. 'Robert Standish' wrote *The Three Bamboos*, London, 1942. Oswald Wynd wrote *Black Fountains*, New York, 1947. Laurens Jan van der Post wrote *A Bar of Shadow*, New York, 1956.

5 See, for instance, W. Plomer, *Double Lives: An Autobiography*, New York, n.d., p. 246 for a frank acknowledgement of this limitation. The implications these limitations had for policy may be studied in C. Thorne, *Allies of a Kind: The United States, Great Britain and the War Against Japan, 1941–1945*, Oxford, 1978, pp. 3–10 and *passim*; and W. R. Louis, *British Strategy in the Far East, 1919–1939*, Oxford, 1971, pp. 1–2, 10, 12, 58ff., 94–5, 259.

6 W. L. Schwartz, *The Imaginative Interpretation of the Far East in Modern French Literature, 1800 – 1925*, Paris, 1927, p. 131.

7 Ashton-Gwatkin, 'The life and times of John Paris', pp. 12–16.

8 Ashton-Gwatkin, 'The life and times of John Paris', p. 13. In 1923 a stage version of *Kimono* had a short, not very successful run in a West-End theatre.

9 As a trained economic and political observer, Ashton-Gwatkin returned from the Far East with a thorough acquaintance with 'the facts' of the Japanese situation. Although he differed from some of his colleagues at the Foreign Office by maintaining a guardedly optimistic view of the prospects for liberal democracy in Japan, he was perfectly capable (in 1920) of warning prophetically against failure 'to take into full account the strength of character and the will to govern, which a French writer has called "'la force romaine du peuple japonais'" 'This "force romaine"', he continued; 'has distinguished the race from the sad records of Oriental degeneracy, has saved its independence from the crushing superiority of Europe, and will probably preserve Japan from ruin when nemesis overtakes her exaggerated prosperity'; for this, and much more, see 'Japan and the War', *Quarterly Review*, 234, 1920, 406 – 7.

10 Miner, *Japanese Tradition*, p. 52.

11 According to Miner, *Japanese Tradition*, p. 50, Plomer modelled 'Mother Kamchatka' on 'the greatest of modern Japanese satires' – *Kappa*, by Akutagwa Ryonosuke. In the same year, 1929, 'John Paris' published *The Island Beyond Japan*, a longer and somewhat laboured fiction which, none-the-less, tried to make many similar points about an Asian people (the 'Thulians'), who are easily recognisable as the Japanese.

12 *The Hidden Flower* might well be called 'Madame Butterfly Fifty Years On'. Like that archetypical 'novel of desertion' it told the story of how an American officer (this time a Virginia-bred captain in the army of occupation) won the affections of a young Japanese woman, brought her to the USA, fathered her child, and, in this variant, betrayed her by submitting spinelessly to a Virginia statute barring miscegenation. In the course of delivering some unsubtle blows at racial prejudice and moral irresponsibility, Buck did a creditable job of lighting up the interior landscape of a middle-class Japanese family trying to cope with the humiliation of defeat and the competing attractions of deep-seated Japanese social traditions and the personal freedom associated with American ways of living.

[213]

13 'Rottang' Hara got his name from the Malay cane whip with which he beat his prisoners. The film *Merry Christmas, Mr Lawrence* offers a cinematic version of van der Post's story.

Reading list

Black, Gavin (Oswald Wynd), *Black Fountains*, New York, 1947.

Boulle, Pierre, *The Bridge over the River Kwai*, translated by Xan Fielding, New York, 1954.

Buck, Pearl S., *The Patriot*, New York, 1939.

__, *The Hidden Flower*, New York, 1952.

Clavell, James, *Shōgun: A Novel of Japan*, New York, 1977.

Fleming, Ian, *You Only Live Twice*, London, 1964.

Marquand, John P., *Stopover Tokyo*, Boston, 1957.

Michener, James, *Sayonara*, London, 1954.

Paris, John Frank (T.A. Ashton-Gwatkin), *Kimono*, London, 1921.

__, *Sayonara*, London, 1924.

__, *Banzai!*, London, 1925.

__, *The Island Beyond Japan*, London, 1929.

__, *Matsu*, London, 1932.

Plomer, William, *Paper Houses*, New York, 1929.

__, *Sado*, London, 1931.

Post, Laurens Jan van der, *A Bar of Shadow*, New York, 1956.

Standish, Robert (Digby Gerahty), *The Three Bamboos*, London, 1942.

Sneider, Vern J., *The Teahouse of the August Moon*, New York, 1954.

Trevanian, *Shibumi*, New York, 1979.

INDEX